TWELVE SERMONS FOR THE
TROUBLED AND TRIED

Twelve Sermons for the

TROUBLED AND TRIED

delivered at the

Metropolitan Tabernacle

BY

CHARLES H. SPURGEON

CURIOSMITH

MINNEAPOLIS

Published by Curiosmith.
P. O. Box 390293, Minneapolis, Minnesota, 55439.
Internet: curiosmith.com.
E-mail: shopkeeper@curiosmith.com.

Previously published by PASSMORE & ALABASTER in 1894.

Scripture verses are from *The Holy Bible*, King James Version.

ISBN 9781935626978

CONTENTS

GOOD NEWS FOR YOU

Sunday Morning, October 5th, 1862, Metropolitan Tabernacle

But a certain Samaritan, as he journeyed, came where he was.
—Luke 10:33.

The good Samaritan is a masterly picture of true benevolence. The Samaritan had no kinship with the Jew, he was purely of foreign origin, yet he pities his poor neighbor. The Jews cursed the Cuthites, and would have no dealings with them, for they were intruders in their land. There was nothing therefore, in the object of the Samaritan's pity that could excite his national sympathies, but everything to arouse his prejudices, hence the grandeur of his benevolence.

It is not my intention this morning, to indicate the delightful points of excellence which Christ brings out in order to illustrate what true charity will perform. I want you only to notice this one fact, that the benevolence which the Samaritan exhibited towards this poor wounded and half-dead man, was available benevolence. He did not say to him, "If you will walk to Jericho, then I will bind up your wounds, pouring in the oil and wine;" or, "If you will journey with me as far as Jerusalem, I will then attend to your wants." Oh, no, he came "where he was," and finding that he could do nothing whatever for his own assistance, the good Samaritan began with him there and then upon the spot, putting no impossible conditions to him, proposing no stipulations which the man could not perform, but doing everything for the man, and doing it for him as he was and where he was.

Beloved, we are all quite aware that a charity of which a man cannot avail himself, is no charity at all. Go among the operatives of Lancashire, and tell them that there is no necessity for any of them to starve, for on the top of Mt. St. Bernard there are hospitable monks who keep a refectory, where they relieve all passers-by; tell them they have nothing to do but to journey to the top of the Alps, and there they will find food enough. Poor souls! they feel that you mock them, for the distance is too great. Penetrate one of our back streets, climb up three pair of stairs into a wretched room, so dilapidated that the stars look between the tiles, see a poor young girl dying of consumption and poverty, tell her if you dare, "If you could get to the sea-side, and if you could eat so much beef-steak, you would no doubt recover." You are shamefully laughing at her—she cannot get these things—they are beyond her reach: she cannot journey to the seaside—she would die ere she reached it. Like the wicked, your tender mercies are cruel. I have noticed this unavailing charity in hard winters. People give away bread and soup tickets to poor people, who are to give sixpence, and then receive soup and bread; and often I have had persons come to me—"Sir, I have a ticket; it would be worth a great deal to me, if I had sixpence to go with to get the relief; but I have not a farthing in all the world, and I cannot make out the good of giving me this ticket at all." This is hardly charity. Think you see Jeremiah, down in the low dungeon: if Ebed melech and Baruch had stood over the top of the dungeon, and called out to him, "Jeremiah, if you will get half way up, we will pull you out," when there was not a ladder, nor any means by which he could possibly get so far, how cruel would have been this charity; but, instead thereof, they took old rags from under the king's treasury, and put them on ropes, and bade him put the rags under his armholes, and sling his arms through the ropes, and then they pulled him up all the way. This was available charity; the other would have been hypocritical pretence. Brethren, if in the description of a good Samaritan, Christ hits him off to the life, as giving to this poor wounded man a charity of which he could avail himself, does it not seem to be strongly probable—nay, even certain—that when Christ comes to deal with sinners, he gives them available mercy—grace which may be of real service to them.

Hence, permit me to say, I do not believe in the way in which some people pretend to preach the gospel. They have no gospel for sinners as sinners, but only for those who are above the dead level of sinnership, and are technically styled *sensible* sinners. Like the priest in this parable; they see the poor sinner, and they say, "He is not conscious of his need, we cannot invite him to Christ;" "He is dead," they say, "it is of no use preaching to dead souls;" so they pass by on the other side, keeping close to the elect and quickened, but having nothing whatever to say to the dead, lest they should make out Christ to be too gracious, and his mercy to be too free. The Levite was not in quite such a hurry as the priest. The priest had to preach, and might be too late for the service, and therefore he could not stop to relieve the man; besides, he might have soiled his cassock, or made himself unclean; and then he would have been hardly fit for the dainty and respectable congregation over which he officiated. As for the Levite, he had to read the hymns; he was a clerk in the church, and he was somewhat in a hurry, but still he could get in after the opening prayer, so he indulged himself with the luxury of looking on. Just as I have known ministers say, "Well, you know we ought to describe the sinner's state, and warn him, but we must not invite him to Christ." Yes, gentlemen, you must pass by on the other side, after having looked at him, for on your own confession you have no *good* news for the poor wretch. I bless my Lord and Master he has given to me a gospel which I can take to *dead* sinners, a gospel which is available for the vilest of the vile. I thank my Master that he does not say to the sinner, "Come half way and meet me," but he comes "where he is," and finding him ruined, lost, obdurate, he meets him on his own ground, and gives him life and peace without asking, or expecting him to prepare himself for grace. Here is, I think, set forth in my text, the available benevolence of the Samaritan; it is mine this morning, to show the available grace of Christ.

I. The sinner is WITHOUT MORAL QUALIFICATION FOR SALVATION, but Christ comes where he is.

I want, if I can, not to talk about this as a matter having to do with the multitude that are abroad, but with us in these pews. I speak not of *them* and *those,* but of *you* and *me.* I want to say to every sinner, "You are in a state in which there is nothing morally that can qualify you for being saved, but Jesus Christ meets you where you now are."

1. Remember first, that when the gospel was first sent into the world, *those to whom it was sent, were manifestly without any moral qualification.* Did you ever read the first chapter of Paul's Epistle to the Romans? It is one of those awful passages in Scripture, not intended to be read in congregations; but to be read and studied in the secrecy of one's chamber. The apostle gives a portrait of the manners and customs of the heathen world, so awful, that unless our missionaries had informed us, that it is exactly the photograph of life in Hindostan at the present moment, infidels might have declared that Paul had exaggerated. Heathendom in the time of Paul, was so desperately wicked that it would be utterly impossible to conceive of a sin, into which men had not fallen; and yet, "We turn unto the Gentiles," said the apostle; and yet the Lord himself commanded, "Go ye into all the world, and preach the gospel to every creature."[1] What! to Sodomites, whose very smallest sin is adultery, and fornication; to thieves and murderers, to murderers of fathers and mothers? Yes, go and preach the gospel *to them!* Manifestly, the fact that the world was steeped up to its very throat in the filth of abominable wickedness, and yet the gospel was sent to it, proves that Christ does not seek for any qualification of morality, or righteousness in man, before the gospel is available to him. He sends the Word to the drunkard, to the swearer, the harlot, the vilest of the vile; for such is the gospel of Christ intended to save.

2. Recollect again, *the Biblical descriptions of those whom Christ came into the world to save, which prove to a demonstration that he comes to the sinner where he is.* How does the Bible describe those whom Christ came to save? As men? No, my brethren; Christ did not come to save men as men, but men as sinners. As sensible

---
1 Mark 16:15.

sinners?—nay, I aver not; they are described as *"dead* in trespasses and sins."* But to the law and to the testimony, let me read you one or two passages; and, while I read them, I hope you may be able to say, "There is hope for me." First, those whom Christ came to save are described in 1 Timothy 1:15, and many other places, as *"sinners."* "This is a faithful saying, and worthy of all acceptation, that Christ Jesus came into the world to save sinners, of whom I am chief." "Sinners," without any adjective before the word; not awakened sinners, not repenting sinners; but sinners as sinners. "Surely," saith one, "I am not shut out." Another account is found in Romans 5:6, "For when we were yet without strength, in due time Christ died"—for whom? those who had some desires after God? some respect to his name? nay, "for *the ungodly."* Now, an ungodly man means a man without God, who cares not for God; "God is not in all his thoughts," and therefore he is not what men call a sensible sinner. "The ungodly are like the chaff which the wind driveth away:" even these are the persons that Christ came to save. In the same chapter, 10ᵀᴴ verse, you find them mentioned as *"enemies"*—"When we were yet enemies, we were reconciled to God by the death of his Son." What say ye to this? they are not described as friends. Christ laid down his life for his friends in one sense; "But God commendeth his love toward us, in that, while we were yet sinners, Christ died for us." Enemies to God were the objects of grace, so that in enmity Christ comes and meets man where he is.

In Ephesians 2:1, we read of them as *"dead* in trespasses and sins"—"and you hath he quickened who were dead in trespasses and sins." Christ, then, does not ask the sinner to make himself alive; the gospel is not only to be preached to those who have some good notions, some good desires, some tremblings of the heavenly life within, but to the dead as dead; to the dead doth Christ come, and meet them in the grave of their sin. Again, (Ephesians 2:3) they are *"children of wrath"*—"we were by nature the children of wrath even as others." Yet the gospel came to such. Can ye see anything hopeful in a child of wrath? I ask you to look over him from head to foot, if this be his name and character; can ye see a spot of goodness as large as a pin's point in the man? And yet such Christ came to save. Once again, they are mentioned as *"accursed."* "Ah," says one sinner, "I have often cursed myself before God, and asked him to curse me." Well, Christ died for the accursed; (Galatians 3:13) "Christ hath redeemed us from the curse of the law, being made a curse for *us;"* that is, for us who were under the curse. And, once more, they are described by the dreadful word *"lost."* They are lost to all hope, to all consideration for themselves; even their own friends have given their case up as hopeless. "The Son of man is come to seek and to save that which was lost." (Luke 19:10.) If I understand those passages which I have read in your hearing, they mean just this—that those whom Christ came to save have no good whatever in them to co-operate towards their salvation, and Christ doth not look upon them in order to find aught that is good in them. I am bold to say, the only fitness for cleansing is filthiness; the only fitness for a Savior is being lost; and the only character under which we come to Jesus is as sinners, lost, dead, and accursed.

3. But, thirdly, it is quite certain from *the work of grace itself,* that the Lord does not expect the sinner to do anything or to be anything in order to meet him, but that he comes to him where he is. See, sinner, Christ *dies* on Calvary, a weight of sin is on his shoulders, and on his heart; in agonies the most awful he shrieks under the desertion of his God. For whom did he die? For the innocent? Wherefore for the innocent? What sacrifice did they need? For those who had some good thing in them? Why all these agonies *for such?* Surely a less price might do for them if they could eke it out themselves. But because Christ died on account of sin, I take it that those whom he died for must be viewed as sinners, and only as such. Inasmuch as he paid a dreadful price, I gather that they must be dreadfully in debt, and that he died for those who had nothing to pay with. But Christ *rose again,* rose again for our justification. For whose justification? For the justification of those who were justified in themselves? Why this were to perform an unnecessary work. No, my brethren, but for those who had no justification of their own, not a shadow of any, who were condemned, utterly condemned on account of their own

works. Moreover, I hear him by the ear of faith *pleading* before the eternal throne. Who does he plead for? For those who have something to plead on their own account?—that were needless. Do men give their money to the rich? Do they spend their charity on those who do not need it? If men have something to plead for themselves, then why does Christ plead for them? No, brethren, he pleads for those who have nothing whatever that they can bring as an argument with which to enforce their prayers. But Christ ascended and *received gifts*. Who for? For those who merited rewards? No, verily, let them get them for themselves. But he received gifts for men; yea, for the rebellious also, that the Lord God might dwell among them. But he *gives the Holy Spirit*. To whom does he give the Holy Spirit? To those that are strong, and good, and can do all themselves? O, my brethren, this were a work of supererogation; but he gives the Holy Spirit to those that are powerless, weak, dead; he gives the Holy Worker to those who are all unholy and full of sin; he puts the omnipotent influence into those who were slaves to the spirit of evil. Brethren, the work of Christ supposes a lost, ruined, rebellious sinner, and so I say, Christ meets the man where he is.

4. Yet more, for I would clear up this point before I leave it, *the godlike character of the grace of God* proves that he meets the sinner where he is. If God forgive little sinners only, then he is little in his mercy. If the Lord does not do something more than men can think, then we have made too much noise about the gospel, and have exalted the cross above measure. Unless there be something extraordinary in divine grace, then I cannot understand such a passage as this, "As high as the heavens are above the earth, so high are my ways above your ways, and my thoughts above your thoughts."[1] I venture to say, brethren, that many of us have thought of forgiving our enemies. It has sometimes been our happy portion to do good to them that hate us. Now, if God would be godlike in his grace—and I am sure he will—he must do something more than that; he must not only forgive his enemies, but they must be enemies of such an atrocious character that no *man* would have forgiven them.

1 See Isaiah 55:9.

"Who is a pardoning God like thee,
Or who hath grace so rich and free."[1]

But where is the meaning of this boast, if the Lord merely pardons sinners who are sensible of their sins, and lament them? The marvel is in this, that while they are yet enemies he calls them by his grace, and invites them to mercy; yea, more, he blots out their sins, and makes them friends; thus meeting the sinner where he is.

5. *The spirit and genius of the gospel utterly forbid the supposition that God requires anything in any man in order to save him.* If salvation be offered to man upon a condition, they who fulfil the condition have a claim to the blessing. This is the old covenant of works. The substance of the legal covenant is, "Do this and I will reward you." When the man has done it, he deserves what has been promised. Yes, and if you make the condition never so easy, yet, mark you, so long as it be a condition, God is bound by his own Word, the condition being fulfilled, to give man what he has earned. This is works and not grace; it is debt and not free favor. But, inasmuch as the gospel is free favor from beginning to end, I am absolutely sure that God asketh nothing; neither good wishes, good desires, nor good feelings of a sinner before he may come to Christ. But that he may know that everything is of grace, the rebel is commanded to come just as he is, bringing nothing, but taking everything from God, who is superabundant in mercy, and therefore meeteth the sinner just where he is.

I say to the sinner, wherever thou mayest be today, if thou be without any virtue, and if thou be filled with all vice, if there be no good points in thy character, but if there be everything that is bad against man and against God; if thou hast committed every crime in the catalogue, if thou hast ruined thy body and damned thy soul, yet still Christ hath said it, "Him that cometh unto me I will in no wise cast out."[2] And if thou comest to him, he can no more cast thee out than if thou hadst been the most virtuous, the most honorable, and the most devout of all living men. Only do thou today believe in the

---

1 *Great God of Wonders* by Samuel Davies.
2 John 6:37.

mercy of God, in Christ, and cast thyself on Him, and thou art saved to the praise and glory of that grace which meets thee just where thou art, and saveth thee from sin.

II. In the second place, there are very many of the lost race of Adam, who say that they are WITHOUT ANY MENTAL QUALIFICATION.

This is their excuse—"But, sir, I never was a scholar. I was sent out as a boy to earn my own living, so that I never had a week's schooling; I am so ignorant that I cannot read my book, and if anybody were to ask me to make a prayer I could not, I have not sense enough." Now, you see the Lord Jesus meets you just where you are. And how does he do this? Why, first, *the saving act is one that requires no mental power.* Faith lays hold on eternal life. Now, a child whose faculties are never so little developed can believe what it is told. The child cannot reason, cannot argue, cannot dispute, cannot split hairs, cannot see a knotty point in theology, but it can believe what it is told. Faith requires so little mental vigor or intellectual clearness, that there have been many who were idiots in other things, who have been made wise unto salvation by the act of faith in Christ. You remember our Lord's own words, "I thank thee, O Father, Lord of heaven and earth, that thou hast hid these things from the wise and prudent, and hast revealed them unto babes."[1] But this never could have happened had not the act which brings us into communion with Christ been the lowest act of the human faculty, that of simply trusting to Christ, as the result of crediting that which is told us upon good testimony.

But then, again, to meet this defect of mental power, remember *the singular simplicity of that which is believed.* Is there anything more simple in the world than the doctrine of the atonement. We deserve to die, Christ dies for us; we are in debt, Christ pays for us. Is not this plain enough for a Ragged School? It is so plain, that many of our learned doctors of divinity try to get it out of the Bible; they think, "If this be the marrow of it all, then any fool can be a theologian;" so they kick against it. What is Unitarianism but a stumbling at the simplicity of the cross. They were Unitarians who stood at the cross when Christ died; they said, "Let him come down from the

1 Luke 10:21.

cross and we will believe on him."[1] That has been the Unitarian character ever since; they will receive Jesus anywhere but on his cross; but up there, dying in man's stead, he is so commonplace, that these great gentlemen run to philosophy and vain deceit sooner than lay hold on that which the commonest may as fully understand as they.

Yet more; to meet any mental deficiency in man, while the truth itself is simple, it is *taught in the Bible under such simple metaphors,* that none can say they cannot understand it. How simple is the metaphor of the brazen serpent, held up before the snake-bitten Israelites, while they are commanded to look and live. Who does not understand that a look at Christ who dies in the stead of men, will make them live? "If any man thirst, let him come unto me and drink."[2] Who does not understand the figure of a fountain flowing in the streets, that every thirsty passer-by may put his lips down and drink? "Behold the Lamb of God." Who does not understand the sacrifice? Here is a lamb killed for the sin of Israel, and so Christ dies for the sin of those who believe in him. The act of faith is simple, the object of faith is plain; the metaphors make it clear, and he is without excuse who does not understand the gospel of Christ.

To crown all, to you, my beloved hearers, Christ *has given you abundance of teachers.* There sits in your pew with you today a man of your own rank and calling, who will explain to you the gospel, if you do not understand it. Here are many of us, who are but too glad if we can roll away the stone from the door of your sepulchre; here are children of God themselves saved by sovereign grace, and if you really do not know the way, do but touch your next neighbor, and say to him, "Can you explain to me yet more clearly what I must do to be saved?" Now, this is meeting you, let your brains be of the very smallest; this is coming down to you though you sit on the lowest step of human intellect. Jesus Christ meets you just where you are.

III. But yet again. I think I hear another say, "I am in despair, for I CANNOT FIND ANY REASON IN MYSELF, OR OUT OF MYSELF, WHY GOD SHOULD FORGIVE SUCH A PERSON AS I AM."

---

1 Matthew 27:42.
2 John 7:37.

So then, you are in a hopeless state, at least you see no hope. The Lord meets you where you are, by putting *the reason of your salvation altogether in himself.* Shall I remind you of one or two texts which will surely satisfy you? "I, even I, am he that blotteth out thy transgressions." What for? "For mine own sake."[1] He cannot pardon you for your sake, you clearly see that; and you feel that he cannot pardon you for other people's sake; but for *"my own sake"* saith he, "that I may glorify myself." Not in you, but in his own mighty breast he finds the motive, that he may make his own mercy illustrious; for his own sake he will do it. Or take another—"For my name's sake, even for my name's sake, will I defer mine anger, that I cut thee not off." Here it is again for his *name's sake,* as if he knew he could not find any other motive, so he puts it all on himself; he pardons that he may honor and glorify his own name. Sinner, thou canst not say that this does not meet thy case: for if thou be the most hellish good-for-nothing sinner that ever cursed God's earth, and polluted the air thou breathest, yet he can save thee, *for his own sake.* There still is room for thee to hope; for the bigger the sinner thou be the more glory to him if he saveth thee; and if salvation be given for a reason only in himself, there is therefore yet a reason by which he can save thee, even thee.

Remember, that *he puts his own design* before your eyes to show you that if you have no reason in yourself, that is no hindrance to his saving you. What is God's design in saving men? When he brings them to heaven, what will be the result of it? Why, that they may love and praise his name for ever, and sing "Unto him that loved us, and washed us from our sins in his blood, unto him be glory."[2] You are just the man; if you are ever saved, and brought to heaven, oh, will not you praise his grace? "Yes," said one old man who had long lived in sin, "if he ever does bring me to heaven, he shall never hear the last of it, for I will praise him throughout eternity." Why, you are the man, do you not see, you are the very man that will answer God's design, for who shall love so much as he who has had much forgiven, and who shall praise so loudly as he whose mighty sins have been

---

1 Isaiah 43:25.

2 See Revelation 1:5, 6.

overcome by the mighty love and goodness and grace of God? Thou canst not say that it does not meet thee, for here is a motive and a reason, though thou canst find none in thyself.

Here is another reason why God should save thee, it is *His own Word*, the Word of him that cannot lie. I will bring up that text again; perhaps there is a heart here that will be able to cast anchor on it— "Him that cometh unto me I will in no wise cast out." You say, "But if I come, I can see no reason why he should save me." I answer, there is a reason in His own promise. God cannot lie. You come; he will not cast you out. He says, "I will in no wise cast out;" but you say, "He may for such-and-such a reason." Now, this is a flat contradiction; the two cannot stand. If there be anything that is necessary in order for a soul to come, and you come without it, yet there is the promise, and as it has no limit in it plead it, and the Lord will not refuse to honor his own Word. If he can cast you out because you have not some necessary qualification, then his Word is not true. Whoever you may be, whatever you may not be, and whatever you may be, if you believe in Jesus Christ, there is a reason in every attribute of God why you should be saved. His truth cries, "Save him, for thou hast said 'I will.'" His power says, "Save him, lest the enemy deny thy might." God's wisdom pleads, "Save him, lest men doubt thy judgment." His love says, "Save him;" his every attribute says, "Save him;" and even Justice, with its hoarse voice, cries, "Save him, for God is faithful and just to forgive us our sins, if we confess our sins."

I am trying to fish in deep waters after some of you that have long escaped the net. I know when I have given free and full invitations, you have said, "Ah! that cannot mean me." You are without faith in Christ, because you think you are not fit. I will be clear of your blood this morning; I will show you that there is no fitness wanted, that you are commanded now to believe in the Lord Jesus Christ as you are, for Jesus Christ's gospel is an available gospel, and comes to you just where you are. Without moral or mental qualification, and without any sort of reason why he should save you, he meets you as such, and bids you trust him.

IV. We proceed to our fourth point. "Oh," says one, "but I am

WITHOUT COURAGE; I dare not believe on Christ, I am such a timid, trembling soul, that when I hear that others trust to Christ I think it must be presumption; I wish I could do the same but I cannot, I am kept under by such a sense of sin, that I dare not. O sir, I dare not, it would look as if I were flying in the face of justice if I were to dare to trust Christ, and then to rejoice in the pardon of my sin." Very well, Christ comes to meet you where you are, by very tender *invitations*. "Ho, every one that thirsteth, come ye to the waters, and he that hath no money; come ye, buy, and eat; yea, come, buy wine and milk without money and without price."[1] "Come unto me, all ye that labour and are heavy laden, and I will give you rest."[2] "The Spirit and the bride say, come. And let him that heareth say, come. And let him that is athirst, come. And whosoever will, let him take the water of life freely."[3] How sweetly he puts it to you. I do not know where more wooing words could be found, than those the Savior uses. Will you not come when Christ beckons, when with his loving face streaming with tears, he bid you come to him. What! is an invitation from him too little a thing for you. O sinner, trembling though thou art, say in thy soul,

> "I'll to the gracious king approach,
>   Whose sceptre pardon gives;
> Perhaps he may command my touch,
>   And then the suppliant lives."

Knowing that you would neglect the invitation, he has put it to you in the light of a *command*. "This is the commandment, that ye believe on Jesus Christ whom he hath sent."[4] "Believe on the Lord Jesus Christ, and thou shalt be saved."[5] "He that believeth and is baptized shall be saved; but he that believeth not shall be damned."[6] He thought you would say, "Ah, but I am not fit to accept the invitation." "Well," says

1 Isaiah 55:1.
2 Matthew 11:28.
3 Revelation 22:17.
4 See 1 John 3:23.
5 Acts 16:31.
6 Mark 16:16.

he, "I will command the man to do it." Like a poor hungry man with bread before him, who says, "Ah, it would be presumption on my part to eat;" but the king says, "Eat, sir, or I will punish you." What a generous and liberal command; even the threat itself has no anger in it. Like the mother, who when the child is near to die, and nothing will save it but the medicine, and the child will not drink, she threatens the child, but only out of love to it that it may be saved. So the Lord doth add *threatenings* to commands; for sometimes a black word will drive a soul to Christ where a bright word would not draw it. Fears of hell sometimes make men flee to Jesus. The weary wing made the poor dove fly to the ark: and the thunderbolts of God's justice are only meant to make thee fly to Christ the Lord.

Beloved, once more, my Master has sweetly met your want of courage by bringing many others, so that you may follow their *example.* As fowlers sometimes have their decoy-birds, so my Master hath decoy-birds that are to draw others to him. Other sinners have been saved, others he has cleansed who did but trust him. There was Lot. Ah, Lot! guilty of drunkenness and incest, and yet a saint of God. David the adulterer and murderer of Uriah, and yet washed "whiter than snow." Manasseh the bloody persecutor, who had cut Esaias in two, sawing him in halves, and yet he was taken among the thorns, and God had mercy on him. What shall I say of Saul of Tarsus, the persecutor of God's people? and the robber dying on the cross for his crimes, and yet saved? Sinner, if these do not induce thee to come, what can overcome thy sinful diffidence? "But," says one, "you have not hit my case yet; I am an outrageous sinner!" Well now, I will hit it this time. In 1 Corinthians, 6:9, hear the Word of the Lord, "Neither fornicators, nor idolaters, nor adulterers, nor effeminate, nor abusers of themselves with mankind, nor thieves, nor covetous, nor drunkards, nor revilers, nor extortioners, shall inherit the kingdom of God. And *such were some of you:* but ye are washed, but ye are sanctified, but ye are justified in the name of the Lord Jesus, and by the Spirit of our God." Why, brethren, what horrible descriptions there are here; there are some of them so bad that when we have read the description, we wish to forget the sin; and yet, and yet, glory be to thine Almighty grace, O God! such hast thou saved, and such thou canst save still. O, timid sinner, can you not trust in Jesus after this? Hear ye the Word of the Lord again (Titus 3:3–5), "For we ourselves also were sometimes foolish, disobedient, deceived, serving divers lusts and pleasures, living in malice and envy, hateful, and hating one another. But after that the kindness and love of God our Savior toward man appeared, not by works of righteousness which we have done, but according to his mercy he saved *us.* "Now, you hateful sinners, and you that hate others; you that are full of malice and envy, here is the gate open even for you, for the kindness and love of God towards man appears in the person of Christ. Listen to another, for God's words are more than mine, and I do hope they will attract some of you (Ephesians 2:1–3): "Dead in trespasses and sins; wherein in time past ye walked according to the course of this world, according to the prince of the power of the air, the spirit that now worketh in the children of disobedience. Among whom also we all had our conversation in times past in the lusts of our flesh, fulfilling the desires of the flesh and of the mind; and were by nature the children of wrath, even as others. But God, who is rich in mercy, for his great love wherewith he loved us, even when we were dead in sins, hath quickened us together with Christ, (by grace ye are saved) and hath raised us up together, and made us sit together in heavenly places in Christ Jesus." What for? "That in the ages to come,"—mark this—"he might show the exceeding riches of his grace in his kindness towards us through Christ Jesus." One more passage, and I will not weary your attention. O that this last passage might comfort some of you, it is Paul who speaks (1 Timothy 1:13), "I was before a blasphemer, and a persecutor, and injurious: but I obtained mercy, because I did it ignorantly in unbelief. And the grace of our Lord was exceeding abundant with faith and love, which is in Christ Jesus. This is a faithful saying," see how he puts it from his own experience, "and worthy of all acceptation;" and therefore worthy of yours, poor sinner; "that Christ Jesus came into the world to save sinners, of whom I am chief." "Ah" says one "but he would not save any more." Let me go on—"Howbeit for this cause I obtained mercy, that in me first Jesus Christ might show forth all longsuffering, for a pattern to them which should hereafter believe on him to life everlasting." So that if you trust as Paul did, you shall be saved as Paul was, for his conversion and salvation are a pattern to all those who should believe in the Lord Jesus Christ, unto life everlasting. So sinner, timid as you are, here Jesus meets you.

O, I wish I could say a word that would lead you poor tearful ones to look to Jesus. O, do not let the devil tempt you to believe that you are too sinful. "He is able to save them to the uttermost that come unto God by him."

"Let not conscience make you linger, nor of fitness fondly dream."[1]

Fitness is not needed—do but come to him. You are black, and you do not feel your blackness as you ought—that makes you all the blacker. Come, then, and be clean. You are sinful, and this is your greatest sin, that you do not repent as you ought; but come to him, and ask him to forgive your impenitence. Come as you are: if he rejecteth one of you, I will bear the blame for ever; if he casteth one of you away that shall trust him, call me a false prophet in the day of the resurrection. But I pawn my life upon it—I stake my own soul's interest on this—that whosoever cometh unto him, he will in no wise cast out.

V. I hear one more complaint. "I am WITHOUT STRENGTH," saith one; "will Jesus come just where I am?" Yes, sinner, just where you are. You say you cannot believe, that is your difficulty. God meets you, then, in your inability. First, he meets you with *his promises.* Soul, thou canst not believe; but when God, that cannot lie, promises, will you not believe, can you not believe then? I do think God's promise—so sure, so stedfast—must overcome this inability of yours.

"Him that cometh to me, I will in no wise cast out." Cannot you believe now? Why, that promise must be true! But next, as if he knew that this would not be enough, he has taken *an oath* with it—and a more awful oath was never sworn—"As I live, saith the Lord, I have no pleasure in the death of him that dieth, but had rather that he should turn unto me and live. Turn ye, turn ye, why will ye die, O

1 *Come, Ye Sinner, Poor and Needy* by Joseph Hart.

house of Israel."[1] Can you not believe now? What, will you doubt God when he swears it, not only make God a liar but—let me shudder when I say it—will you think that God can perjure his own self? God forbid you should so blaspheme. Remember, he that believeth not hath made God a liar, because he believeth not on the Son of God. Do not do this. Surely you can believe when the promise and the oath compel you to faith. But yet more, as if he knew that even this were not enough, he has given you of *his Spirit.* "If ye being evil know how to give good gifts unto your children, how much more shall your heavenly Father give the Holy Spirit to them that ask him."[2] Surely with this you can believe. "But," saith one, "I will try." No, no, do not try, that is not what God commands you to do; no trying is wanted; believe Christ now, sinner. "But," saith one, "I will think of it." Do not think of it, do it now, do it at once for this is God's gospel. There are some of you standing in these aisles and sitting in these pews, who I feel in my soul will never have another invitation, and if this be rejected today, I feel a solemn motion in my soul—I think it is of the Holy Ghost—that you will never hear another faithful sermon, but you shall go down to hell impenitent, unsaved, except ye trust in Jesus *now.* I speak not as a man, but I speak as God's ambassador to your souls, and I command you, in God's name, trust Jesus, trust *now.* At your peril reject the voice that speaks from heaven, for "he that believeth not shall be damned." How shall ye escape if ye neglect so great salvation. When it comes right home to you, when it thrusts itself in your way, oh, if ye will neglect it how can ye escape? With tears I would invite you, and, if I could, would compel you to come in. Why will ye not? O souls, if ye will be damned, if ye make up your mind that no mercy shall ever woo you, and no warnings shall ever move you, then, sirs, what chains of vengeance must you feel that slight these bonds of love. You have deserved the deepest hell, for you slight the joys above. God save you. He will save you, if you trust in Jesus. God help you to trust him even now, for Jesus' sake. Amen.

1 Ezekiel 33:11.
2 Matthew 7:11.

A SERMON FOR THE MOST MISERABLE OF MEN

LORD'S-DAY MORNING, JANUARY 31ST, 1869, METROPOLITAN TABERNACLE

My soul refused to be comforted.—PSALM 77:2.

In this refusal to be comforted, David is not to be imitated. His experience in this instance is recorded rather as a warning than as an example. Here is no justification for those professors who, when they suffer bereavements or temporal losses, repine bitterly, and reject every consoling thought. We have known persons who made mourning for departed ones the main business of life, years after the beloved relative had entered into rest. Like the heathen, they worship the spirits of the dead. The sufferer has a right to mourn, a right which Jesus Christ has sealed, for "Jesus wept," but that right is abused into a wrong, when protracted sorrow poisons the springs of the heart, and unfits the weeper for the duties of daily life. There is a "hitherto" beyond which the floods of grief may not lawfully advance. "What," said the Quaker, to one who wore the weeds of mourning many years after the death of her child, and declared that she had suffered a blow from which she should never rally—"What, friend, hast thou not forgiven God yet?" Much of unholy rebellion against the Most High will be found as a sediment at the bottom of most tear-bottles. Sullen repining and protracted lamentation indicate the existence of idolatry in the heart. Surely the beloved object must have been enshrined in that throne of the heart which is the Lord's alone, or else the taking away of the beloved object, though it caused poignant sorrow, would not have excited such an unsubmissive spirit. Should it not be the endeavor of God's children to avoid excessive and continued grief, because it verges so closely upon the two deadly sins of rebellion and idolatry? Sorrow deserves sympathy, but when it springs from a want of resignation, it merits censure more. When believers refuse to be comforted, they act as mere worldlings might do with some excuse, for when unbelievers lose earthly comforts they lose their all; but for the Christian to pine and sigh in inconsolable anguish over the loss of a creature good, is to belie his profession, and degrade his name. He believes of his trial that the Lord has done it, he calls God his Father, he knows that all things work together for good, he is persuaded that a far more exceeding and eternal weight of glory is being wrought out for him, how then can he sit down in sullen silence, and say, "I will not be comforted!" surely then the truths which he professes to believe have never entered into his soul; he must be a mere speculative theoriser, and not a sincere believer. Beloved, shame on us, if with such a faith as ours we do not play the man. If the furnace be hot, let our faith be strong; if the burden be heavy, let our patience be enduring. Let us practically admit that he who lends has a right to reclaim his own; and as we blessed the giving, so let us bless the taking hand. At all times let us praise the Lord our God. Though he slay us, let us trust him; much more, let us bless him when he only uses the rod.

Our text, however, might very fittingly describe individuals who, although free from outward trial or bereavement, are subject to deep depression of spirits. There are times with the brightest eyed Christians when they can hardly brush the tears away. Strong faith and joyous hope at times subside into a fearfulness which is scarcely able to keep the spark of hope and faith alive in the soul; yea, I think the more rejoicing a man is at one time the more sorrowful he will be at others. They who mount highest descend lowest. There are cold-blooded individuals who neither rejoice with joy unspeakable nor groan with anguish unutterable; but others of a more excitable temperament, capable of lofty delights, are also liable to horrible sinkings of heart, and just because they have gazed in ecstasy within the gates of pearl, they are too apt to make a descent to the land of deathshade, and to stand shivering on the brink of hell. I know this, alas! too well. In the times of our gloom, when the soul is well nigh overwhelmed, it is our duty to grasp the promise and to rejoice in the Lord; but it is not easy to do so. The duty is indisputable, but the fulfilment of it impossible. In vain for us at such seasons the star of promise and the candle of experience: the darkness which may be felt seems to smother all cheering lights. Barnabas, the son of consolation, would be hard put to it to cheer the victims of depression when their fits are on them. The oil of joy is poured out in vain for those heads upon which the dust and ashes of melancholy are heaped up. Brethren, at such times the unhappy should wisely consider whether their disturbed minds ought not to have rest from labor. In these days, when everybody travels by express and works like a steam-engine, the mental wear and tear are terrible, and the advice of the Great Master to the disciples to go into the desert and rest awhile is full of wisdom, and ought to have our earnest attention. Rest is the best, if not the only medicine for men occupied in mental pursuits and subject to frequent depression of spirit. Get away, ye sons of sadness, from your ordinary avocations for a little season if you possibly can, and enjoy quiet and repose—above all, escape from your cares by casting them upon God: if you bear them yourself, they will distract you, so that your soul will refuse to be comforted; but if you will leave them to God, and endeavor to serve him without distraction, you will overcome the drooping tendency of your spirits, and you will yet compass the altar of God with songs of gladness. Let none of us give way to an irritable, complaining, mournful temperament. It is the giving way which is the master-mischief; for it is only as we resist this devil that it will flee from us. Let not your *heart* be troubled. If the troubles outside the soul toss your vessel and drive her to and fro, yet, at least, let us strain every nerve to keep the seas outside the bark, lest she sink altogether. Cry with David, "Why art thou cast down, O my soul? and why art thou disquieted within me?"[1] Never mourn unreasonably. Question yourself about the causes of your tears; reason about the matter *till* you come to the same conclusion as the psalmist, "Hope thou in

1 Psalm 42:11.

God: for I shall yet praise him." Depend upon it, if thou canst believe in God, thou hast, even in thy soul's midnight, ten times more cause to rejoice than to sorrow. If thou canst humbly lie at Jesus' feet, there are more flowers than thorns ready to spring up in thy pathway; joys lie in ambush for thee; thou shalt be compassed about with songs of deliverance. Therefore, companions in tribulation, give not way to hopeless sorrow; write no bitter things against yourselves; salute with thankfulness the angel of hope, and say no more, "My soul refused to be comforted."

My main bent, this morning, to which I have set my whole soul, is to deal with these mourners who are seeking Christ, but up till now have sought him in vain. Convinced of sin, awakened and alarmed, these unhappy ones tarry long outside the gate of mercy, shivering in the cold, pining to enter into the banquet which invites them, but declining to pass through the gate which stands wide open for them. Sullenly—no, I will not use so hard a word—tremblingly they refuse to enter within mercy's open door, although infinite love itself cries to them, "Come, and welcome: enter, and be blessed."

I. Concerning so deplorable a state of heart, alas! still so common, we will remark in the first place that IT IS VERY WONDERFUL.

It is a most surprising thing that there should be in this world persons who have the richest consolation near to hand, and persistently refuse to partake of it. It seems so unnatural, that if we had not been convinced by abundant observation, we should deem it impossible that any miserable soul should refuse to be comforted. Doth the ox refuse its fodder? Will the lion turn from his meat? Or the eagle loathe its nest? The refusal of consolation is the more singular because *the most admirable comfort is within reach.* Sin can be forgiven; sin has been forgiven; Christ has made an atonement for it. God is graciously willing to accept any sinner that comes to him confessing his transgressions, and trusting in the blood of the Lord Jesus. God waiteth to be gracious. He is not hard nor harsh; he is full of mercy; he delights to pardon the penitent, and is never more revealed in the glory of his Godhead than when he is accepting the unworthy through the righteousness of Jesus Christ. There is so much comfort in the word of God that it were as easy to mete the heavens above, or set the limits of space, as to measure the grace revealed therein. You may seek, if you will, to comprehend all the sweetness of divine love, but you cannot, for it passeth knowledge. Like the vast expanse of the ocean is the abounding goodness of God made manifest in Jesus Christ. Wonderful is it, then, that men refuse to receive what is so lavishly provided. It is said that some years ago, a vessel sailing on the northern coast of the South American continent, was observed to make signals of distress. When hailed by another vessel, they reported themselves as "Dying for water!" "Dip it up then," was the response, "you are in the mouth of the Amazon river." There was fresh water all around them, they had nothing to do but to dip it up, and yet they were dying of thirst, because they thought themselves to be surrounded by the salt sea. How often are men ignorant of their mercies! How sad, that they should perish for lack of knowledge!

But suppose after the sailors had received the joyful information, they had still refused to draw up the water which was in boundless plenty all around them, would it not have been a marvel? Would you not at once conclude that madness had taken hold upon the captain and his crew? Yet, so great, dear friends, is the madness of many who hear the gospel, and know that there is mercy provided for sinners, that unless the Holy Spirit interferes they will perish, not through ignorance, but because, for some cause or other, like the Jews of old, they judge themselves "unworthy of everlasting life," and exclude themselves from the gospel, refusing to be comforted. This is the more remarkable because *the comfort provided is so safe.* Were there suspicions that the comforts of the gospel would prove delusive, that they would only foster presumption, and so destroy the soul, men would be wise to start back as from a poison-cup; but many have satisfied themselves at this life-giving stream, not one has been injured, but all who have partaken have been eternally blessed. Why, then, doth the thirsty soul hesitate, while the river, clear as crystal, flows at his feet? Moreover, *the comfort of the gospel is most suitable*, it is *fully adapted* to the sinful, the weak, and the broken-hearted, adapted to those who are crushed by their need of mercy, and adapted equally as much to those who are least sensible of their want of it. The gospel bears a balm in its hand suited to the sinner in his worst estate, when he has no good thing about him, and nothing within which can, by possibility, be a ground of hope. Does not the gospel declare that Christ died for the ungodly? Is it not a faithful saying and worthy of all acceptation, that Christ Jesus came into the world to save sinners, of whom, said the apostle, "I am chief?" Is not the gospel intended even for those who are dead in sin? Read we not such words as these, "God, who is rich in mercy, for his great love wherewith he loved us, even when we where dead in sins, hath quickened us together in Christ (by grace are ye saved)?"[1] Are not the invitations of the gospel, so far as we can judge, just the kindest, tenderest, and most attractive that could be penned and addressed at the worst emergency in which a sinner can be placed? "Ho, every one that thirsteth, come ye to the waters, and he that hath no money; come ye, buy, and eat; yea, come, buy wine and milk without money and without price."[2] "Let the wicked forsake his way, and the unrighteous man his thoughts: and let him return unto the Lord, and he will have mercy upon him; and to our God, for he will abundantly pardon."[3] No qualifying adjectives are used to set forth a degree of goodness in the person invited, but the wicked are bidden to come and the unrighteous are commanded to turn to God. The invitation deals with base, naked, unimproved sinnership. Grace seeks for misery, unworthiness, guilt, helplessness, and nothing else. Not because we are good, but because the Lord is gracious, we are bidden to believe in the infinite mercy of God in Christ Jesus, and so to receive comfort. Strange that where consolation is so plentiful—where comfort is so safe, where the heart-cheer is so suitable, souls should be found by thousands who refuse to be comforted.

This fact grows the more remarkable because *these persons greatly need comfort,* and from what they say, and I trust also from what they feel, you might infer that comfort was the very thing they would

1 Ephesians 2:4, 5.
2 Isaiah 55:1.
3 Isaiah 55:7.

clutch at as a drowning man at a rope. Why, they scarcely sleep at night by reason of their fears. By day their faces betray the sorrow, which, like a tumultuous sea rages within. They can scarcely speak a cheerful sentence. They make their household miserable; the infection of their sorrow is caught by others. You would think that the very moment the word "hope" was whispered in their ears, they would leap towards it at once; but it is not so. You may put the gospel into what shape you please, and yet these poor souls who need your pity, though, I fear, they must also have your blame, refuse to be comforted. Though the food be placed before them, their soul abhorreth all manner of meat, and they draw near unto the gates of death; yea, you may even put the heavenly cordial into their very mouths, but they will not receive the spiritual nutriment; they pine in hunger rather than partake in what divine love provides.

Need I enlarge on this strange infatuation? It is a monstrosity unparalleled in nature. When the dove was weary, she recollected the ark, and flew into Noah's hand at once; these are weary and they know the ark, but they will not fly to it. When an Israelite had slain, inadvertently, his fellow, he knew the city of refuge, he feared the avenger of blood, and he fled along the road to the place of safety; but these know the refuge, and every Sabbath we set up the sign-posts along the road, but yet they come not to find salvation. The destitute waifs and strays of the streets of London find out the night refuge and ask for shelter; they cluster round our workhouse doors, like sparrows under the eaves of a building on a rainy day; they piteously crave for lodging and a crust of bread; yet crowds of poor benighted spirits, when the house of mercy is lighted up and the invitation is plainly written in bold letters, "Whosoever will, let him turn in hither,"[1] will not come, but prove the truth of Watts' verse—

> "Thousands make a wretched choice
> And rather starve than come."

'Tis strange, 'tis passing strange, 'tis wonderful!![2]

---

1 See Proverbs 9:16.
2 *Othello, the Moor of Venice* by William Shakespeare.

II. Secondly, this wonderful madness has a method in it, and MAY BE VARIOUSLY ACCOUNTED FOR.

In many, their refusal to be comforted arises from *bodily and mental disease*. It is in vain to ply with scriptural arguments those who are in more urgent need of healing medicine, or generous diet, or a change of air. There is so close a connection between the sphere of the physician and the divine, that they do well to hunt in couples when chasing the delusions of morbid humanity; and I am persuaded there are not a few cases in which the minister's presence is of small account until the physician shall first of all wisely have discharged his part. I shall not, this morning, therefore, further allude to characters out of my line of practice, but I shall speak of those whose refusal to accept comfort arises from moral rather than physical disease.

In some the monstrous refusal is suggested by a *proud dislike to the plan of salvation*. They would be comforted, ay, that they would, but may they not do something to earn eternal life? May they not at least contribute a feeling or emotion? May they not prepare them-selves for Christ? Must salvation be all gratis? Must they be received into the house of mercy as paupers? Must they come with no other cry but "God be merciful to me a sinner?" Must it come to this—to be stripped, to have every rag of one's own righteousness torn away, as well righteousness of feeling as righteousness of doing? Must the whole head be confessedly sick, and the whole heart faint, and the man lie before Jesus as utterly undone and ruined, to take everything from the hand of the crucified Savior? Ah! then, saith flesh and blood, I will not have it. The crest is not easy to cleave in twain; the banner of self is upheld by a giant standard-bearer; it floats on high long after the battle has been lost. But what folly! Forsooth, for the sake of indulging a foolish dignity we will not be comforted. O sir, down with you and your dignity: I beseech you, bow down now before the feet of Jesus, and kiss the feet which were nailed for your sins. Roll yourself and your glory in the dust. What are you but an unclean thing, and what are your righteousnesses but filthy rags? O take Christ to be your all-in-all, and you shall have comfort this very morning; let not pride prompt a fresh refusal, but be wise and submit to sovereign grace.

In others it is not pride, but *an unholy resolve to retain some favorite sin.* In most cases when the Christian minister tries to heal a wound that has long been bleeding, he probes and probes again with his lancet, wondering why the wound will not heal. It seems to him that all the circumstances augur a successful healing of the wound. He cannot imagine why it still continues to bleed, but at last he finds out the secret, "Ah, here I have it; here is an extraneous substance which continually frets and aggravates the wound. It cannot heal while this grit of sin lies within it." In some cases we have found out that the sorrowing person indulged still in a secret vice, or kept the society of the ungodly, or was undutiful to parents, or unforgiving, or slothful, or practised that hideous sin, secret drunkenness. In any such case, if the man resolves, "I will not give up this sin," do you wonder if he is not comforted? Would not it be an awful thing if he were? When a man carries a corroding substance within his soul, if his wound is filmed over, an internal disease will come of it and prove deadly. I pray God none of you may ever get comfort till you get rid of every known sin and are able to say—

> "The dearest idol I have known,
>   Whate'er that idol be,
> Help me to tear it from its throne,
>   And worship only thee."[1]

There must be a plucking out of the right eye and a losing of the right arm, if we are to inherit eternal life: foolish indeed is he, who for the sake of some paltry sin—a sin which he himself despises, a sin which he would not dare to confess into the ears of another—continues to reject Christ. Might I take such a one by the hand and say, "My brother, my sister, give it up. Oh, for God's sake, hate the accursed thing, and come now with me! Confess to Jesus, who will forgive all your foolishness and accept you this morning, so that no longer you shall refuse to be comforted."

Some refuse to be comforted because of *an obstinate determination only to be comforted in a way of their own selecting.* They have

---

1 *Walking with God* by William Cowper.

read the life of a certain good man who was saved with a particular kind of experience. "Now," say they, "if I feel like that man, then I shall conclude I am saved." Many have hit upon the experience of Mr. Bunyan, in "Grace Abounding;" they have said, "Now, I must be brought just as John Bunyan was, or else I will not believe." Another has said, "I must tread the path which John Newton trod—my feet must be placed in the very marks where his feet went down, or else I cannot believe in Jesus Christ." But, my dear friend, what reason have you for expecting that God will yield to your self-will, and what justification have you for prescribing to the Great Physician the methods of his cure? Oh, if he do but bring me to heaven, I will bless him, though he conduct me by the gates of hell. If I be but brought to see the King in his beauty, in the land which is very far off, it shall make no trouble to my heart by what method of experience he brings me there. Come, lay aside this foolish choosing of yours, and say, "Lord, do but have mercy on me, do but give me to trust thy dear Son, and my whims and my fancies shall be given up."

I fear, in a great many, there is another reason for this refusing to be comforted, namely, *a dishonoring unbelief in the love and goodness and truthfulness of God.* They do not believe God to be gracious; they think him a tyrant, or if not quite that, yet one so stern that a sinner had need plead and beg full many a day before the stern heart of God will be touched. Oh, but you do not know my God! What is he? He is love. I tell you he wants no persuading to have mercy any more than the sun needs to be persuaded to shine, or a fountain to pour out its streams. It is the nature of God to be gracious. He is never so godlike as when he is bestowing mercy. "Judgment is his strange work;" it is his left-handed work; but mercy, the last manifested of his attributes, is his Benjamin, the child of his right hand. He delights to exercise it. Is it not so written, "He delighteth in mercy?"[1] Alas! alas! alas! that God should be slandered by those to whom he speaks so lovingly! "As I live, saith the Lord," here he takes an oath, and will you not believe him? "As I live, saith the Lord God, I have no pleasure in the death of the wicked; but that the wicked should turn from his

1 Micah 7:18.

way and live." "Turn ye, turn ye! Why will ye die, O house of Israel?"[1] He even seems to turn beggar to his own creatures, and to plead with them to come to him. His bowels yearn as he cries, "How shall I give thee up, Ephraim? how shall I deliver thee, Israel? how shall I make thee as Admah? how shall I set thee as Zeboim? Mine heart is turned within me, my repentings are kindled together. I will not execute the fierceness of mine anger, I will not return to destroy Ephraim: for I am God, and not man."[2] O do not, I pray you, be unbelieving any longer, but believe God's word and oath, and accept the comfort which he freely offers to you this morning in the words of his gospel.

Some, however, have refused comfort so long, that they have grown into *the habit of despair*. Ah! it is a dangerous habit, and trembles on the brink of hell. Every moment in which it is indulged a man grows inured to it. It is like the cold of the frigid zone, which benumbs the traveller after awhile, till he feels nothing, and drops into slumber, and from that into death. Some have despaired and despaired until they had reason for despair, and until despair brought them into hell. Despair has hardened some men's hearts till they have been ready to commit sins which hope would have rendered impossible to them. Beware of nursing despondency. Does it creep upon you today through unbelief? O shake it off if possible! Cry to the Holy Spirit, the Comforter, to loose you from this snare of the fowler; for, depend upon it, doubting God is a net of Satan, and blessed is he who escapes its toils. Believing in God strengthens the soul and brings us both holiness and happiness, but distrusting, and suspecting, and surmising, and fearing, hardens the heart, and renders us less likely ever to come to God. Beware of despair; and may you, if you have fallen into this evil habit, be snatched from it as the brand from the burning, and delivered by the Lord, who looseth his prisoner.

III. Thirdly, this remarkable piece of folly ASSUMES DIVERS FORMS.

If I were to give a catalogue of the symptoms of this disease which I have met with, and have jotted down in my memory, I should need

---

1 Ezekiel 33:11.
2 Hosea 11:8, 9.

not an hour, but a month; for as each man hath something peculiar to himself, so each form of this melancholy bears about it a measure of distinctness. I can scarcely put them under divers heads and species: they are too many and too mixed. I think they say a sheep has so many diseases that you cannot count them; and I am sure men have a great many more mental maladies than I can tell. You might as well count the sands on the sea-shore as enumerate the soul's diseases. But certain forms are very common. For instance, one is *a persistent misrepresentation of the gospel*, as though it claimed some hard thing of us. Persons have been sitting in these seats now for years, who have heard us say, and who know the truth of it, from God's word, that all that is asked of the sinner is that he should trust in the work which Jesus Christ has wrought out—should trust Christ, in fact. We have in all manner of ways, as numerous and varied as our ingenuity could suggest, sought to show that there is nothing for the sinner to do, that he is to be nothing, but just get out of the way, and let Christ and the grace of God be everything; we have tried to show that to trust in Christ, which is the great saving act, is looking to him, resting on him, depending on him; we have multiplied figures and metaphors to make this plain, and yet as soon as ever we begin to talk to some of these who refuse to be comforted, they say, "But I am afraid, sir, that I have never been sufficiently made to feel the evil of sin." Now, did we ever say that feeling of sin was the great saving grace? Does not the word of God put it over and over again, that believing saves the soul, not feeling? Yet these people virtually deny the gospel, and set up another gospel; a gospel of feeling in the place of a gospel of trusting. "Oh! but," they will then say, "I have had these desires so many times before, and they have all gone, and I cannot expect that I should be accepted now." This is another denial of the gospel again. They make it out that God will only accept those who have not experienced good desires before, and repressed them. They reduce the gospel into this kind of thing: Ho, you who never had desires before, and never repressed them, you may come; whereas the gospel saith, "Whosoever will, let him take the water of life freely."[1] I could not give you all the

1 Revelation 22:17.

shapes and ways in which they will evade and mystify the gospel, but assuredly they use as much ingenuity to make themselves unhappy, as the most ardent spirit that ever lived ever used to discover a country or to win a crown.

Another shape of this malady is this: *many continually and persistently underestimate the power of the precious blood of Jesus.* Not, if you brought them to look, that they would dare affirm that Jesus could not save, or that his blood could not pardon sin, but, virtually, it comes to that. "Oh, I am such a sinner!" And what if you are? Did not Christ come to save sinners, even the very chief? What has the greatness of your sinnership to do with it? Is not Christ a greater Savior than you are a sinner; towering high the mountain of his mercy far outtops the hills of your guiltiness? Yes, but you do not think so. Ay, and herein you limit the efficacy of an infinite atonement, and so dishonor the blood of Jesus Christ. There are some who will then say, "But I have sinned such-and-such a sin." What, and cannot the blood of Jesus wash that away? "All manner of sin and blasphemy shall be forgiven unto men."[1] There is no sin which thou canst by any possibility have committed, which Jesus cannot pardon, if thou wilt come to him and trust him; for "the blood of Jesus Christ, God's dear Son, cleanseth us from all sin."[2] Why, believe me, sinner, though thy sin is such that of itself it will damn thee to all eternity, beyond all hope, though it is such that could thy tears for ever flow, not a particle of it could ever be washed out, yet in a moment it shall vanish if thou dost but now trust in that bleeding Savior. There is nothing in thy sin that now can obstruct the power of the bleeding Savior. God will at once forgive thee. But I know that thou wilt still slander my Lord Jesus, and refuse his comfort. I pray him therefore to forgive thee this wrong, and bring thee, by his Holy Spirit, into a saner mind, to believe that he is able and willing, and to doubt no more.

Many cast their doubts into the shape of *foolish inferences drawn from the doctrine of predestination.* I do not find that the doctrine of predestination impresses people in the way of sadness in any way

---

1 Matthew 12:31.

2 1 John 1:7.

except that of religion. Everybody believes that there is a predestination about the casting of lots, and yet the spirit of gambling is rife everywhere, and men in crowds subscribe to the public lotteries, which to our shame are still tolerated. They know that only two or three can win a large prize, yet away goes the money, and nobody stands at the office door and says, "I shall not invest my money, because if I am to get a prize I shall get a prize, and if I am not to win a prize I shall not do so." Men are not such fools when they come to things of common life as they are when they deal with religion. This predestination sticks in the way of many as a huge stumbling-block when they come to the things of God. The fact is, there is nothing in predestination to stumble a man; the evil lies in what he chooses to make of it. When a man wants to beat a dog, they say he can always find a stick to do it with; and when a man wants to find excuses for not believing in Christ, he can always discover one somewhere or other. For this cause so many run to this predestination doctrine, because it happens to be a handy place of resort. Now, God has a people whom he will save, a chosen and special people, redeemed by the blood of Christ; but there is no more in that doctrine to deny the other grand truth that whosoever believeth in Jesus Christ is not condemned, than there is in the fact that Abyssinia is in Africa, to contradict the doctrine that Hindostan is in Asia. They are two truths which stand together, and though it may not always be easy for us to reconcile them, it would be more difficult to make them disagree. There never seems to me to be any need to reconcile the two truths, nor, indeed, any practical difficulty in the matter; the difficulty is metaphysical, and what have lost sinners to do with metaphysics? Fixed is everything, from the motion of a grain of dust in the summer's wind to the revolution of a planet in its orbit, and yet man is as free as if there was no God, as independent an actor as if everything were left to chance. I see indelible marks both of predestination and free agency everywhere in God's universe. Then why do you ask questions about your election when God says, "whosoever will?" It is foolish to stand and ask whether you are ordained to come when the invitation bids you come. Come, and you are ordained to come; stay away, and you deserve to perish.

Yonder is the gate of the hospital for sick souls, and over it is written, "Whosoever will, let him come," and you stand outside that house of mercy, and say, "I do not know whether I am ordained to enter." There is the invitation, man! Why are you so mad? Would you talk like that at Guy's or at Bartholomew's Hospital? Would you say to the kind persons who picked you up in the street, and carried you to the hospital, "Oh, for goodness' sake, do not take me in, I do not know whether I am ordained to go in or not?" You know the hospital was built for such as are sick and wounded, and when you are taken in you perceive that it was built for you. I do not know how you are to find whether you were ordained to enter the hospital or not, except by getting in; and I do not know how you are to find out your election to salvation, except by trusting Jesus Christ, who bids you trust, and promises that if you do so you shall be saved. You may smile, but these things which to some of us are like spiders' nets, through which we break, are like nets of iron to those desponding ones whose soul refuseth to be comforted.

I have known others, and here I shall close this list, who have tried to find a hole in which to hide their eyes from the comforting light in the thought of *the unpardonable sin*. The greatest divines who have written on this subject have never been able to prove anything about it, except that all the other divines are wrong. I have never yet read a book upon the subject which did not, one-half of it, consist in proving that all who had written before knew nothing at all on the subject, and I have come to the conclusion, when I have finished each treatise, that the writer was about as right as his predecessors, and no more. Whatever the unpardonable sin may be, and perhaps it is different in every person—perhaps it is a point of sin in each one, a filling up of his measure, beyond which there is no more hope of mercy—whatever it is, there is one thing that is sure, that no man who feels his need of Christ, and sincerely desires to be saved, can have committed that sin at all. If you had committed that sin, it would be to you death. "There is a sin which is unto death." Now, death puts an end to feeling. You would be given up to hardness and to incorrigible impenitence. The reason why you could not be saved would be because your will would become fast set against all good, and you never would will to be saved. For there is no difficulty in salvation when the will is made right; and if thou hast a will, and God has made thee willing to come to Christ and to be saved, thou hast no more committed the unpardonable sin than has the angel Gabriel who stands at God's right hand. If thy heart palpitates still with fear, if thy soul still trembles before the law of God, and dreads his wrath, then still art thou within the bounds of mercy; and the silver trumpet sounds this morning sweet and shrill, "Whosoever will, let him take of the water of life freely." "Believe in the Lord Jesus Christ, and thou shalt be saved."

IV. We will not continue that dreary catalogue, but turn to a fourth consideration, namely, that this refusal to be comforted INVOLVES MUCH OF WRONG.

Much of it we can readily forgive; still we must mention it. When you hear the gospel and refuse to be comforted by it, there is a wrong done to the minister of God. He sympathizes with you, he desires to comfort you, and it troubles him when he puts before you the cup of salvation, and you refuse to take it. Now, I do not say that we in our private persons claim any great respect from you, but I do say that to reject God's ambassador may not be a light sin, and to cause the man whom God sends to speak words of mercy to you to go with a heavy heart again and again to his knees, may be such a sin as will rankle in your soul in years to come, if it be not repented of.

But worse than that, you wrong God's gospel. Every time you refuse to be comforted, you do as good as say, "The gospel is of no use to me; I do not esteem it; I will not have it." You put it away as though it were a thing of nought. You wrong this precious Bible. It is full of consoling promises, and you read it, and you seem to say, "It is all chaff." You act as if you had winnowed it and found no food in it. It is a barren wilderness to you. Oh, but the Bible does not deserve to have such a slur cast upon it.

You do wrong to the dear friends who try to comfort you. Why should they so often bring you with loving hands the words of comfort and you put them away?

Above all, you do wrong to your God, to Jesus, and to his Holy Spirit. The crucifixion of Christ is repeated by your rejection of Christ. That unkind, ungenerous thought, that he is unwilling to forgive, crucifies him afresh. Grieve not the Holy Spirit—

> "He's waited long, is waiting still;
> You use no other friend so ill."[1]

He is the Spirit of consolation, and when you refuse the consolation, you virtually reject him, reject him to your shame.

Think, dear friends, wherever you may be this morning, your refusing to be comforted is very wrong, because it is depriving the church of what you might do for it. Oh, if you became a cheerful Christian, what a mother in Israel you might be! I think I hear you sing as the virgin did of old, "He hath remembered the low estate of his handmaiden."[2] How would you rejoice with Hannah that "He raiseth up the poor out of the dust, and lifteth the needy out of the dunghill, that he may set him with princes."[3] How would your exultant psalm go up to heaven, "He hath filled the hungry with good things, and the rich he hath sent empty away."[4]

The world—what a wrong you are doing to it! Why, that part of the world which comes under your influence is led to say, "Religion makes that woman miserable: it is religion which makes that man so sad." You know it is not so. But they put it down to it—they say, "Religion drives people mad." I would sooner loose this right hand, and this right eye too, than have such a thing said of my religion. I cannot bear, when I do anything wrong that men should say, "That's your Christianity." If they lay the blame on me, who so well deserved it, then let me bear it; but to lay it on the cross of Christ—oh! this makes a man shudder.

V. I will close with this remark—that SUCH A REFUSAL SHOULD NOT BE PERSISTED IN.

---

1 *Behold, a Stranger at the Door* by Joseph Grigg.
2 Luke 1:48.
3 Psalm 113:7, 8.
4 Luke 1:53.

It is unreasonable to be sad when you might rejoice; it is *unreasonable* to be wretched when mercy provides every cause for making you happy. Why art thou sad, and why is thy countenance fallen? If there were no Savior, no Holy Spirit, no Father willing to forgive, you might go your way and put an end to your existence in despair; but while all this grace is ready for you, why not take it? One would think you were like Tantalus, placed up to his neck in water, which, when he tried to drink thereof, receded from his lips; but you are in no such condition. Instead of the water flowing away from you, it is rippling up to your lips; it is inviting you but to open your mouth and receive it.

While it is unreasonable to continue such a persistence, it is also *most weakening* to you. Every hour that you continue sad you spoil the possibilities of your getting out of that sadness. You are dissolving the strength even of your bodily frame; and, as for your soul, the pillars thereof are being shaken.

And, mark you, it is most dangerous, too; for may be—oh, I pray God it may not be!—it may be, that God, who gives you light, when he sees you shut your eyes again, will say, "Let his sun be darkened and his moon be turned into blood. The creature which I made for light rejects it, and no light shall ever come to it henceforth, even for ever." The King who kills the fatlings and makes ready the feast, and brings you to the table, if he sees you still refuse to partake, may swear in his wrath that you shall not eat of his supper. I have known parents, when their children cried for nothing, take care to give them something to cry for; and, may be, if you are miserable when there is no cause for it, you may have cause for it—cause that will never end. Oh! by the blood and wounds of Jesus, by the overflowing heart of God, by the eternal promises of grace, by the covenant which God hath made with sinners in the person of his Son, by the Holy Ghost the Comforter, put not from you the consolation which God provides; say no longer, "My soul refuseth to be comforted;" but cast yourself at Jesus' feet, and trust in him, and you are saved. God bless you and grant this prayer for Jesus' sake. Amen.

COMPASSION FOR SOULS

LORD'S-DAY MORNING, FEBRUARY 5TH, 1871, METROPOLITAN TABERNACLE

She went, and sat her down over against him a good way off, as it were a bow shot; for she said, Let me not see the death of the child. And she sat over against him, and lift up her voice, and wept.
—GENESIS 21:16.

Briefly let us rehearse the circumstances. The child Isaac was, according to God's word, to be the heir of Abraham. Ishmael, the elder son of Abraham, by the bondwoman Hagar, resided at home with his father till he was about eighteen years of age; but when he began to mock and scoff at the younger child whom God had ordained to be the heir, it became needful that he and his mother should be sent away from Abraham's encampment. It might have seemed unkind and heartless to have sent them forth, but God having arranged to provide for them sent a divine command which at once rendered their expulsion necessary, and certified its success. We may rest assured that whatever God commands he will be quite certain to justify. He knew it would be no cruelty to Hagar or Ishmael to be driven into independence, and he gave a promise which secured them everything which they desired. "Also of the son of the bondwoman will I make a great nation;"[1] and again, "I have blessed him, and will make him fruitful, and will multiply him exceedingly; twelve princes shall he beget, and I will make him a great nation."[2] Had they

1 Genesis 21:13.
2 Genesis 17:20.

both been able to go forth from Abraham's tent in faith they might have trodden the desert with a joyous footstep, fully assured that he who bade them go, and he who promised that he would bless them, would be certain to provide all things needful for them. Early in the morning they were sent forth on their journey, with as much provision as they could carry, and probably they intended to make their way to Egypt, from which Hagar had come. They may have lost their way; at any rate, they are spoken of as wandering. Their store of food became exhausted, the water in the skin bottle was all spent; both of them felt the fatigue of the wilderness, and the heat of the pitiless sand; they were both faint and weary, and the younger utterly failed. As long as the mother could sustain the tottering, fainting footsteps of her boy, she did so; when she could do so no longer, he swooned with weakness, and she laid him down beneath the slight shade of the desert tamarisk, that he might be as far as possible screened from the excessive heat of the sun. Looking into his face and seeing the pallor of coming death gathering upon it, knowing her inability to do anything whatever to revive him, or even to preserve his life, she could not bear to sit and gaze upon his face, but withdrew just far enough to be able still to watch with all a mother's care. She sat down in the brokenness of her spirit, her tears gushed forth in torrents, and heartrending cries of agony startled the rocks around. It was needful that the high spirit of the mother and her son should be broken down before they received prosperity: the mother had been on a former occasion graciously humbled by being placed in much the same condition, but she had probably relapsed into a haughty spirit, and had encouraged her boy in his insolence to Sarah's son, and therefore she must be chastened yet again; and it was equally needful that the high-spirited lad should for a little bear the yoke in his youth, and that he who would grow up to be the wild man, the father of the unconquerable Arab, should feel the power of God ere he received the fulfilment of the promise given to him in answer to Abraham's prayer. If I read the text aright, while the mother was thus weeping, the child, almost lost to all around, was nevertheless conscious enough of his own helpless condition, and sufficiently mindful of his father's God to cry in his soul to heaven for help; and the Lord heard not so much the mother's weeping (for the feebleness of her faith, which ought to have been stronger in memory of a former deliverance, hindered her prayer), but the silent, unuttered prayers of the fainting lad went up into the ears of Elohim, and the angel of Elohim appeared, and pointed to the well. The child received the needed draught of water, was soon restored, and in him and his posterity the promise of God received and continues to receive a large fulfilment. I am not about to speak upon that narrative except as it serves me with an illustration for the subject which I would now press upon you.

Behold the compassion of a mother for her child expiring with thirst, and remember that such a compassion ought all Christians to feel towards souls that are perishing for lack of Christ, perishing eternally, perishing without hope of salvation. If the mother lifted up her voice and wept, so also should we; and if the contemplation of her dying child was all too painful for her, so may the contemplation of the wrath to come, which is to pass upon every soul that dies impenitent, become too painful for us, but yet at the same time it should stimulate us to earnest prayer and ardent effort for the salvation of our fellow men.

I shall speak, this morning, upon *compassion for souls, the reasons which justify it, the sight it dreads, the temptation it must fight against, the paths it should pursue, the encouragement it may receive.*

I. Compassion for souls—the reasons which justify it, nay, compel it.

It scarce needs that I do more than rehearse in bare outline the reasons why we should tenderly compassionate the perishing sons of men. For first, observe, *the dreadful nature of the calamity which will overwhelm them.* Calamities occurring to our fellow men naturally awaken in us a feeling of commiseration; but what calamity under heaven can be equal to the ruin of a soul? What misery can be equal to that of a man cast away from God, and subject to his wrath world without end? Today your hearts are moved as you hear the harrowing details of war. They have been dreadful indeed; houses burnt, happy families driven as vagabonds upon the face of the earth, domestic circles and quiet households broken up, men wounded, mangled, massacred by thousands, and starved, I was about to say, by millions; but the miseries of war, if they were confined to this world alone, were nothing compared with the enormous catastrophe of tens of thousands of spirits accursed by sin, and driven by justice into the place where their worm dieth not, and their fire is not quenched. The edge of the sword grows blunt at last, the flame of war dies out for want of fuel, but, lo! I see before me a sword which is never quiet, a fire unquenchable. Alas! that the souls of men should fall beneath the infinite ire of justice. All your hearts have been moved of late with the thought of famine, famine in a great city. The dogs of war, and this the fiercest mastiff of them all, have laid hold upon the fair throat of the beautiful city which thought to sit as a lady for ever and see no sorrow; you are hastening with your gifts, if possible to remove her urgent want and to avert her starvation; but what is a famine of bread compared with that famine of the soul which our Lord describes when he represents it as pleading in vain for a drop of water to cool its tongue tormented in the flame? To be without bread for the body is terrible, but to be without the bread of life eternal, none of us can tell the weight of horror which lies there! When Robert Hall in one of the grand flights of his eloquence pictured the funeral of a lost soul, he made the sun to veil his light, and the moon her brightness; he covered the ocean with mourning and the heavens with sackcloth, and declared that if the whole fabric of nature could become animated and vocal, it would not be possible for her to utter a groan too deep, or a cry too piercing to express the magnitude and extent of the catastrophe. Time is not long enough for the sore lamentation which should attend the obsequies of a lost soul. Eternity must be charged with that boundless woe, and must utter it in weeping and wailing and gnashing of teeth. Not the tongues of prophets, nor of seraphs, could set forth all the sorrow of what it is to be condemned from the mouth of mercy, damned by the Savior who died to save, pronounced accursed by rejected love. The evil is so immense that imagination finds no place, and understanding utterly fails. Brethren, if our bowels do not yearn for men who are daily hastening towards destruction, are we men at all?

I could abundantly justify compassion for perishing men, even on the ground of *natural feelings*. A mother who did not, like Hagar, weep for her dying child—call her not "mother," call her "monster." A man who passes through the scenes of misery which even this city presents in its more squalid quarters, and yet is never disturbed by them, I venture to say he is unworthy of the name of man. Even the common sorrows of our race may well suffuse our eyes with tears, but the eternal sorrow, the infinite lake of misery—he who grieves not for this, write him down a demon, though he wear the image and semblance of a man. Do not think the less of this argument because I base it upon feelings common to all of woman born, for remember that grace does not destroy our manhood when it elevates it to a higher condition.

In this instance what nature suggests grace enforces. The more we become what we shall be, the more will compassion rule our hearts. The Lord Jesus Christ, who is the pattern and mirror of perfect manhood, what said he concerning the sins and the woes of Jerusalem? He knew Jerusalem must perish; did he bury his pity beneath the fact of the divine decree, and steel his heart by the thought of the sovereignty or the justice that would be resplendent in the city's destruction? Nay, not he, but with eyes gushing like founts, he cried, "O Jerusalem, Jerusalem, how often would I have gathered thy children together as a hen gathereth her chickens under her wings! and ye would not."[1] If you would be like Jesus, you must be tender and very pitiful. Ye would be as unlike him as possible if ye could sit down in grim content, and, with a Stoic's philosophy, turn all the flesh within you into stone. If it be natural, then, and above all, if it be natural to the higher grace given nature, I beseech you, let your hearts be moved with pity, do not endure to see the spiritual death of mankind. Be in agony as often as you contemplate the ruin of any soul of the seed of Adam.

Brethren, *the whole run and current, and tenor and spirit of the gospel* influences us to compassion. Ye are debtors, for what were ye if compassion had not come to your rescue? Divine compassion, all undeserved and free, has redeemed you from your vain conversation.

1 Matthew 23:37.

Surely those who receive mercy should show mercy; those who owe all they have to the pity of God, should not be pitiless to their brethren. The Savior never for a moment tolerates the self-righteous isolation which would make you despise the prodigal, and cavil at his restoration, much less the Cainite spirit which cries, "Am I my brother's keeper?"[1] No doctrine is rightly received by you if it freezes the genial current of your Christian compassion. You may know the truth of the doctrine, but you do not know the doctrine in truth if it makes you gaze on the wrath to come without emotions of pity for immortal souls. You shall find everywhere throughout the gospel that it rings of brotherly love, tender mercy, and weeping pity. If you have indeed received it in its power, the love of Christ will melt your spirit to compassion for those who are despising Christ, and sealing their own destruction.

Let me beseech you to believe that it is *needful* as well as justifiable that you should feel compassion for the sons of men. You all desire to glorify Christ by becoming soul-winners—I hope you do—and be it remembered that, other things being equal, he is the fittest in God's hand to win souls who pities souls most. I believe he preaches best who loves best, and in the Sunday-school and in private life each soul-seeker shall have the blessing very much in proportion to his yearning for it. Paul becomes a savior of many because his heart's desire and prayer to God is that they may be saved. If you *can* live without souls being converted, you shall live without their being converted; but if your soul breaketh for the longing that it hath towards Christ's glory and the conversion of the ungodly, if like her of old you say, "Give me children, or I die,"[2] your insatiable hunger shall be satisfied, the craving of your spirit shall be gratified. Oh! I would to God there should come upon us a divine hunger which cannot stay itself except men yield themselves to Jesus; an intense, earnest, longing, panting desire that men should submit themselves to the gospel of Jesus. This will teach you better than the best college training how to deal with human hearts. This will give the stammering

1 Genesis 4:9.
2 Genesis 30:1.

tongue the ready word; the hot heart shall burn the cords which held fast the tongue. You shall become wise to win souls, even though you never exhibit the brilliance of eloquence or the force of logic. Men shall wonder at your power—the secret shall be hidden from them, the fact being that the Holy Ghost shall overshadow you, and your heart shall teach you wisdom, God teaching your heart. Deep feeling on your part for others shall make others feel for themselves, and God shall bless you, and that right early.

But I stand not here any longer to justify what I would far rather commend and personally feel.

> "Did Christ o'er sinners weep,
>   And shall our cheeks be dry?
> Let floods of consecrated grief
>   Stream forth from every eye."[1]

Is God all love, and shall God's children be hard and cold? Shall heaven compassionate and shall not earth that has received heaven's mercy send back the echo of compassion? O God, make us imitators of thee in thy pity towards erring men.

II. We shall pass on to notice THE SIGHT WHICH TRUE COMPASSION DREADS.

Like Hagar, the compassionate spirit says, "Let me not see the death of the child,"[2] or as some have read it, "How can I see the death of the child?" To contemplate a soul passing away without hope is too terrible a task! I do not wonder that ingenious persons have invented theories which aim at mitigating the terrors of the world to come to the impenitent. It is natural they should do so, for the facts are so alarming as they are truthfully given us in God's word, that if we desire to preach comfortable doctrine and such as will quiet the consciences of idle professors, we must dilute the awful truth. The revelation of God concerning the doom of the wicked is so overwhelming as to make it penal, nay, I was about to say damnable, to be indifferent and careless in the work of evangelizing the world.

---

1 *Did Christ o'er Sinners Weep?* by Benjamin Beddome.
2 Genesis 21:16.

I do not wonder that this error in doctrine springs up just now when abounding callousness of heart needs an excuse for itself. What better pillow for idle heads than the doctrine that the finally impenitent become extinct? The logical reasoning of the sinner is, "Let us eat and drink, for tomorrow we die,"[1] and the professing Christian is not slow to feel an ease of heart from pressing responsibilities when he accepts so consolatory an opinion. Forbear this sleeping draught, I pray you, for in very deed the sharp stimulant of the truth itself is abundantly needful; even when thus bestirred to duty we are sluggish enough, and need not that these sweet but sleep-producing theories should operate upon us.

For a moment, I beseech you, contemplate that which causes horror to every tender heart; behold, I pray you, a soul lost, lost beyond all hope of restitution. Heaven's gates have shut upon the sanctified, and the myriads of the redeemed are there, but that soul is not among them, for it passed out of this world without having washed its robes in Jesus' blood. For it there are no harps of gold, no thrones of glory, no exultation with Christ; from all the bliss of heaven it is for ever excluded. This punishment of loss were a heavy enough theme for contemplation. The old divines used to speak much of the *poena damni*, or the punishment of loss; there were enough in that phase of the future to make us mourn bitterly, as David did for Absalom. My child shut out of heaven! My husband absent from the seats of the blessed! My sister, my brother not in glory! When the Lord counts up his chosen, my dear companion outside the gates of pearl, outside the jewelled battlements of the New Jerusalem! O God, 'tis a heartbreaking sorrow to think of this. But then comes the punishment added to the loss. What saith the Savior? "Where their worm dieth not, and the fire is not quenched."[2] "These shall go away into everlasting punishment."[3] And yet again, "And shall cut him asunder, and appoint him his portion with the hypocrites."[4] And

---

1 1 Corinthians 15:32.

2 Mark 9:44.

3 Matthew 25:46.

4 Matthew 24:51.

yet again, "Into outer darkness: there shall be weeping and gnashing of teeth."[1] "Metaphors," say you. It is true, but not meaningless
metaphors. There is a meaning in each expression—and rest assured
though man's metaphors sometimes exaggerate, God's never do; his
symbols everywhere are true; never is there an exaggeration in the language of inspiration. Extravagances of utterance! He uses them not;
his figures are substantial truth. Terrible as the scriptural emblems of
punishment are, they set forth matters of undoubted fact, which if a
man could look upon this day, the sight might blanch his hair, and
quench his eye. If we could hear the wailings of the pit for a moment,
we should earnestly entreat that we might never hear them again. We
have to thank God that we are not allowed to hear the dolorous cries
of the lost, for if we did they would make our life bitter as gall. I cast
a veil over that which I cannot paint; like Hagar, I cannot bear to look
at the dread reality which it breaks my heart to think upon.

How all this gathers intensity, when it comes to be our own child,
our own friend! Hagar might perhaps have looked upon a dying
child, but not upon her dying Ishmael. Can you bear now to think
for a moment of the perdition of your own flesh and blood? Does not
your spirit flinch and draw back with horror instinctively at the idea
of one of your own family being lost? Yet, as a matter of stern fact,
you know that some of them will be lost if they die as they are now
living? At God's right hand they cannot stand unless they be made
new creatures in Christ Jesus. You know that, do not try to forget it.

It will greatly add to your feeling of sorrow if you are forced to
feel that the ruin of your child or of any other person may have been
partly caused by your example. It must be a dreadful thing for a father
to feel, "My boy learned to drink from me; my child heard the first
blasphemous word from his father's lips." Or mother, if your dying
daughter should say, "I was led into temptation by my mother's example," what a grief will this be! O parents, converted late in life, you
cannot undo the evil which you have already done; God has forgiven
you, but the mischief wrought in your children's characters is indelible, unless the grace of God step in. I want you to seek after that grace

1 Matthew 25:30.

with great earnestness. As you must confess that you have helped to train your child as a servant of sin, will you not long to see your evil work undone before it ends in your child's eternal destruction?

If we shall have to feel that the ruin of any of our friends or relations is partly occasioned by our own personal neglect of religion, it will cause us bitter pangs. If our example has been excellent and admirable in all respects, but that we have forgotten the Lord and his Christ, it will have been none the less injurious to men's souls. I sometimes think that these examples are the very worst in their effect. Immoral, ungodly men can hardly work the same measure of mischief as moral but unchristian men. I will tell you why. The ungodly quote the orderly life of the moralist as an argument that there can be goodness apart from Christianity, and this often helps men to rest satisfied apart from Christ Jesus. And what, O moralist, though you never taught your child a vice, if you taught it unbelief, and if your example helped to harden its heart in bold rebellion against God! Ah! then, how will you blame yourself when you are converted, or curse yourself if both you and your child perish.

Dear friends, it makes a terrible addition to the sight of a soul being lost if we have to feel we were under responsibility concerning it, and have been in any measure unfaithful. I cannot bear the idea of any of my congregation perishing, for in addition to the compassion I hope I feel, I am influenced by a further additional consideration, for I am set as a watchman to your souls. When any die, I ask myself, "Was I faithful? Did I speak all the truth? And did I speak it from my very soul every time I preached?" John Walsh, the famous Scotch preacher, was often out of bed in the coldest night, by the hour together, in supplication; and when some one wondered that he spent so many hours upon his knees, he said, "Ah, man, I have three thousand souls to give account of in the day of judgment, and I do not know but what it is going very ill with some of them." Alas! I have more than that to give account of, and well may I cry to God that I may not see you perish. O may it never be that you shall go from these pews to the lowest hell. You, too, my fellow Christian, have your own responsibilities, each one in your measure—your children, your school classes, your servants, ay, and your neighbors, for if you are not doing any good and do not assume any responsibility towards the regions in which you dwell, that responsibility rests upon you none the less. You cannot live in a district without being responsible to God for doing something towards the bettering of the people among whom you reside. Can you endure it then, that your neighbors should sink into hell? Do not your hearts long for their salvation?

Is it not an awful thing that a soul should perish with the gospel so near? If Ishmael had died, and the water had been within bow-shot, and yet unseen till too late, it had been a dreadful reflection for the mother. Would she not have torn her hair with double sorrow? And yet many of you are being lost with the gospel ringing in your ears; you are perishing while Christ is lifted up before you; you are dying in the camp through the serpent's bite, though the brazen serpent is yonder before your eyes, and with many tears we cry to you, "Look unto Jesus Christ, and live!" Ah, woe is me, woe is me, if you perish when salvation is brought so close home to you. Some of you are very near the kingdom of God; you are very anxious, very concerned, but you have not believed in Jesus; you have much that is good, but one thing you lack. Will you perish for lack of only one thing? A thousand pities will it be if you make shipwreck in the harbor's mouth and go to hell from the gates of heaven.

We must add to all this, the remembrance that it is not one soul which is lost, but tens of thousands are going down to the pit. Mr. Beecher said in one of his sermons, "If there were a great bell hung high in heaven which the angels swung every time a soul was lost, how constantly would its solemn toll be heard!" A soul lost! The thunder would not suffice to make a knell for a lost spirit. Each time the clock ticks a soul departs out of this world, perhaps oftener than that, and out of those who make the last journey how few mount to the skies; what multitudes descend to endless woe! O Christians, pull up the sluices of your souls, and let your hearts pour out themselves in rivers of compassion.

III. In the third place, I said I would speak upon COMPASSION

FOR THE SOULS OF MEN—THE TEMPTATION IT MUST RESIST.

We must not fall into the temptation to imitate the example of Hagar too closely. She put the child under the shrubs and turned away her gaze from the all too mournful spectacle. She could not endure to look, but she sat where she could watch in despair. There is a temptation with each one of us to try to forget that souls are being lost. I can go home to my house along respectable streets, and naturally should choose that way, for then I need not see the poverty of the lowest quarters of the city, but am I right if I try to forget that there are Bethnal Greens and Kent Streets, and such like abodes of poverty? The close courts, the cellars, the crowded garrets, the lodging-houses—am I to forget that these exist? Surely the only way for a charitable mind to sleep comfortably in London is to forget how one half of the population lives; but is it our object to live comfortably? Are we such brute beasts that comfort is all we care for, like swine in their stye? Nay, brethren, let us recall to our memories the sins of our great city, its sorrows and griefs, and let us remember also the sins and sorrows of the wide, wide world, and the tens of thousands of our race who are passing constantly into eternity. Nay, look at them! Do not close those eyes! Does the horror of the vision make your eyeballs ache? Then look until your heart aches too, and your spirit breaks forth in vehement agony before the Lord. Look down into hell a moment; open wide the door; listen, and listen yet again. You say you cannot, it sickens your soul; let it be sickened, and in its swooning let it fall back into the arms of Christ the Savior, and breathe out a cry that he would hasten to save men from the wrath to come. Do not ignore, I pray you, what does exist. It is a matter of fact that in this congregation many are going down to hell, that in this city there are multitudes who are hastening as certainly to perdition as time is hastening to eternity. It is no dream, no fiction of a fevered brain that there is a hell. If you think so, then why dare you call yourselves Christians? Renounce your Bible, renounce your baptism, renounce your profession if one spark of honesty remains in you. Call not yourselves Christians when you deny the teaching of your Master. Since assuredly there is a dreadful hell, shut not your eyes to it, put not the souls of your fellows away among the shrubs, and sit not down in supineness. Come and look, come and look, I say, till your hearts break at the sight. Hear the cries of dying men whose consciences are awakened too late. Hear the groans of spirits who are feeling the sure consequences of sin, where sin's cure will never avail them. Let this stir you, my brethren, to action—to action immediate and intense. You tell me I preach dreadful things; ay, and they are wanted, they are wanted. Was there ever such a sleepy age as this? Were there ever such sleepy persons as ourselves? Take heed lest you take sad precedence of all others in the accusations of conscience, because knowing the gospel, and enjoying it, you nevertheless use so little exertion in spreading it abroad among the human race. Let us shun the temptation which Hagar's example might suggest.

IV. I will now speak upon THE PATH WHICH TRUE COMPASSION WILL BE SURE TO FOLLOW; and what is that?

First of all, *true pity does all it can*. Before Hagar sat down and wept, she had done her utmost for her boy; she had given him the last drop from the bottle; she had supported his tottering footsteps, she had sought out the place under the shrubs where he might be a little sheltered; she had laid him down gently with soothing words, and then, but not till then, she sat herself down. Have we done all that it is possible for us to do for the unconverted around us? There are preventable causes of men's ruin. Some causes you and I cannot touch, but there are some we ought at once to remove. For instance, it is certain that many perish through ignorance. It ought never to be that a soul should perish of ignorance within a mile of where a Christian lives. I would even allot a wider area in regions where the people dwell not so thickly. It should at least be the resolve of each Christian, "Within this district where I live, so far as my ability goes, everybody shall know the gospel by some means or other. If I cannot speak to each one I will send something for him to read; it shall not be said that a man lost his way for ever because he had no Bible." The Holy Ghost alone can lead men into the truth, but it is our part to put the letter of the word before all men's eyes.

Prejudice, too, is another preventable cause of unbelief. Some will not hear the gospel, or listen to it, because of their notions of its sternness, or of the moroseness of its professors. Such a prejudice may effectually close their hearts; be it yours to remove it. Be kind to the ungodly; be loving, be tender, be affable, be generous to them, so that you may remove all unnecessary antipathy to the gospel of Jesus. Do them all the good you can for their bodies, that they may be the more likely to believe in your love towards their souls. Let it be said by each one here, "If a soul perishes, I, at least, will have done all in my power to reclaim it."

But what next does compassion do? Having done all it can, it sits down and weeps over its own feebleness. I have not the pathos wherewith to describe to you the mother sitting there and pouring out her tears, and lifting up her plaintive voice over her child. The voice of a broken heart cannot be described, it must be heard. But, ah! there is wonderful power with God in the strong crying and tears of his people. If you know how to weep before the Lord, he will yield to tears what he will not yield to anything besides. O ye saints, compassionate sinners; sigh and cry for them; be able to say, as Whitefield could to his congregation, "Sirs, if ye are lost, it is not for want of my weeping for you, for I pour out my soul day and night in petitions unto God that ye may live." When Hagar's compassion had wailed itself out, she looked unto God, and God heard her. Take care that your prayers be abundant and continuous for those who are dying without hope.

And then what else doth Hagar teach us? She stood there ready to do anything that was needful after the Lord had interposed. The angel opened her eyes; until then she was powerless, and sat and wept, and prayed, but when he pointed to the well, did she linger for a minute? Was she unprepared with the bottle wherewith to draw water? Did she delay to put it to her child's lips? Was she slack in the blessed task? Oh, no! with what alacrity did she spring to the well; with what speed did she fill the bottle; with what motherly joy did she hasten to her child, and give him the saving draught! And so I want every member here to stand ready to mark the faintest indication of grace in any soul. Watch always for the beginning of their conversion, be ready with the bottle of promise to carry a little comfort to their parched lips; watch with a mother's earnestness, watch for the opportunity of doing good to souls; yearn over them, so that when God shall work you shall work with him *instanter*, and Jesus shall not be hindered because of your carelessness and want of faith. This is the path which the true Christian should pursue. He is earnest for souls, and therefore he lays himself out for them. If we did really know what souls are, and what it is for them to be cast away, those of us who have done very little or nothing would begin to work for Christ directly. It is said in old classic story, that a certain king of Lydia had a son who had been dumb from his birth, but when Lydia was captured, a soldier was about to kill the king, when the young man suddenly found a tongue, and cried out, "Soldier, would you kill the king?" He had never spoken a word before, but his astonishment and fear gave him speech. And methinks if ye had been dumb to that moment, if ye indeed saw your own children and neighbors going down into the pit, you would cry out, "Though I never spoke before I will speak now. Poor souls, believe in Christ, and ye shall be saved." You do not know how such an utterance as that, however simple, might be blessed. A very little child once found herself in company with an old man of eighty, a fine old man who loved little children, and who took the child upon his knee to fondle it. The little one turning round to him said, "Sir, I got a grandpa just like you, and my grandpa love Jesus Christ, does you?" He said, "I was eighty-four years of age and had lived always among Christian people, but nobody ever thought it worth his while to say as much as that to me." That little child was the instrument of the old man's conversion. So have I heard the story. He knew he had not loved the Savior, and he began to seek him, and in his old age he found salvation. If as much as that is possible to a child it is possible to you. O dear brother, if you love Jesus, burst the bonds of timidity, or it may be of supineness; snap all fetters, and from this day feel that you cannot bear to think of the ruin of a soul, and must seek its salvation if there be in earth or heaven ways and means by which you can bring a blessing to it.

V. But I must close, and the last point shall be THE ENCOURAGEMENT WHICH TRUE COMPASSION FOR SOULS WILL ALWAYS RECEIVE.

First take the case in hand. The mother compassionated, God compassionated too. You pity, God pities. The motions of God's Spirit in the souls of his people are the footfalls of God's eternal purposes about to be fulfilled. It is always a hopeful sign for a man that another man prays for him. There is a difficulty in getting a man to hell whom a child of God is drawing towards heaven by his intercessions. Satan is often defeated in his temptations by the intercession of the saints. Have hope then that your personal sense of compassion for souls is an indication that such souls God will bless. Ishmael, whom Hagar pitied, was a lad about whom promises had been made large and broad; he could not die; *she* had forgotten that, but God had not. No thirst could possibly destroy him, for God had said he would make of him a great nation. Let us hope that those for whom you and I are praying and laboring are in God's eternal purpose secured from hell, because the blood of Christ has bought them, and they must be the Lord's. Our prayers are ensigns of the will of God. The Holy Ghost leads us to pray for those whom he intends effectually to call.

Moreover, those we pray for, we may not know it, but there may be in their souls at this time a stirring of divine life. Hagar did not know that her son was praying, but God did. The lad did not speak, but God heard his heart cry. Children are often very reticent to their parents. Often and often have I talked with young lads about their souls, who have told me that they could not talk to their fathers upon such matters. I know it was so with me. When I was under concern of soul the last persons I should have elected to speak to upon religion would have been my parents, not out of want of love to them, nor absence of love on their part; but so it was. A strange feeling of diffidence pervades a seeking soul, and drives it from its friends. Those whom you are praying for may be praying too, and you do not know it; but the time of love will come when their secret yearnings will be revealed to your earnest endeavors.

The lad was preserved after all, the well of waters was revealed, and the bottle put to his lips. It will be a great comfort to you to believe that God will hear importunate prayers. Your child will be saved, your husband will be brought in yet, good woman, only pray on.

Your neighbor shall be brought to hear the truth and be converted, only be earnest about it.

I do not know how to preach, this morning; the tongue cannot readily speak when the heart feels too much. I pray that we may have a great revival of religion in our midst as a church; my spirit longs and pants for it. I see a great engine of enormous strength, and a well-fashioned machine: the machine cannot work of itself, it has no power in it, but if I could get the band to unite the machine with the engine, what might be done! Behold, I see the omnipotence of God, and the organization of this church. O that I could get the band to bind the two together! The band is living faith. Do you possess it? Brethren, help me to pass it round the fly wheel, and oh, how God will work, and we will work through his power, and what glorious things shall be done for Christ! We must receive power from on high, and faith is the belt that shall convey that power to us. The divine strength shall be manifest through our weakness. Cease not to pray. More than you ever have done, intercede for a blessing, and the Lord will bless us: he will bless us, and all the ends of the earth shall fear him. Amen.

FOR THE TROUBLED

Lord's-day Morning, January 12th, 1873, Metropolitan Tabernacle

Thy wrath lieth hard upon me, and them hast afflicted me with all thy waves.—Psalm 88:7.

It is the business of a shepherd not only to look after the happy ones among the sheep, but to seek after the sick of the flock, and to lay himself out right earnestly for their comfort and succor. I feel, therefore, that I do rightly when I this morning make it my special business to speak to such as are in trouble. Those of you who are happy and rejoicing in God, full of faith and assurance, can very well spare a discourse for your weaker brethren; you can be even glad and thankful to go without your portion, that those who are depressed in spirit may receive a double measure of the wine of consolation. Moreover, I am not sure that even the most joyous Christian is any the worse for remembering the days of darkness which are stealing on apace, "for they are many." Just as the memories of our dying friends come o'er us like a cloud, and "damp our brainless ardors," so will the recollection that there are tribulations and afflictions in the world sober our rejoicing, and prevent its degenerating into an idolatry of the things of time and sense. It is better for many reasons to go to the house of mourning than to the house of feasting; the quassia cup has virtues in it which the wine cup never knew; wet thy lips with it, young man, it will work thee no ill. It may be, O thou who art today brimming with happiness, that a little store of sacred cautions and consolations may prove no sore to thee, but may by and by stand thee in good stead. This morning's discourse upon sorrow may suggest a few thoughts to thee which, being treasured up, shall ripen like summer fruit, and mellow by the time thy winter shall come round.

But to our work. It is clear to all those who read the narratives of Scripture, or are acquainted with good men, that the best of God's servants may be brought into the very lowest estate. There is no promise of present prosperity appointed to true religion, so as to exclude adversity from believer's lives. As men, the people of God share the common lot of men, and what is that but trouble? Yea, there are some sorrows which are peculiar to Christians, some extra griefs of which they partake because they are believers, though these are something more than balanced by those peculiar and bitter troubles which belong to the ungodly, and are engendered by their transgressions, from which the Christian is delivered. From the passage which is open before us, we learn that sons of God may be brought so low as to write and sing psalms which are sorrowful throughout, and have no fitting accompaniment but sighs and groans. They do not often do so; their songs are generally like those of David, which if they begin in the dust mount into the clear heavens before long; but sometimes, I say, saints are forced to sing such dolorous ditties that from beginning to end there is not one note of joy. Yet even in their dreariest winter night, the saints have an aurora in their sky, and in this Eighty-eighth Psalm, the dreariest of all psalms, there is a faint gleam in the first verse, like a star-ray falling upon its threshold—"O Jehovah, God of my salvation." Heman retained his hold upon his God. It is not all darkness in a heart which can cry, "My God;" and the child of God, however low he may sink, still keeps hold upon his God. "Though he slay me, yet will I trust in him,"[1] is the resolution of his soul. Jehovah smites me, but he is my God. He frowns upon me, but he is my God. He tramples me into the very dust, and lays me in the lowest pit, as among the dead, yet still he is my God, and such will I call him till I die: even when he leaves me I will cry, "My

1 Job 13:15.

God, my God, why hast thou forsaken me?"[1] Moreover, the believer in his worst time still continues to pray, and prays, perhaps, the more vigorously because of his sorrows. God's rod flogs his child not from him, but to him. Our griefs are waves which wash us to the rock. This psalm is full of prayer, it is as much sweetened with supplication as it is salted with sorrow. It weeps like Niobe, but it is on bended knees, and from uplifted eyes. Now, while a man can pray he is never far from light; he is at the window, though, perhaps, as yet the curtains are not drawn aside. The man who can pray has the clue in his hand by which to escape from the labyrinth of affliction. Like the trees in winter, we may say of the praying man, when his heart is greatly troubled, "his substance is in him, though he has lost his leaves." Prayer is the soul's breath, and if it breathes it lives, and, living, it will gather strength again. A man must have true and eternal life within him while he can continue still to pray, and while there is such life there is assured hope. Still the best child of God may be the greatest sufferer, and his sufferings may appear to be crushing, killing, and overwhelming; they may also be so very protracted as to attend him all his days, and their bitterness may be intense; all of which and much more this mournful psalm teaches us.

Let us, in pursuit of our subject, first give *an exposition of the text;* and then *a brief exposition of the benefits of trouble.*

I. I will endeavor, in a few observations, to EXPOUND THE TEXT.

In the first place, its strong language suggests the remark that *tried saints are very prone to overrate their afflictions.* I believe we all err in that direction, and are far too apt to say, "I am the man that hath seen affliction." The inspired man of God, who wrote our text, was touched with this common infirmity, for he overstates his case. Read his words, "Thy wrath lieth hard upon me." I have no doubt Heman meant wrath in its worst sense. He believed that God was really angry with him, and wrathful with him, even as he is with the ungodly; but that was not true. As we shall have to show by-and-by, there is a very grave difference between the anger of God with his children and the anger of God with his enemies; and we do not think

---

1 Psalm 22:1.

Heman sufficiently discerned that difference, even as we are afraid that many of God's children even now forget it, and therefore fear that the Lord is punishing them according to strict justice, and smiting them as though he were their executioner. Ah, if poor bewildered believers could but see it, they would learn that the very thing which they call wrath is only love, in its own wise manner, seeking their highest good. Besides, the Psalmist saith, "Thy wrath *lieth hard upon me.*" Ah, if Heman had known what it was to have God's wrath lie hard on him, he would have withdrawn that word, for all the wrath that any man ever feels in this life is but as a laying on of God's little finger. It is in the world to come that the wrath of God lies heavy on men. Then when God putteth forth his hand and presses with omnipotence upon soul and body to destroy them for ever in hell, the ruined nature feels in its never-ending destruction what the power of God's anger really is. Here the really sore pressure of wrath is not known, and especially not known by a child of God. It is too strong a speech if we weigh it in the scales of sober truth. It out-runs the fact, even though it were the most sorrowful living man that uttered it. Then Heman adds, "Thou hast afflicted me with *all* thy waves;" as though he were a wreck with the sea breaking over him, and the whole ocean, and all the oceans, were running full against him as the only object of their fury. His barque has been driven on shore and all the breakers are rolling over him; one after another they leap upon him like wild beasts, hungry as wolves, eager as lions to devour him: it seemed to him that no wave turned aside, no billow spent its force elsewhere, but all the long line of breakers roared upon him, as the sole object of their wrath. But it was not so. *All* God's waves have broken over no man, save only the Son of Man. There are still some troubles which we have been spared, some woes to us unknown. Have we suffered all the diseases which flesh is heir to? Are there not modes of pain from which our bodies have escaped? Are there not also some mental pangs which have not wrung our spirit? And what if we seem to have traversed the entire circle of bodily and mental misery, yet in our homes, households, or friendships we have surely some comfort left, and therefore from some rough billow we are screened. All

God's waves had not gone over thee, O Heman, the woes of Job and Jeremiah were not thine. Among the living none can literally know what *all* God's waves would be. They know, who are condemned to feel the blasts of his indignation, they know in the land of darkness and of everlasting hurricane; they know what all God's waves and billows are; but we know not. The metaphor is good and admirable, and correct enough poetically, but as a statement of fact it is strained. We are all apt to aggravate our grief: I say this here as a general fact, which you who are happy can bear to be told, but I would not vex the sick man with it while he is enduring the weight of his affliction. If he can calmly accept the suggestion of his own accord, it may do him good, but it would be cruel to throw it at him. True as it is, I should not like to whisper it in any sufferer's ear, because it would not console but grieve him. I have often marvelled at the strange comfort persons offer you when they say, "Ah, there are others who suffer more than you do." Am I a demon then? Am I expected to rejoice at the news of other people's miseries? Far otherwise, I am pained to think there should be sharper smarts than mine, my sympathy increases my own woe. I can conceive of a fiend in torment finding solace in the belief that others are tortured with a yet fiercer flame, but surely such diabolical comfort should not be offered to Christian men. It shows our deep depravity of heart, that we can decoct comfort out of the miseries of others; and yet I am afraid we rightly judge human nature when we offer it water from that putrid well. There is, however, a form of comfort akin to it, but of far more legitimate origin, a consolation honorable and divine. There was ONE upon whom God's wrath pressed very sorely, ONE who was in truth afflicted with all God's waves, and that ONE is our brother, a man like ourselves, the dearest lover of our souls; and because he has known and suffered all this, he can enter into sympathy with us this morning whatever tribulation may beat upon us. His passion is all over now, but not his compassion. He has borne the indignation of God, and turned it all away from us: the waves have lost their fury, and spent their force on him, and now he sitteth above the floods, yea, he sitteth King for ever and ever. As we think of him, the Crucified, our souls may not only derive consolation from his sympathy and powerful succor, but we may learn to look upon our trials with a calmer eye, and judge them more according to the true standard. In the presence of Christ's cross our own crosses are less colossal. Our thorns in the flesh are as nothing when laid side by side with the nails and spear.

But, secondly, let us remark that *saints do well to trace all their trials to their God.* Heman did so in the text: "*Thy* wrath lieth hard upon me, *thou* hast afflicted me with all *thy* waves." He traces all his adversity to the Lord his God. It is God's wrath, they are God's waves that afflict him, and God makes them afflict him. Child of God, never forget this; all that thou art suffering of any sort, or kind, comes to thee from the divine hand. Truly, thou sayest, "my affliction arises from wicked men," yet remember that there is a predestination which, without soiling the fingers of the Infinitely Holy, nevertheless rules the motions of evil men as well as of holy angels. It were a dreary thing for us if there were no appointments of God's providence which concerned the ungodly; then the great mass of mankind would be entirely left to chance, and the godly might be crushed by them without hope. The Lord, without interfering with the freedom of their wills, rules and overrules, so that the ungodly are as a rod in his hand, with which he wisely scourges his children. Perhaps you will say that your trials have arisen not from the sins of others, but from your own sin. Even then I would have you penitently trace them still to God. What though the trouble spring out of the sin, yet it is God that hath appointed the sorrow to follow the transgression, to act as a remedial agency for your spirit. Look not at the second cause, or, looking at it with deep regret, turn your eye chiefly to your heavenly Father, and "hear ye the rod and who hath appointed it." The Lord sends upon us the evil as well as the good of this mortal life; his is the sun that cheers and the frost that chills; his the deep calm and his the fierce tornado. To dwell on second causes is frequently frivolous, a sort of solemn trifling. Men say of each affliction, "It might have been prevented *if* so and so had occurred." Perhaps if another physician had been called in, the dear child's life had still been spared; possibly if I had moved in such a direction in business I might not have been a loser. Who is to judge of what might have been? In end-less conjectures we are lost, and, cruel to ourselves, we gather material for unnecessary griefs. Matters happened not so; then why conjecture what would have been had things been different? It is folly. You did your best, and it did not answer: why rebel? To fix the eye upon the second cause will irritate the mind. We grow indignant with the more immediate agent of our grief, and so fail to submit ourselves to God. If you strike a dog he will snap at the staff which hurts him, as if *it* were to blame. How doggish we sometimes are, when God is smiting us we are snarling at his rod. Brother, forgive the man who injured thee,—his was the sin, forgive it, as thou hopest to be forgiven; but thine is the chastisement, and it comes from God, therefore endure it and ask grace to profit by it. The more we get away from intermediate agents the better, for when we reach to God grace will make submission easy. When we know "it is the Lord," we readily cry, "let him do what seemeth him good." As long as I trace my pain to accident, my bereavement to mistake, my loss to another's wrong, my discomfort to an enemy, and so on, I am of the earth earthy, and shall break my teeth with gravel stones; but when I rise to my God and see his hand at work, I grow calm, I have not a word of repining, "I open not my mouth because thou didst it."[1] David preferred to fall into the hands of God, and every believer knows that he feels safest and happiest when he recognizes that he is even yet in the divine hands. Cavilling with man is poor work, but pleading with God brings help and comfort. "Cast thy burden on the Lord" is a precept which it will be easy to practise when you see that the burden came originally from God.

But now, thirdly, *afflicted children of God do well to have a keen eye to the wrath that mingles with their troubles.* "Thy *wrath* lieth hard upon me." There is Heman's first point. He does not mention the waves of affliction till he has first spoken of the wrath. We should labor to discover what the Lord means by smiting us; what he purposes by the chastisement, and how far we can answer that purpose. We must use a keen eye clearly *to distinguish* things. There is an anger and an anger, a wrath and a wrath. God is never angry with his

1 Psalm 39:9.

children in one sense, but he is in another. As men, we have all of us disobeyed the laws of God, and God stands in relationship to all of us as a judge. As a judge, he must execute upon us the penalties of his law, and he must, from the necessity of his nature, be angry with us for having broken that law. That concerns all the human race. But the moment a man believes in the Lord Jesus Christ his offences are his offences no longer; they are laid upon Christ Jesus, the substitute, and the anger goes with the sin. The anger of God towards the sins of believers has spent itself upon Christ. Christ has been punished in their stead; the punishment due to their sin has been borne by Jesus Christ. God forbid that the Judge of all the earth should ever be unjust, it were not just for God to punish a believer for a sin which has been already laid upon Jesus Christ. Hence the believer is altogether free from all liability to suffer the judicial anger of God, and all risk of receiving a punitive sentence from the Most High. The man is absolved—shall he be judged again? The man has paid the debt—shall he be brought a second time before the judge, as though he were still a debtor? Christ has stood for him in his place and stead, and therefore he boldly asks, "Who shall lay anything to the charge of God's elect? It is God that justifieth. Who is he that condemneth? It is Christ that died, yea rather, that is risen again, who is even the right hand of God, who also maketh intercession for us." Now, then, the Christian man takes up another position; he is adopted into the family of God: he has become God's child. He is under the law of God's house. There is in every house an economy, a law by which the children and servants are ruled. If the child of God breaks the law of the house the Father will visit his offence with fatherly stripes,—a very different kind of visitation from that of a judge. There are felons in prison today who in a short time will feel the lash on their bare backs that is one thing; but yonder disobedient child is to receive a whipping from his father's hand, that is quite another thing. Wide as the poles asunder are the anger of a judge and the anger of a father. The father loves the child while he is angry, and is mainly angry for that very reason; if it were not his child he would probably take no notice of its fault, but because it is his own boy who has spoken an untruth or committed an act of disobedience he feels he must chastise him, because he loves him. This needs no further explanation. There is a righteous anger in God's heart towards guilty impenitent men; he feels none of that towards his people. He is their father, and if they transgress he will visit them with stripes, not as a legal punishment, since Christ has borne all that, but as a gentle paternal chastisement, that they may see their folly and repent of it; and that awakened by his tender hand, they may turn unto their Father and amend their ways. Now, child of God, if you are suffering today in any way whatever, whether from the ills of poverty or bodily sickness, or depression of spirits, recollect there is not a drop of the judicial anger of God in it all. You are not being punished for your sins as a judge punishes a culprit;—never believe such false doctrine, it is clean contrary to the truth as it is in Jesus. Gospel doctrine tells us that our sins were numbered on the Great Scapegoat's head of old, and carried away once for all, never to be charged against us again.

But we must use the eye of our judgment in looking at our present affliction to *see and confess* how richly, as children, we deserve the rod. Go back to the time since you were converted, dear brother and sister, and consider;—do you wonder that God has chastened you? Speaking for myself, I wonder that I have ever escaped the rod at any time. If I had been compelled to say "All the day long have I been plagued, and chastened every morning," I should not have marvelled, for my shortcomings are many. How ungrateful have we been, how unloving, and how unlovable, how false to our holiest vows, how unfaithful to our most sacred consecrations. Is there a single ordinance over which we have not sinned? Did we ever rise from our knees without having offended while at prayer? Did we ever get through a hymn without some wandering of mind or coldness of heart? Did we ever read a chapter which we might not have wept over because we did not receive the truth in the love of it into our soul as we ought to have done? O, good Father, if we smart, richly do we deserve that we should yet smart again.

When you have confessed your ill-desert, let me exhort you to use those same eyes zealously to *search out the particular sin* which has caused the present chastisement. "Oh," says one, "I do not think I should ever find it out." You might. Perhaps it lies at the very door. I do not wonder that some Christians suffer: I should wonder if they did not. I have seen them, for instance, neglect family prayer and other household duties; and their sons have grown up to dishonor them. If they cry out, "What an affliction," we would not like to *say,* "Ah, but you might have expected it; you were the cause of it;" but such a saying would be true. When children have left the parental roof, and gone into sin, we have not been surprised when the father has been harsh, sour, and crabbed in temper. We did not expect to gather figs of thorns, or grapes of thistles. We have seen men whose whole thought was "Get money, get money," and yet they have professed to be Christians. Such persons have been fretful and unhappy, but we have not been astonished. Would you have the Lord deal liberally with such surly curmudgeons? No, if they walk frowardly with him, he will show himself froward to them. Brother, the roots of your troubles may run under your doorstep where your sin lies. Search and look.

But sometimes the cause of the chastisement lies further off. Every surgeon will tell you that there are diseases which become troublesome in the prime of life, or in old age, which may have been occasioned in youth by some wrong doing, or by accident, and the evil may have lain latent all those years. So may the sins of our youth bring upon us the sorrows of our riper years, and faults and omissions of twenty years ago may scourge us today. I know it is so. If the fault may be of so great an age, it should lead us to more thorough search, and more frequent prayer. Bunyan tells us that Christian met with Apollyon, and had such a dark journey through the Valley of the Shadow of Death, because of slips he made when going down the hill into the Valley of Humiliation. It may be so with us. Perhaps when you were young you were very untender towards persons of a sorrowful spirit; you are such yourself now—your harshness is visited upon you. It may be that, when in better circumstances, you were wont to look down upon the poor and despise the needy; your pride is chastened now. Many a minister has helped to injure another by believing a bad report against him, and by and by he has himself been the victim of slander. "With what measure ye mete it shall be measured to you again."[1] We have seen men who could ride the high horse among their fellow-creatures, and speak very loftily, and when they have been brought very, very low, we have understood the riddle. God will visit his children's transgressions. He will frequently let common sinners go on throughout life unrebuked; but not so his children. If you were going home today, and saw a number of boys throwing stones and breaking windows, you might not interfere with them, but if you saw your own lad among them, I will be bound you would fetch him out, and make him repent of it. If God sees sinners going on in their evil ways, he may not punish them *now*—he will deal out justice to them in another state; but if it be one of his own elect, he will be sure to make him rue the day. Perhaps the reason of your trouble may not be a sin committed, but a duty neglected. Search and look, and see wherein you have been guilty of omission. Is there a sacred ordinance which you have neglected, or a doctrine you have refused to believe?

Perhaps the chastisement may be sent by reason of a sin as yet undeveloped, some latent proneness to evil. The grief may be meant to unearth the sin, that you may hunt it down. Have you any idea of what a devil you are by nature? None of us know what we are capable of if left by grace. We think we have a sweet temper, an amiable disposition! We shall see!! We fall into provoking company, and are so teased and insulted, and so cleverly touched in our raw places, that we become mad with wrath, and our fine amiable temper vanishes in smoke, not without leaving blacks behind. Is it not a dreadful thing to be so stirred up? Yes it is, but if our hearts were pure no sort of stirring would pollute them. Stir pure water as long as you like and no mud will rise. The evil is bad when seen, but it was quite as bad when not seen. It may be a great gain to a man to know what sin is in him, for then he will humble himself before his God, and begin to combat his propensities. If he had never seen the filth he would never have swept the house; if he had never felt the pain the disease would have lurked within, but now that he feels the pain he will fly to the remedy.

1 Matthew 7:2.

Sometimes, therefore, trial may be sent that we may discern the sin which dwelleth in us, and may seek its destruction. What shall we do this morning if we are under the smitings of God's hand, but humble ourselves before him, and go as guilty ones desiring to confess most thoroughly the particular sin which may have driven him to chastise us, appealing to the precious blood of Jesus for pardon and to the Holy Spirit for power to overcome our sin.

When you have so done let me give one word of caution before I leave this point. Do not let us expect when we are in the trouble to perceive any immediate benefit resulting from it. I have tried myself when under sharp pain to see whether I have grown a bit more resigned or more earnest in prayer, or more rapt in fellowship with God, and I confess I have never been able to see the slightest trace of improvement at such times, for pain distracts and scatters the thoughts. Remember that word, "Nevertheless, *afterward* it yieldeth the peaceable fruit of righteousness."[1] The gardener takes his knife and prunes the fruit trees to make them bring forth more fruit; his little child comes trudging at his heels and cries, "Father, I do not see that the fruit comes on the trees after you have cut them." No, dear child, it is not likely you would, but come round in a few months when the season of fruit has come, and then shall you see the golden apples which thank the knife. Graces which are meant to endure require time for their production, and are not thrust forth and ripened in a night. Were they so soon ripe they might be as speedily rotten.

II. Now, as time is failing me, I will take up the second part of my discourse, and handle it with great brevity. I want to give a very short EXPOSITION OF THE BENEFITS OF TROUBLE. This is a great subject. Many a volume has been written upon it, and it might suffice to repeat the catalogue of the benefits of trial, but I will not so detain you.

Severe trouble in a true believer has the effect of loosening the roots of his soul earthward and tightening the anchor-hold of his heart heavenward. How can he love the world which has become so

1 Hebrews 12:11.

drear to him? Why should he seek after grapes so bitter to his taste? Should he not now ask for the wings of a dove that he may fly away to his own dear country, and be at rest for ever? Every mariner on the sea of life knows that when the soft zephyrs blow men tempt the open sea with outspread sails, but when the black tempest comes howling from its den they hurry with all speed to the haven. Afflictions clip our wings with regard to earthly things, so that we cannot fly away from our dear Master's hand, but sit there and sing to him; but the same afflictions make our wings grow with regard to heavenly things, we are feathered like eagles, we catch the soaring spirit, a thorn is in our nest, and we spread our pinions towards the sun.

Affliction frequently opens truths to us, and opens us to the truth,—I know not which of these two is the more difficult. Experience unlocks truths which else were closed against us; many passages of Scripture will never be made clear by the commentator; they must be expounded by experience. Many a text is written in a secret ink which must be held to the fire of adversity to make it visible. I have heard that you see stars in a well when none are visible above ground, and I am sure you can discern many a starry truth when you are down in the deeps of trouble which would not be visible to you elsewhere. Besides, I said it opened us to the truth as well as the truth to us. We are superficial in our beliefs: we are often drenched with truth, and yet it runs off from us like water from a marble slab; but affliction, as it were, ploughs us and sub-soils us, and opens up our hearts, so that into our innermost nature the truth penetrates and soaks like rain into ploughed land. Blessed is that man who receives the truth of God into his inmost self; he shall never lose it, but it shall be the life of his spirit.

Affliction, when sanctified by the Holy Spirit, brings much glory to God out of Christians, through their experience of the Lord's faithfulness to them. I delight to hear an aged Christian giving his own personal testimony of the Lord's goodness. Vividly upon my mind flashes an event of some twenty-five years ago; it is before me as if it had occurred yesterday, when I saw a venerable man of eighty, grey and blind with age, and heard him in simple accents, simple as the language of a child, tell how the Lord had led him, and had dealt well with him, so that no good thing had failed of all that God had promised. He spoke as though he were a prophet, his years lending force to his words. But suppose he had never known a trial, what testimony could he have borne? Had he been lapped in luxury and never endured suffering, he might have stood there dumb and have been as useful as if he had spoken. We must be tried or we cannot magnify the faithful God, who will not leave his people.

Again, affliction gives us through grace the inestimable privilege of conformity to the Lord Jesus. We pray to be like Christ, but how can we be if we are not men of sorrows at all, and never become the acquaintance of grief? Like Christ, and yet never traverse through the vale of tears! Like Christ, and yet have all that heart could wish, and never bear the contradiction of sinners against thyself, and never say, "My soul is exceeding sorrowful, even unto death!"[1] O, sir, thou knowest not what thou dost ask. Hast thou said, "Let me sit on thy right hand in thy kingdom?" It cannot be granted to thee unless thou wilt also drink of his cup and be baptized with his baptism. A share of his sorrow must precede a share of his glory. O, if we are ever to be like Christ, to dwell with him eternally, we may be well content to pass through much tribulation in order to attain to it.

Once more, our sufferings are of great service to us when God blesses them, for they help us to be useful to others. It must be a terrible thing for a man never to have suffered physical pain. You say, "I should like to be the man." Ah, unless you had extraordinary grace, you would grow hard and cold, you would get to be a sort of cast-iron man, breaking other people with your touch. No; let my heart be tender, even be soft, if it must be softened by pain, for I would fain know how to bind up my fellow's wound. Let mine eye have a tear ready for my brother's sorrows even if in order to that, I should have to shed ten thousand for mine own. An escape from suffering would be an escape from the power to sympathise, and that were to be deprecated beyond all things. Luther was right, when he said affliction was the best book in the minister's library. How can the man of God

1 Matthew 26:38.

sympathise with the afflicted ones, if he knows nothing at all about their troubles? I remember a hard, miserly churl, who said that the minister ought to be very poor, that he might have sympathy with the poor. I told him I thought he ought to have a turn at being very rich too, so that he might have sympathy with the very rich; and I suggested to him that perhaps, upon the whole, it would be handiest to keep him somewhere in the middle, that he might the more easily range over the experience of all classes. If the man of God who is to minister to others could be always robust, it were perhaps a loss; if he could be always sickly it might be equally so; but for the pastor to be able to range through all the places where the Lord suffers his sheep to go, is doubtless to the advantage of his flock. And what it is to ministers that it will be to each one of you, according to his calling, for the consolation of the people of God.

Be thankful then, dear brethren, be thankful for trouble; and above all be thankful because it will soon be over, and we shall be in the land where these things will be spoken of with great joy. As soldiers show their scars and talk of battles when they come at last to spend their old age in the country at home, so shall we in the dear land to which we are hastening, speak of the goodness and faithfulness of God which brought us through all the trials of the way. I would not like to stand in that white-robed host and hear it said, "These are they that come out of great tribulation, all except that one." Would you like to be there to see yourself pointed at as the one saint who never knew a sorrow? O no, for you would be an alien in the midst of the sacred brotherhood. We will be content to share the battle, for we shall soon wear the crown and wave the palm.

I know while I am preaching some of you have said, "Ah, these people of God have a hard time of it." So have you. The ungodly do not escape from sorrow by their sin. I never heard of a man escaping from poverty through being a spendthrift, I never heard of a man who escaped from headache or heartache by drunkenness; or from bodily pain by licentiousness. I have heard the opposite; and if there be griefs to the holy there are others for you. Only mark this, ungodly ones, mark this. For you these things work no good. You pervert them to mischief; but for the saints they work eternal benefit. For you your sorrows are punishments; for you they are the first drops of the red hail that shall fall upon you for ever. They are not so to the child of God. You are punished for your transgressions, and he is not. And let us tell you, too, that if this day you happen to be in peace, and prosperity, and plenty, and happiness,—yet there is not one child of God here, in the very deeps of trouble that would change places with you under any consideration whatever. He would sooner be God's dog, and be kicked under the table, than be the devil's darling and sit at meat with him. "Let God do as he pleases," we say, "for a while here; we believe our worst state to be better than your best." Do you think we love God for what we get out of him, and for nothing else? Is that your notion of a Christian's love to God? We read in Jeremiah of certain who said they would not leave off worshipping the Queen of Heaven. "For when," said they, "we worshipped the Queen of Heaven, we had bread in plenty, but now we starve." This is how the ungodly talk, and that is what the devil thought was Job's case. Says he: "Does Job fear God for naught? Hast thou not set a hedge about him, and all that he has?"[1] The devil does not understand real love and affection; but the child of God can tell the devil to his face that he loves God if he covers him with sores and sets him on the dunghill, and by God's good help he means to cling to God through troubles ten-fold heavier than those he has had to bear, should they come upon him. Is he not a blessed God? Ay, let the beds of our sickness ring with it: he is a blessed God. In the night watches, when we are weary, and our brain is hot and fevered, and our soul is distracted, we yet confess that he is a blessed God. Every ward of the hospital where believers are found, should echo with that note. A blessed God? "Ay, that he is," say the poor and needy here this morning, and so say all God's poor throughout all the land. A blessed God? "Ay," say his dying people, "as he slays us we will bless his name. He loves us, and we love him; and, though all his waves go over us, and his wrath lieth sore upon us, we would not change with kings on their thrones if they are without the love of God."

1 Job 1:9, 10.

O, sinner, if God smites a child of his so heavily, he will smite you one day; and if those he loves are made to smart, what will he do with those who rebel against him and hate him? "Kiss the Son, lest he be angry, and ye perish from the way, when his wrath is kindled but a little. Blessed are all they that put their trust in him."[1] The Lord bless you, and bring you into the bonds of his covenant, for Christ's sake. Amen.

---

1 Psalm 2:12.

GOOD NEWS FOR THE LOST

LORD'S-DAY MORNING, MARCH 9TH, 1873, METROPOLITAN TABERNACLE

For the Son of man is come to seek and to save that which was lost.
—LUKE 19:10.

The promises of God are like stars, there is not one of them but has in its turn guided tempest-tossed souls to their desired haven: but as among the stars which stud the midnight sky there are constellations which above all others attract the mariner's gaze, and are helpful to the steersman, so there are certain passages in Scripture which have not only directed a few wise men to Jesus, but have been guiding stars to myriads of simple minds who have through their help found the port of peace. I could mention a number of texts this morning, which I might compare to the pointers of the Great Bear or to the Southern Cross, because they have directly pointed the penitent eye to Jesus, the pole star; and by looking to him sinners have found "the way, the truth, and the life."[1] This text is one of the notable stars, or rather, its words form a wonderful constellation of divine love, a very Pleiades of mercy. The words and syllables seem to glisten to my eye with a supernal splendor. I bless God for every letter of this thrice blessed text: "The Son of man is come to seek and to save that which was lost." But as stars are of small service when the sky is all beclouded, or the air dense with fog, so it may be even such a bright gospel light as our text will not yield comfort to souls surrounded with the clinging mists of doubts and fears. At such times

---

1 John 14:6.

mariners cry for fair weather, and ask that they may be able to see the stars again: so let us pray the Holy Spirit to sweep away with his divine wind the clouds of our unbelief, and enable each earnest eye in the light of God to see the light of peace. O that many awakened minds may find pardon and eternal life in the Savior this morning. God grant that in answer to the prayers now silently breathed by many, the blessing of salvation may come to this house.

I. There are four things I shall try to set forth this morning for the comfort of seeking sinners. The first is this:—I would have all anxious hearts consider HOW THE OBJECTS OF MERCY ARE HERE DESCRIBED: "The Son of man is come to seek and to save *that which was lost."* I feel inexpressibly grateful for this description—*"that which was lost!"* There cannot be a case so bad as not to be comprehended in this word "lost." I am quite unable to imagine the condition of any man of woman born so miserable as not to be contained within the circumference of these four letters—"lost." The man may have gone to a perfect extravagance of vice; he may have ruined himself body and soul; he may be upon the very verge of hell, and feel as if he were slipping into the pit; but this word descends to the lowest depth of his misery, for he is "lost." Here and there upon our iron-bound coasts there are harbors of refuge, but, unfortunately, some of them are only available for large vessels at certain times of the tide. At high-water, a vessel of large tonnage may enter them and find security, but if the tide run out strongly, even though the harbor be there, there is not water enough to enable vessels of great draught to enter. Behold, my text is a harbor of refuge available at all tides, and even at the lowest ebb the biggest ships of heaviest tonnage may enter here. No matter, though the sinner should need a fathomless ocean of mercy to float in, there is depth enough for him here; and if the wind be blowing horribly this morning, and the storms be out, and all the fiends out with the storms, yet, if the tempest-tost soul can but make sail for this divine harbor—there is no bar at the mouth—no shallow water in the channel, there is no fear of its being able to enter. This harbor's mouth is exceeding deep in mercy, for the text speaks of "that which was lost." Souls lost through sin and folly are sought and saved by the Son of man.

Let us consider how men are lost. We know first that they are lost by *nature*. However much men may rebel against the doctrine, it is a truth of inspiration that we are lost even when we are born, and that the word "lost" has to do, not only with those who have gone into sin grossly and wickedly, but even with all mankind. Did you ever notice the other place where this text occurs? It is in the eighteenth chapter of Matthew and the eleventh verse, and it occurs there in a very significant relationship. Let me read you the words. Christ is speaking about little children, and he says, "Take heed that ye despise not one of these little ones; for I say unto you, That in heaven their angels do always behold the face of my Father which is in heaven. For the Son of man is come to save that which was lost." The Lord had placed a little child in the midst of the disciples, and had declared that they must be converted and become as little children, and yet he uttered these words in that connection. From that passage it is clear that, by nature, little children are lost, and they owe their salvation to the Lord Jesus, when God is pleased to carry them to heaven in infancy. Jesus is come to seek and to save those who are lost by nature; and it is most certain that no man now perishes through Adam's sin only, and no man is cast into hell because of natural depravity alone; his own personal sin and unbelief cast him there.

A far more terrible matter for us practically is this, that we are, apart from divine grace, lost by our own *actions*. Our nature has revealed itself in our character; our inward inclinations have developed themselves in our conduct, and we have lost ourselves by our own act and deed. We have erred and strayed from God's ways wilfully and wickedly like lost sheep, and now the word "lost" belongs to us by our own overt acts, as well as through Adam's fall.

And in addition to that, we are lost because our actual sin and our natural depravity have co-worked to produce in us an *inability* to restore ourselves from our fallen condition. We are not only wanderers, but we have no will to come home; we are prodigal sons, but we never say, "I will arise, and go to my father," until the grace of God puts it into our hearts to do so; we are like sheep which wander and wander and wander, but will never by any chance return, unless the Good Shepherd of souls shall seek us. If this world of ours could suddenly be left to itself, could forget the centripetal force which holds it in alliance with the sun, and could set out upon a fearful journey into the darkness of far-off space, if it should travel so far away that no longer could a single beam of light reach it from the sun, and it were altogether in darkness, it is quite certain that it could never find the sun again; for who could light a candle upon the earth wherewith we might search for the sun? The sun can only be seen by its own light. Where upon earth would be found the bands and cords with which to draw us back to the sun? The world could only be drawn by an influence from the sun itself; the central orb must give the motive power. So, when a soul wanders from God, it has no light in it with which to see God, and no force in it to draw God to itself. God must enlighten and draw the soul to him. So that, in this three-fold sense, we are lost by nature, by practice, and by an utter inability to find out our God, and to return to him. Yet, terrible as this lost estate is, "The Son of man is come to seek and to save that which was lost."

In addition to this, we are all lost by the *condemnation* which our sin has brought upon us. We are sometimes told by inaccurate talkers that we are in a state of probation. My brethren, nothing can be more unscriptural than such a statement. We have long ago been proved and found wanting. Our probation is over. We are now, if unrenewed, in a state of condemnation. The trial is not now pending: it is over, and we are condemned already for our sins; the fearful sentence of condemnation hangs over every man here who has not believed in the Lord Jesus. The sinner is lost in that sense. It is but a matter of time, and that time in God's hands, and the condemned man will be taken out to execution, and the punishment of divine wrath will fall upon his guilty head. We are lost because we are under legal sentence, and are unable to escape from it. We cannot make atonement to God for the wrong we have done, nor avoid his righteous jurisdiction. No mortifications of the body, no lamentations of the spirit, can wipe out a single sin.

"Could my tears for ever flow;
Could my zeal no respite know:
All for sin could not atone,
Christ must save, and Christ alone."[1]

So that, being before the bar of God regarded as condemned criminals, unregenerate men are lost indeed.

More than this, there are certain persons in the world who are lost in a more apparent sense than others are—I mean that they are lost *to society*, to respect, and perhaps to decency. That was the case with Zacchaeus, in connection with whom our text was spoken. I do not know what may have been his parentage. Possibly he was born of most reputable folk, but he showed a vicious mind, and he turned aside from the good old paths; he loved low company, and despised his father's seriousness. There was great grief in that household on his account. Zacchaeus was lost to his parents; they had hoped he would have been a credit to their name, but instead thereof he was a dishonor; they trusted that he would be the staff of their old age, but now he was a scourge to them. They scarcely dared to whisper his name in any company, for he had joined with the men of Belial, and mingled with the lewdest sort in the city; and by and by, as men go from bad to worse, Zacchaeus had taken up with the low and infamous trade of a tax-gatherer, and he so pushed his way in it by his sharpness and hardness of heart, that he became chief of the odious band of the extortionate oppressors of the people. The Pharisees, of course, never looked at him: they passed him by as though he were a dog, while the ordinary people of Jericho, when he was out of hearing, cursed him. Had he not exacted upon one—had he not oppressed another? His very name had a ban set upon it. He was lost to society. But the Son of man sought him and saved him, lost as he was. Society, to this day, has its rules, by the breach of which persons become outcasts. These rules are, some of them, commendable, but others are arbitrary, one-sided, cruel and hypocritical. We have sometimes heard men of the world ridicule what they are pleased to call the cant of the Church, but we take leave to say that there is no cant so desperately

1 *Rock of Ages* by Augustus M. Toplady.

canting as the cant of the world. There occurred, not long ago, an instance of the world's relentless cruelty to those whom it is fashionable to brand with dishonor. A person who had, perhaps, fallen into sin in her earlier days, was restored to a respectable position; she was received in society among the noblest, but on a sudden, dastardly lips revealed a secret, and a sin committed far back was raked up against her; henceforth the world put away the woman, never asking her if she had repented, or taking her after-conduct into consideration. The world is so pure and chaste and immaculate, that it shut out the erring one as if she had been a leper. Though itself reeking with foulest abominations, society feigns a virtuousness pure as the lily and chaste as the snow. The world is cold, hard, cruel, towards a certain class of offenders. It receives into its embraces men who are, every inch of them, unclean; but a betrayed, deceived, broken-hearted woman, the world shakes off as if she were a viper. This is the society which boasts its gallantry! This is the just, fair-dealing world! It caresses its noble rakes, but casts off the most penitent among the betrayed. Ah, hypocritical, canting world! Ah, hollow, lying world, to pretend to a virtue which thou dost not know! Rail not at the inconsistencies of religious men while thine own are so glaring! Cruel tyrant, learn mercy and do justice, ere thou becomest a judge of the servants of the Lord. Now, the Son of man is come to seek and to save those whom the world puts outside its camp. The world says "No;" "Shame on her;" "We will not speak to her;" but Christ Jesus says, "I have come to pardon her, and to restore her, and she shall love me much, because much has been forgiven her!" There are other cases in which men by their crimes most justly place themselves outside the pale of society; and for the preservation of order they are separated from the company of honest men. Now even these should have a door of hope left to them, and a way of return. The cry too often is "Down with him; down with him; he has sinned against his fellow men: put him aside, what care we what becomes of him." But the Son of man who is infinitely pure and holy, who has a genuine horror of sin, so that he really hates it and loathes it, yet does not loathe sinners, but has come to seek and to save them. The sweep of divine compassion is not limited by the customs of mankind: the boundaries of Jesu's love are not to be fixed by Pharisaical self-righteousness, "The Son of man is come to seek and to save that which was lost."

Putting all that we have said into a few words, we would thus speak: I may be addressing persons here who feel that they have broken God's laws, perhaps by no means publicly or in any of the grosser vices, but they have broken the laws of God; they feel that they have, and are sorrowing in their hearts because of it; they fear also that they have sinned in a such a way that it cannot be possible for them to be forgiven. At the same time the hardness of their hearts astounds them; they feel themselves to be altogether bad, and that no good thing dwells within them; they therefore despair of being saved. Beloved friends, "The Son of man is come to seek and to save that which was lost." Does not the description suit *you?* are you not among the lost? Well then, you are among such as Jesus Christ came to save. And if perchance there should be one here who has fallen into the grosser vices, some one who has sullied his name, and degraded himself to the very lowest degree, I am bound not to restrict the text, and I do not desire to do so: "The Son of man is come to seek and to save that which was lost." O ye lost ones! O ye ruined and destroyed ones! The Son of man is come to seek and to save you! The Greek word here used for lost is a form of that word which has by certain modern discoverers been translated "annihilated," with a view to buttressing their unscriptural theory of the annihilation of the wicked. It is one of those instances in which the absurdity of such an interpretation ought to be evident even to themselves. The Son of man has not come to seek and to save that which is annihilated—that would be rank nonsense. But the word is very forcible, and signifies a destruction very terrible, a ruin of the most solemn kind. To be lost is to be fallen altogether, to be destroyed as to all good, to be utterly undone, yet the Lord Jesus Christ is come to seek and to save such as are in this wretched plight. Why, this text sounds to me like the ringing of joyful Sabbath bells which sometimes mariners have heard at sea. Ships are sometimes surrounded with a dense fog, and the mariners know not whether they are near the land or on the wide ocean—they lie becalmed with no stir in the air, no stir in the sea, the ship has been like a lost thing, without power of motion or knowledge of her whereabouts, and then suddenly the mariners have heard bells ringing in the blessed Sabbath, and as the silver sounds have pierced the gloomy mist the mariners have known that they were somewhere near Old England's happy shores. My text rings out most sweetly, and through the fogs of your soul's despair and doubt, I trust the glad message will reach you, "The Son of man is come to seek and to save that which was lost."

II. Now, let us turn to another point. There is very much of con-solation in our text for the guilty, in the second place, if they notice HOW THE SAVIOR IS HERE DESCRIBED, "The *Son of man* is come to seek and to save that which was lost." As the Son of man he is come. And here note, first of all, *his Deity*. You say, "Deity, how is that? The text says 'the Son of man.'" Yes, and that is the point upon which I ground my remark. No prophet or apostle needed to call himself by way of distinction the son of man. It would be ridiculous for any one of us to speak of himself emphatically as the son of man; it would be an affectation of condescension supremely absurd. Therefore when we hear our Lord particularly and especially calling himself by this name, we are compelled to think of it as contrasted with his higher nature, and we see a deep condescension in his choosing to be called the Son of man, when he might have been called the Son of God. O my soul, he who is come to save thee, is so plainly God that he sees reason to remind thee that he is also the Son of man, lest thou should-est doubt it. No angel's arm is stretched out for thy help, but the arm of him who created all worlds.

In speaking of himself as the Son of man, our Lord shows us that he has come to us in a *condescending character*. Not in flames of fire has Jesus descended from heaven; not in his chariot of wrath, girt with the sword of vengeance, does Jehovah Jesus come to men. He is come upon his errand of mercy as one who has lain upon a woman's breast, who has known weakness, suffering, and want; as one who knows by personal experience the lowliness of your estate. Oh, sin-ner, is it not joy to know that the Son of God has come to save you as the Son of man? "The Son of man"—that describes also the *tenderness* of his character. A man can sympathise with a man: Jesus the tender-hearted One, was full of sympathy, and in loving gentleness he is come to save sinners. He is no stern Rhadamanthus, no judge of severe countenance, no Draco with bloody edicts, but Jesus, the Man of Sorrows and the acquaintance of grief. It is as your brother, touched with a feeling of your infirmities, that Jesus comes to you. He has, moreover, come in his *mediatorial character*, for "There is one Mediator between God and man, the Man Christ Jesus."[1] He can put his hand upon you, and, at the same time, lay his hand upon God. He who bridges the gulf between the misery of fallen manhood and the eternal dignity of the unsullied God, is come to save the lost. What a joy is this!

Our Lord is come in his *representative character*, for he calls himself the Son of man, as if to note that he is man for men, the representative man, the Son of man. He is come as the covenant substitute, representing man. He has suffered in our stead, died in our stead, paid our debts in our stead, risen in our stead, and gone to heaven as our forerunner. It is the Son of man who in all things has acted for men, who is "come to seek and to save that which was lost."

Now, it seems to me, dear friends, if the Spirit of God would only help poor troubled hearts to see it, that the wording of this part of my text, though very simple, is full of the richest consolation. Soul, what an attractive Savior hast thou to deal with! God is a consuming fire: thou canst not, O guilty one, go to him: but Jesus is thy brother, thy friend, the Friend of Sinners, who received them and ate with them; and he it is, great as he is, who is "come to seek and to save that which was lost." I tell thee what I would have thee do. Go to him without fear or trembling; ere yon sun goes down and ends this day of mercy, go and tell him thou hast broken the Father's laws—tell him that thou art lost, and thou needest to be saved; tell him that he is a man, and appeal to his manly heart, and to his brotherly sympathies. Pour out thy broken heart at his feet: let thy soul flow over in his presence, and I tell thee he cannot cast thee away; though thy prayer be feeble

---

1 1 Timothy 2:5.

as the spark in the flax, he will not quench it; and though thy heart be bruised like a reed, he will not break it. May the Holy Spirit bless you with a desire to go to God through Jesus Christ; and encourage you to do so by showing that he is meek and lowly of heart, gentle, and tender, and full of pity.

III. I pass on to our third point, and that also is full of comfort, though I will only touch upon it. You that seek salvation should joyfully observe HOW OUR LORD'S PAST ACTION IS DESCRIBED: "The Son of man is come." Note, not "shall come," but "is come." His coming is a fact accomplished. We could not have said this before the days of Bethlehem's wondrous birth; we should have had to say the Son of man "will come," and then you would have needed extraordinary faith to believe that the Son of God would become the Son of man to save you. But he "*is* come." That part of the salvation of a sinner which is yet to be done is not at all so hard to be believed as that which the Lord has already accomplished. That Jesus Christ, after being incarnate, and after having suffered for sin, should pardon sinners for whom he has died does not seem to me to be extraordinary; but the extraordinary matter lies in this, that he should come from heaven, that he should be born in Bethlehem, that he should tarry here on earth, that he should go up to the cross and down to the grave, and bear and suffer in the sinner's stead: yet, our Lord has done that. The greatest part of the work he has accomplished. Your salvation, if you believe in Jesus, is comparatively an easy matter: he has but to apply that which is already prepared, and hand over to your faith that which he has laid by in store.

The state of the case since Jesus has come may be illustrated thus: Certain of our fellow countrymen were the prisoners of the Emperor Theodore, in Abyssinia, and I will suppose myself among them. As a captive, I hear that the British Parliament is stirring in the direction of an expedition for my deliverance, and I feel some kind of comfort, but I am very anxious, for I know that amidst party strifes in the House of Commons many good measures are shipwrecked. Days and months pass wearily on, but at last, I hear that Sir Robert Napier has landed with a delivering army. Now my heart leaps for joy. I am shut up within the walls of Magdala, but in my dungeon I hear the sound of the British bugle, and I know that the deliverer is come. Now I am full of confidence, and am sure of liberty. If the general is already come my rescue is certain. Mark well, then, O ye prisoners of hope, that Jesus is come. Do you not hear it? The gospel bugle is sounding. Blessed are the people who know the joyful sound! The captain of our salvation is come, he is at our dungeon gates! He has come to our rescue! He is come! He is come!

Jesus has come; and by his Holy Spirit he is still here, and we may depend upon it, that if he has actually come to the work, he means to go through with it, for he never draws back his hand. When he said he would save men, it was certain he would do so; but now he has come to do it, it is more than certain. Behold the Lord of glory has disrobed himself for work, he has hung up his royal robes and put on a workman's garb, a human toiler's dress; he means work, stern, persevering work. He has cast his azure mantle across the sky, and come down here to the city of David robed in mortal clay to wear the garment without seam. O, sirs, he means to do his Father's business; he is in real earnest, be sure of that—he has come to do it, and means to accomplish his design of love. Besides, he is not like a foolish one who comes to his work and leaves his tools behind him: Jesus would not come unprepared. The Son of man is an infinitely wise Savior, and you may depend upon it, having come with his Father's consent and anointed with the Holy Ghost, he is come with everything that is wanted to accomplish his purpose. He is come to do a work which he can do and will do, and in which he will not be baffled though all the powers of earth and hell should contend with him. "The Son of man is come to seek and to save that which was lost." My heart rejoices as I feel how sure it is that the lost ones will be saved. If we had heard the sons of the morning sing in solemn symphony, "God himself has come to scatter the primeval darkness, to bring order out of chaos, and to create life in the earth which lieth without form and void," we should have felt certain of the result. If God had come to create, he would create; and it would have been no matter of surprise to us to have seen the round earth glowing in the morning light, verdant with new-born vegetation, and populous with variety of life. We are sure that what God comes to do he will do. In the night when Israel was pursued by the Egyptians, and overtaken at the sea, even at the Red sea, it was a sign of victory when the Lord came to deliver his people. The pillar of cloud went to the rear, turning its black side on the foe, and its bright side on the chosen. God was come to smite Pharaoh, and to rebuke the proud tyrant; and oh, you might be sure he would do it—failure was out of the question. When, next morning, the placid deep swept over the angry armies, and all was peace where Pharaoh and his hosts had raged so furiously, and instead of the shoutings of men-at-arms were heard the sweet voices of damsels, singing, "Sing unto the Lord, for he hath triumphed gloriously,"[1] it was but natural it should be so, for if God came to avenge his Israel, who could stand before him? The Son of man *is come* to save. Rejoice, ye heavens, and be glad, O earth! He will do all his pleasure. Neither earth nor hell can stand against him. Seeking he will save, yea, he will save that which is lost. All glory be unto his name.

IV. The last point is to be this—there is much of deepest comfort in THE DESCRIPTION WHICH IS HERE GIVEN OF OUR LORD'S WORK. He is come "to seek and to save;" the enterprise is one, but has two branches. I would have you first notice what our Lord has not come to do. He has not come to aid those who, in their own esteem, are almost as good as they ought to be, to become a little better, and so to enter heaven by their own efforts. I believe that such is the general persuasion of mankind. If they were to put their beliefs into plain English their notion is as nearly as possible what I have said. According to them you are to attend a place of worship regularly, and say prayers, and give to the poor, and be as good as ever you can; and then, inasmuch as there will be a little bit in which you will be lacking, you are to trust to Jesus Christ to make up the rest. Now, mark my word, this is a gross and fatal delusion. There is not between the two covers of this Bible one single word of hope held out to any man who believes in that manner—nay, more, there is this solemn utterance, that Christ has not come to save people of that sort at all,

1 Exodus 15:1.

for thus it is written: "The whole have no need of a physician, but they that are sick: I came not to call the righteous, but sinners to repentance."[1] As many as are of the works of the law are under the curse. If any of you are very good people, and have no sins, and have done no wrong, and are nearly as good as you ought to be, and only need just to say a little about the blood of Christ, Christ has not come to save such as you are, he has "come to seek and to save that which was lost." If you are not lost you have no part nor lot in this matter.

Moreover, the Lord Jesus has not come to aid us in self-sufficient endeavors to save ourselves. I wonder how Christian people can sing that verse—

"A charge to keep I have,
A God to glorify;
A never-dying soul to save,
And fit it for the sky."[2]

It might suit a Jew at the foot of Sinai, but a Christian should have none of it. If we have to save our own souls it is all over with us. What! we fit our souls for the sky! We, save our own souls! Why, this is the clean opposite of the gospel of Jesus Christ. The theory of some is that there is much natural goodness in men, and they have only to work it out and gradually improve themselves into a state of grace. No, sir, you are on the wrong tack. Do you know what is the very first ceremony of the Christian religion? "Yes," say you, "baptism." So it is. And what is baptism? "Buried with Christ in baptism." Who are buried, then? Living people? No! but dead people. The very first lesson of the gospel after believing in Christ is that you are, before the law, dead, through having been crucified with Christ, and therefore you must be buried. There is no improving your old nature, mending it up and beautifying it into perfection—the thing is hopeless, and it must die and be buried. The scripture does not say, "Ye must be improved," but, "Ye must be born again." That is quite another thing. You must be made new creatures in Christ Jesus. "Old things

1 Mark 2:17.
2 *A Charge to Keep I Have* by Charles Wesley.

are passed away; behold, all things are become new."[1] A new creation is wanted, not an improvement of the old creature. For what saith the apostle?—"The carnal mind is enmity against God, and is not reconciled to God, neither indeed can be."[2] There he ends it,—"Neither, indeed, can be." It is all over with the flesh, for corruption has seized upon it. This the believer accepts as fact, "because," says the apostle, "we thus judge, that if One died for all, then all died." The death of Jesus, as a punishment for sin, was *our* death, and we died in him; so that we now live as new men, and risen men, and not as though the old life had been improved into something better. The old nature is put into the place of death, and then the man receives life in Christ; that is how we are saved, not by improving yourself into something better, but by being new created by the divine power of the Holy Spirit. "Very discouraging," says one. Yes! and such discouragement is much needed now-a-days. If I saw a man trying to climb to the top of a mountain by a path which was quite impassable and full of dangers, I should be his true friend if I discouraged him from dashing himself to pieces. The way to heaven is not by our own works. Ye who think that ye can climb to heaven by the way of Sinai should look to the flames that Moses saw, and sink, and tremble, and despair. There is no road to God by the way of Sinai. There, at Calvary, is the way, all crimson with the Savior's blood. Salvation is ours through his atoning sacrifice: "For the Son of man is come to seek and to save that which was lost."

Now, having cleared away the rubbish, let us come to the truth. Jesus is come to *seek* the lost. He did that *personally*. There was a lost woman at Samaria, and Jesus said he must needs go through Samaria; there was a lost man at Jericho, and Jesus said he must abide in that man's house. What he did personally, he now does under the dispensation of the Holy Spirit, in his *providence*. Sometimes providence takes away a child, lays a man on a bed of sickness, deprives him of his wealth, and all these trials are intended to bring him to Jesus. It is Jesus seeking him. It is an odd thing, my friend, that you should

---

1 2 Corinthians 5:17.

2 Romans 8:7.

be here this morning: you did not reckon upon being here: strange circumstances brought you. Suppose the Lord means to save you this morning? Then the providence which brought you to this spot is Jesus seeking you.

As our Lord seeks souls by his providence he also seeks them by the *Word*. It is very wonderful how the Word of God will come home to people. It is a part of every preacher's business who is sent of God, so to preach that persons in the congregation may perceive that he speaks of them. What remarkable things have happened in our ministry and in the ministries of all who are sent of God. Why, they speak to people as if they knew them; though they never saw them before, they tell their case and picture their state. God guides his servants and gives them words that they never thought of till the time came to utter them, so that on the spur of the moment they pick out the character as well as if they had known the man from childhood. Thus Jesus seeks the sinner. If there be anything in this sermon which suits your case, dear friend, do not talk about what relation it may have to anybody else, but be sure Jesus is seeking *you*. You are a lost one: you have come here in such a condition of heart that you cannot deny your lost state. Jesus is seeking you. Look how the Lord served Zacchaeus. It seemed an odd thing that when the Lord was under the tree, he should look up and say, "Zacchaeus, make haste, and come down:" but Jesus does the same thing still in the preaching of the gospel. He applies the word with power to individual consciences, and makes men perceive that he speaks of them. God has a message of love to their souls; and they are compelled to hear it: they cannot shut their ears to it: they must receive it, for the *Spirit of God* comes with it and sends it home with power to their soul. That is Jesus seeking sinners.

But whom Jesus seeks he saves. There is the second part of it—"To seek and to save." And how is the saving done? That is done, first of all, by the complete pardon of all the sinner's sins. The very instant that a man trusts Christ with all his heart, the past is blotted out as if it had never existed: all the sins he has ever done in thought, in word, in deed, however crimson in dye, go at once, they are sunk as in the sea, never to be found again. And this is done upon this one solitary condition, that the man believe in Jesus; and even that is not a condition, for he that bade him believe enables him to believe, and gives him the faith which saves his soul.

Then the sinner is saved in another way. From the moment that a man believes in Jesus his nature becomes different from what it was before: he receives a new heart—another influence takes possession of him; another love engrosses him. When a man is absorbed by some master-passion what a different man he becomes. The passion for wealth will work marvels; we have known idle persons become very diligent, and profuse voluptuaries become even self-denying and mortifying to their flesh, in their ambition to acquire riches. Now, God gives us another passion, the passion of gratitude to Christ, and love to the God that saved us, and that becomes a master-principle and rules the entire man. He who loved self now loves God and lives for him. And is that change possible to the most degraded? Yes, possible with God. If a man has committed every crime in the whole catalogue of villainy, and his heart has become hard as the nether millstone, and his disposition altogether base and mean, and grovelling, and sensual, and devilish, the Spirit of God can turn that man in a single moment into a lover of that which is true and right and just, can break his heart concerning the past, make him angry with himself for having lived as he has done, and can passionately inflame him with the desire to be perfectly holy; and that passion within the man can carry him on until he loves his fellow-creatures as himself, and makes great sacrifices for them; and all for the sake of Jesus, that blessed, crucified Son of man, who came "to seek and to save that which was lost." We do not preach that Christ forgives men and then lets them live as before; but we assert that the moment he gives the pardon of sin, he gives the new nature too. The gospel hospital is not merely a place where lepers are harbored, but where lepers are healed: "The Son of man is come to seek and to save that which was lost."

Brethren, let us cry to Jesus this morning to save us. I will put myself down among the lost by nature and by practice. If there is no one else here that is lost by nature I am such, and I bless my Lord that he is "come to seek and to save" me, a lost man. Brothers and sisters, some of you have known his love for many years. Did you not come at first to him as lost ones? And will you not confess this morning that were it not for his infinite mercy you would still be as lost as ever? What a mercy it is to know we are lost, and to trust to Christ who saves the lost. What a blessing to be among the dead who died in Christ, whose life is a new life in him: "for ye are dead, and your life is hid with Christ in God."[1] Martin Luther speaks in his book on Galatians of cutting the devil's head off with his own sword: "There," says Martin to the devil, "thou sayest I am a great sinner. I thank thee for that, for Jesus Christ came into the world to save sinners, and so I feel he came to save me." And if the devil saith to any one of you this morning, "You are lost altogether;" off with his head, my brother, with his own sword, and this very day rejoice that "the Son of man is come to seek and to save that which was lost."

Is there anyone here who is not lost, anyone in this congregation who needs no saving? Well, then, I cannot say in God's name a single word of consolation to you; ye are rich and increased in goods and have need of nothing, so ye say. But this is what the Lord saith to you: "He hath put down the mighty from their seat, and he hath exalted them of low degree: he hath filled the hungry with good things, and the rich he hath sent empty away."[2] That is the only gospel for you; but every poor, heavy-laden, troubled heart, and every soul that feels itself to be lost by nature, has this gracious word, "The Son of man is come to seek and to save that which was lost."

The last word is this: Let us who are saved seek the lost ones. Jesus did it: O follower of Jesus, do likewise! Is there any work that you could undertake amongst the worst of people? Undertake it. Never be ashamed of mingling with the poorest of the poor, and the vilest of the vile, for Christ's sake. I always feel intense satisfaction at the remembrance of such useful members of our church as Brother Orsman, engaged as he is from day to day in the very worst part of London, in Golden Lane, seeking that which is lost. I hope there are

1 Colossians 3:3.
2 Luke 1:52, 53.

many here imitating him. I know there are some. There is room for many more laborers in that department to seek those that are lost—pre-eminently lost. You need not, however, go to Golden Lane, or Seven Dials, there are plenty of lost people around you—lost people who come to the Tabernacle, lost people who go to church, and lost people who go nowhere on the Sabbath. Go and seek them. If you are saved yourself, I beseech you by the blood that bought you, by the Christ who loved you, and by the Christ whom you love, go out this very day to seek and to save that which was lost. Amen and Amen.

PORTION OF SCRIPTURE READ BEFORE SERMON—LUKE 19:1–27.

GOOD CHEER FOR OUTCASTS

Thursday Evening, June 15th, 1876, Metropolitan Tabernacle

He gathereth together the outcasts of Israel.—Psalm 147:2.

Does not this show us the great gentleness and infinite mercy of God? And as we know most of God in the person of our Lord Jesus Christ, should it not charm us to remember that when he came on earth he did not visit kings and princes, but he came unto the humble and simple folk. He did not seek out Pharisees, wrapped up in their own supposed righteousness, but he sought out the guilty, for he said, "They that are whole have no need of the physician, but they that are sick."[1] The Son of man has come to seek and to save that which was lost. It would have seemed natural that our Lord Jesus, when he came here, should first of all, have addressed himself to the most respectable people he could find, and should have sent his message to the rabbis of Jerusalem, to the senators at Rome, to the philosophers of Greece; instead of which the common people heard him gladly, and he rejoiced in spirit while he said, "I thank thee, O Father, Lord of heaven and earth, because thou hast hid these things from the wise and prudent, and hast revealed them unto babes. Even so, Father: for so it seemed good in thy sight."[2]

I think you may judge of a man's character by the persons whose affection he seeks. If you find a man seeking only the affection of those who are great, depend upon it he is ambitious and self-seeking;

---

1 Mark 2:17.
2 Luke 10:21.

but when you observe that a man seeks the affection of those who can do nothing for him, but for whom he must do everything, you know that he is not seeking himself, but that pure benevolence sways his heart. When I read in the text that the Lord gathers together the outcasts of Israel, and when I see that the text is truly applicable to the Lord Jesus Christ, because this is just what he did, I see another illustration of the gentleness of his heart, who said, "Take my yoke upon you, for I am meek and lowly of heart, and ye shall find rest unto your souls."[1] Be glad tonight, dear friends, that we gather around such a Savior as this, from whom all pride and self-seeking are absent, and who, coming down among us in gentleness and meekness, comes to gather those whom no man cares for—those who are judged to be worthless and irreclaimable. He comes to gather together the outcasts of Israel.

Applying this text to our Lord Jesus Christ we not only see his gentleness, but we also clearly see an illustration of his love to men, as men. If you seek only after rich men the suspicion arises, and it is more than a suspicion, that you rather seek their wealth than them. If you aim only at the benefit of wise men, it is probably true that it is their wisdom which attracts you, and not their manhood: but the Lord Jesus Christ did not love men because of any advantageous circumstances, or any commendable incidents of their condition: his love was to manhood. He loved his own chosen people as men, not as this or that among men. He has no respect for rank, nor care for wealth. A man is a man with Christ whether the "guinea-stamp" be there or no: he died not for titles and dignities, but for men. "Not yours, but *you*," our Lord Jesus could truly say. Where Jesus Christ sees a man, though he be an outcast, an outlaw, one condemned by the law of his own country, he sees a human being there—a creature capable of awful sin and terrible misery, but yet, renewed by grace, capable of bringing wondrous glory to the Most High. Our Lord Jesus Christ, by gathering together the outcasts, proves to demonstration that it is not the things which surround men, but the men themselves that he cares for. He considers not so much *where* a man is, but

1 Matthew 11:29.

what he is; not what he has learned, or what he is thought of, or what he has done; but what he is. The man is the jewel, the immortal soul is the pearl of great price, which Jesus seeks as a merchantman seeks goodly pearls.

Another thing is also clear. If Jesus gathers together the outcasts of Israel, it proves his power over the hearts of men. There is a certain class of men who follow that which is morally good because the Lord has given them a noble disposition. Thank God, he has in mercy been pleased to give some men a desire after that which is beautiful and true. They, too, are merchantmen seeking goodly pearls, and it is not difficult, when the heart is brought into such a desirable state, for the excellence and beauty of Jesus Christ to attract it. But here is the tug of war: there are men still left in the guilt and filthiness of human nature who have no desire after that which is good, but whose entire longings are after evil, only evil, and that continually. These have no more eye to anything that is high and noble than the swine hath for the stars. The minister of Christ may appeal to them, but he will appeal in vain; and providence may warn them by the deaths of others, and by personal sickness, but they are not to be separated from the earth to which they are glued. Yet our Lord Jesus can gather together even these, the outcasts of Israel. Such is his power that he does not stay till he sees good desires in men, but he imparts those desires to those who have them not. Such are the charms of his cross that blind eyes are made to see by its beauty; such is the music of his voice that deaf ears are opened by its music; such is the majesty of his life that the dead hear his voice, and they that hear are made to live. No groundwork of goodness is asked or expected from any man that Christ may come and act upon it; but he takes man in his ruin, and in the extremity of his depravity, and begins with him there and then. When the good Samaritan came to the wounded man, he did not wait for him to make the first advance, or come a little towards him, but he came unto him where he was, and poured into his wounds the oil and the wine: so the Lord comes where human nature is, and, bad as its condition is, he stoops to it, and he gathers together the outcasts of Israel. Oh, it is a wonderful thing this, that there should be attractions about the Lord Jesus Christ which can draw to him those whom nothing else that is good can possibly stir! You may preach virtue to the sinner; but he does not practically yield to its charms; you may preach to the drunkard, to the unchaste, to the immoral, the beauties and excellences of honesty and of all the virtues and the graces, but little good will come of it; the result is infinitesimal. You may charm very wisely upon those subjects, but these deaf adders do not care for charming. We have heard of a divine who said that he had preached honesty till he had not an honest person left in the parish, and preached of virtue till he did not know where Diogenes with his lantern could find it. Nothing worth having comes of preaching when Christ is not its theme. You may preach the law, and men will be frightened by it, but they will forget their fears; yet if Jesus Christ be preached he draws all men unto him. The most wicked will listen to the news of him who is able to save unto the uttermost them that come unto God by him. The most obdurate have been known to weep when they have heard the story of his grief and of his love, the proudest have found themselves suddenly humbled at his feet, whereof some of us are witnesses, for we marvelled to find the hardness and loftiness of our hearts suddenly removed by a sense of his goodness. I do not believe that we preachers have half enough, or a tenth enough, faith in Jesus Christ. If we could preach Jesus Christ to a company of convicted felons should we be wrong in hoping to see the larger part of them converted on the spot? If we had but faith enough to preach to them as we should, aiming directly, distinctly, and believingly at their souls, might we not look for great results? We go so timidly, so doubtingly to work. We pray that God would save *some* out of our congregations, and that he would be pleased to bless the word here and there: but, such a splendid gospel as we have to preach should not be preached so, nor should we so pray about it. When Moses lifted up the brazen serpent in the wilderness it was not with this prayer— "Lord, grant that one or two of those who are bitten of the serpent may look and live;" but Moses came out boldly with his serpent high upon the pole; he believed that thousands would look: they did look, and they lived. May we after the same manner proclaim Jesus who "gathereth together the outcasts of Israel."

Now, with this introduction, I would speak upon the text a little more particularly, and we shall observe with brevity, first, *to whom the text applies,*—"He gathereth together *the outcasts* of Israel." Secondly, we shall consider *in what sense he may be said to gather them;* and then, thirdly, *what lesson this teaches us.*

I. First, then, TO WHOM MAY THIS TEXT APPLY—"He gathereth together *the outcasts of Israel?*" It refers to several classes in different ways.

First, it is a fact that our Lord Jesus did gather together some of the very *poorest and most despised among men,* who might under some respects be regarded as outcasts; and it is certain that, to this day, the gospel comes in the largest measure of power to the poor of this world. Often, too, it comes with amazing power to those who are despised by others, or are regarded as being of inferior degree. You know that at this time it is boastfully said by the enemies of the gospel, that the culture, the brain, the intellect, the education of England is all on the side of scepticism. I am not sure about it. When people say that they possess a deal of brain, I am not certain that their claim is correct, unless it be that as sheep have a good deal of brain, and yet are not the wisest animals in the world, so these gentlemen also are no wiser than they should be. As to those gentlemen who so evidently claim to be the cultured people, who monopolize all the sweetness and the light, I am not clear that they have all the modesty. It does seem to me that if they talked in a lower key it would be as well; and if they thought a little less of their own culture, and allowed a little more to other people, we might have more faith in this wonderful "culture" of theirs. Some of us have failed to see the deep thought and the profound learning we were told to look for in the books of the sceptical cultured mind, and therefore we are the less patient when we hear the perpetual bragging of our foes. Still, let it stand so. We will not quarrel with it. Suppose it to be so—that none but foolish people embrace the old-fashioned faith—the Puritanism, which they say is nearly dead—the old evangelism which they ridicule as being exploded: be it so, that we are an inferior order of people, with very little brain, and all that.

Well, we are not out of heart on that account, because we find that it so happened in our Savior's day, and has happened all days since, that the wisdom of the world has been at enmity with God; and it has also turned out that the foolishness of God has been wiser than men, and God has mastered human wisdom by the foolishness of preaching. By that gospel which wise men laughed at as being folly God has brought carnal wisdom to naught. The Lord Jesus Christ looks with love on those whom others look down upon with scorn.

> "He takes the fool, and makes him know
> The wonders of his dying love,
> To lay aspiring wisdom low,
> And all our pride reprove."

I am thankful when I meet with poor saints, and see what a grip humble men and women get of the promises of God. Laboring men, humble shepherds, and the like, have often been more distinguished for deep insight into the mysteries of grace than learned doctors of divinity. Where there has been little in the cupboard, and the provision on the table has been but slender, there has been more enjoyment of the favor of God than amongst the great ones of the earth. They may regard those who still stand by the old-fashioned truth as being outcasts from the commonwealth of letters, and not worthy to be named amongst the cultured intellects of the age, but if the Lord will but gather us continually to his bosom and refresh us with himself, we shall be well content. The text should be a source of joy to us if any of us happen to be extremely poor—so poor that even Christian men are so ungenerous as to give us the cold shoulder, or if we happen to be the despised ones of our family. Here and there, sad to say it, there will be in families a better one than the rest, less thought of than the others—a Joseph whom his brothers hate, because he loves his God. Well, you may become as a stranger to your mother's children, and you may have no one to give you a good word, yet may you put this verse under your tongue as a sweet morsel—"He gathereth together the outcasts of Israel." Those who are lowest in the esteem of men are still remembered by the Lord.

The text may be applied very well to those *who have made themselves outcasts by their wickedness and are deservedly cast out of society.* May God grant that none of us may be or may have been amongst that number; but if I should be addressing any such at this time, I have a word for them. If there should be some such here tonight who do not often attend places of worship, but have dropped in from curiosity I may suppose your case to be that of one who has broken a mother's heart and brought a father's grey hairs to the grave with grief. You have lived such a life that your own brothers could scarcely be expected to acknowledge you. You have sinned, and sinned terribly. Man or woman—for woman also becomes an outcast, she is too severely treated, as a general rule, and oftener becomes an outcast than the man who deserves it more—if I address such, it is a great joy to me to know that our Lord Jesus Christ can save the most wicked of the wicked, the most fallen of the fallen, the most depraved of the depraved. If you have sunk so low that there is not much to choose between you and a devil, and some men and women do get as low as that, yet Jesus Christ can lift you up. If your life-story is such that it would be a pity it should ever be told, and most grievous that it should ever have been enacted, yet Jesus can wash all the stains of your life away, and save you, even you. Only one such may be present here tonight, but I make no apology for concentrating my whole thoughts upon one single person. I leave the ninety and nine to go after the one lost sheep, that in the one lost one may be revealed the richness and freeness of the grace of God in Jesus Christ. Come, then, outcast, come to your Redeemer and find pardon. "Though your sins be as scarlet they shall be as snow: though they be red like crimson they shall be as wool."[1] Jesus is able to wash away every transgression from those who are steeped in guilt. Countless iniquities dissolve and disappear before the presence of his mighty love, for he, even Jesus, gathereth together the outcasts of Israel. Is there no helper on earth? Yet is there one in heaven. Is there no friend below? Yet is there one above. Is there nothing that can now save you? Do you meditate suicide? Stay, stay your hand, for Jesus is "able to save to the

1 Isaiah 1:18.

uttermost"—*to the uttermost*—"them that come unto God by him."[1] Let the prayer go up, "God be merciful to me a sinner";[2] and go thy way with hope in thy soul, for "he gathereth together the outcasts of Israel."

A third class of persons consists of *those who judge themselves to be outcasts,* though as to outward actions they certainly do not deserve the character. Many who have written about John Bunyan have been surprised at the description which he gives of his own life, for it does not appear that, with the sole exception of the use of blasphemous language, John Bunyan was one of the very worst of mankind; but he thought himself to be so. Now it often happens—I do not say always, but I think it is generally so—that when the Spirit of God comes with power to the conscience and awakens it, the man judges himself to be the very chief of sinners. For see, it may be that you have never gone into actual vice; you have never been a blasphemer or dishonest, you have, on the contrary, from the instructions of your childhood, been led into the path of right; and yet when you are awakened you may feel yourself to be vilest of the vile. Everything that is lovely and of good report has been found in you, you do not know the time in which you would not have been shocked to hear a blasphemous word, and yet when the Holy Spirit arouses you, you will plead guilty among the very worst. I know that, in my own case, I had a horror of ungodliness, and yet when the Spirit of God came to me I felt myself to be far worse than the swearer or the drunkard, for this reason—that I knew that many who indulged in those open sins did so ignorantly, did so from the imitation of those in whose society they had been brought up; but as for me, with a godly parentage, with a mother's prayers and tears, with light and knowledge, understanding the letter of the gospel, having read the Bible from my youth up, I felt that my sins were blacker than those of others, because I had sinned against light and knowledge. And you must have felt the same, I am persuaded; perhaps you are even now feeling it. You recollect that night when you stifled conviction, when conscience had an earnest

1 Hebrews 7:25.
2 Luke 18:13.

battle with you, and it seemed that you must yield to God and to his Christ; but you deliberately did violence to the inward principle, and resolved to go on in sin. Do you remember that? If you do, it will sting you as doth a serpent now that you are under conviction of sin, and you will feel yourself to be the very chief of sinners on account of it, though no public sin may ever have stained your life. Well, I should not wonder, if such be your condition, that you also judge that there is no salvation for you—that God might save your mother, your brother, or your friend, but not you. You believe the blood of Jesus to be very precious, but you think it never will be applied to you. You heard the other day of the conversion of a friend, and you felt glad, but at the same time you thought, "Grace will never come to me." When the preacher has exhorted his hearers to believe in Jesus Christ you have said, "Ah, but I—I cannot. I am in a condition in which that gospel does not avail me." You think yourself an outcast. You feel that you deserve to be. You are not content to be so, but, at the same time, you could not blame the Lord if he left you to perish. You feel that your transgressions have been so great that if he should leave you out of his gracious plans, and grace should come to others and not to you, you could only bow your head in bitterest sorrow, and say, "Thou art just, O God." Now, listen, thou who hast condemned thyself. The Lord absolves thee. Thou who hast shut thyself out as an outcast, thou shalt be gathered; for whereas they call thee an outcast, whom no man seeketh after, thou shalt be called Hephzibah, for the Lord's delight is in thee. Only believe thou in Jesus Christ, and cast thyself upon him.

Outcasts of this sort are the people who most gladly welcome Christ. People who have nowhere else to go but to him—people so cast down, so full of sin, so everything but what they ought to be— these are the people to whom Christ is very precious. "Oh," says one, "but I do not feel like that. I cannot feel my guilt as I should." Very well, then, you are one of the outcasts among the outcasts: you do not think yourself to be so good even as they are. You are in your own esteem one of the veriest outcasts of them all, because you lack even the feeling of your needs. You say, "I have a hard heart. I cannot see sin as others have seen it who have found Christ: I wish I could. I smite my breast and mourn that I cannot mourn, for if aught is felt it is only pain to find that I cannot feel. I seem made of hell-hardened steel which will not melt or break." Well, I see what you are, but "such were some of us," we also knew our insensibility, and lamented that we could not lament. But he gathered us, and there stands the text, "He gathereth together the outcasts of Israel." If you have not a broken heart, only Christ can give it you. If you cannot come to him *with* it, come to him *for* it. If you cannot come to him wounded, come to him that he may wound you and make you whole. You need bring nothing to Jesus. I would like to whisper in your ear just this— that those people who think themselves insensible generally think so because they are more than usually sensitive; and those who think that they do not feel are usually those who feel most. I do not think we are ever good judges of our own feeling in this matter. The day may come when, in looking back, you will say, "I did after all mourn over sin, when I thought that I did not; I had such a sense of how black it was, that I felt I was not mourning enough! even when I was deeply mourning." Brother, you never will mourn enough. Enough! Would oceans full of tears be enough to mourn the guilt of sin? No, but, blessed be God, we are not asked to repent or to mourn up to a certain standard. O outcast soul, trust thou in Jesus, and he will save thee.

I must not dwell, however, on this class, but proceed further to notice that there is another sort of people who are even more truly the outcasts of Israel, whom Jesus gathers. I mean *the backsliders from the church*—the outcasts of Israel who have been put out, and properly put out, for their unholy lives and inconsistent actions: those whom the church is obliged, alas, to look upon as diseased members that must be removed; sickly sheep that infect the flock, and that must be put away; lepers that must be set aside from the camp. O wanderer, banished from a church, there is a word in the gospel to thee also, even to the backslider! The Lord calls back his wandering children. Though his church does right to put out those who do dishonor to his holy name, yet she would do wrong if she did not follow her Lord in saying, "Return, ye backsliding children." It is not easy to persuade one who has been a backslider to come back to his first love. The return journey is uphill, and flesh and blood do not assist us in it. Many new converts come, but the old wanderers remain outside, and sometimes they do this because they fancy they will not be welcome. But if you are sincerely repenting of the sin which has put you away from the church, the church of Christ will be glad to receive you; and if you be indeed the Lord's believing one, though you have defiled yourself yet he does not forget you. He does earnestly remember you still, and he bids you come in all your defilement and wash in his atoning blood; for the fountain that he has opened is not only for strangers, when they are at first brought nigh, but it is opened "for the house of David and for the inhabitants of Jerusalem,"[1] for those who know the Lord, that they may be daily purged from their transgressions, and be cleansed from the filthiness of their backslidings. The Lord gathers together those who have been carried captive by their sins, and makes them once more to dwell in the land of uprightness, and all his wandering sheep he brings back to himself.

The expression of the text may certainly be applied to *those who have loved the Lord for years, but who have fallen into great depression of spirit.* We happen, every now and then, to meet with some of the best of God's people who get into the Slough of Despond, and stick there by the month together—ay, by the year together. There are believers who take periodically to despondency, as birds do to moulting, and when the fit is on them you cannot cheer or comfort them. Then they write bitter things against themselves, and call themselves all the ugly names in the dictionary, until they make us smile to hear them, because we know how mistaken they are. We are admiring their consistency, and they are mourning over their foolishness. We see their generosity towards the cause of God, and their devotion to everything that is good; yet they say there is nothing good in them. We know where they are; for we have been laid in iron ourselves, and set fast in the very same stocks. What a mercy it is that, when you who love the Lord thus sit down and commune with your

1 Zechariah 13:1.

despondencies—I mean you, Miss Much-afraid, you, Mr. Ready-to-halt, and you, Mr. Feeblemind,—my Lord does not leave you, nor judge you as you judge yourselves, but he is pleased to gather together in mercy those who think themselves outcasts in Israel.

Lastly, upon this point, there are some who become outcasts through their love to Christ, and of these the text is peculiarly true. I mean *those who suffer for righteousness' sake, till they are regarded as the offscouring of all things.* Who that serves God faithfully has escaped the trial of cruel mockings? The names of those who are eminently useful are generally used as footballs for an ungodly world. The world is not worthy of them, and yet their enemies think they are hardly worthy to live in the world. We do not hear much about persecution now-a-days, but in private life there is a world of it; the cold shoulder is given where once friendship was sought; hard, cruel, cutting things are said where once admiration was expressed; and separations take place between very friends because of Christ. It is still true in the Christian's case that a man's foes are they of his own household. But if you should become an outcast upon the face of the earth for Christ's sake, there is this for your comfort—"The Lord doth build up Jerusalem, he gathereth together the outcasts of Israel." Of the persecuted he makes pillars in his holy temple for ever. Blessed are those who are outcasts for Christ! Rich are those who are so honored as to be permitted to become poor for him! Happy they who have had this grace given them to be permitted to lay life itself down for Jesus Christ's sake!

II. Now a few words upon the second point—IN WHAT SENSE THE LORD JESUS GATHERS TOGETHER THESE OUTCASTS OF DIFFERENT CLASSES. Of course I should have to vary the explanation to suit each case, but as that would take a long time, let me say that the Lord Jesus has several ways of gathering together the outcasts.

He gathers them *to hear the gospel.* Preach Jesus Christ and they will come. Both outcast saints and outcast sinners will come to hear the charming sound of his blessed name. They cannot help it. Nothing draws like Jesus Christ. Jesus Christ next gathers them *to himself.* The parable of the wedding feast is repeated over again,

"Go out into the highways and hedges, and compel them to come in, that my house may be filled."[1] "Bring in hither the poor, and the maimed, and the halt, and the blind."[2] In this sort the Lord Jesus Christ gathers multitudes where he is faithfully preached. He gathers all sorts of characters, and especially the odds and ends of society—the despised of men and the despised of themselves. He gathers them to himself. And oh, what a blessed gathering-place that is where there is cleansing for their filthiness, health for their disease, clothing for their nakedness, and all-sufficient supplies for their abundant necessities. He gathers them to himself, which is to gather them to God—to gather them to blessedness and peace through reconciliation with the Father. "To him shall the gathering of the people be."[3]

When he has done that, he gathers them *into the divine family*. He takes the outcasts and makes them children of God—heirs with himself. From the dunghill he lifts them, and sets them among princes. He takes them from the swine-trough, and puts the ring on their fingers and the shoes on their feet, and they sit down at the Father's table to feast and to be glad. Jesus Christ, as the good Shepherd, gathers the lost sheep, the lame, the halt, the diseased, and feeds them, and makes them to lie down, and restores their souls, and finally leads them to the rich pastures of the glory-land.

In due time the Lord gathers together the outcasts *into his visible church*. As David enrolled a company of men that were in debt, and discontented, so does Jesus Christ still gather the indebted ones and the malcontents and makes them his soldiers; and these are known as the church militant. Surely as David did great exploits by those Pelethites and Cherethites, and Gittites, and strange men of foreign extraction whom he gathered to himself, so does Jesus of Nazareth do great things by those great sinners whom he greatly forgives—those hard-hearted ones whom he so strangely changes and makes to be the Old Guard of his army. Yes, he gathers them into his church, and he gathers them *into his work*. The outcasts of Israel he uses for his own glory.

1 Luke 14:23.
2 Luke 14:21.
3 Genesis 49:10.

And when he has done that, he gathers them *into heaven*. What a surprise it must be for any man to find himself in heaven, when he remembers where he once was; but for the outcast to remember the ale-bench on which he sat and soaked himself in liquor till he degraded himself below the brute beast, and now to be cleansed in the Redeemer's blood, and to sit among the angels—this will be surprising grace indeed. "Oh, to think," one might well say, "that I who was once in lewd company, polluted and defiled, am now made to wear a crown, and sit at the Redeemer's feet!" When we reach heaven, brethren, I do not suppose that we shall forget all the past; and sometimes it must burst in upon us as a strangely divine instance of love that Christ should have brought *us* there, and set *us* among the peers of his realm. And yet he means to do it; and you, Mrs. Much-afraid—you will be there; and you who think "surely Satan will have me!" you will be there. You who are stumbling over every straw; you who seem stopped by every little gully in the road, and who fancy, "Surely, there is no grace in my heart," and yet you are still holding on, "faint, yet pursuing," you who touch the hem of Christ's garment, but have such very little faith that you are afraid that you have none at all, you shall get up from that mourning and moaning, you shall rise from that despondency and distress; and among the sweetest music of heaven shall be your songs of gratitude and joy. "He gathereth together the outcasts of Israel."

III. Well, now, WHAT IS THE LESSON OF THIS? I think there are three lessons, and I will just hint at them.

One is this—*encouragement to those who are unworthy, or who think themselves so, to go to Jesus Christ tonight.* I have been trying to think of all I know, and I have lifted up my heart to the Holy Spirit to guide me that I may cheer some discouraged one. It was my object last Sunday night to comfort the broken-hearted, and I do not seem to have got out of that vein yet. I believe there are some here whom God has sent me after who really believe themselves to be out of the region of hope. My dear friend, if God gathers together the outcasts, why should he not gather you? And if it be true that Jesus Christ does not look for goodness, but that he only considers our sin and misery, why should he not look upon you? May I urge you to go and try my Master; and if you go to him, confessing your unworthiness and trusting yourself with him, if he does not save you I would like to know it, because you will be the first person I have ever heard of that did trust himself with Jesus and was rejected. It shall not be the case, whatever your condition may be, however desperate your state. You think your condition to be worse than I have pictured it to be, and you fancy that I cannot know anything about how bad you are. Well, I do not know your special form of rebellion, but you are the very person I mean for all that. I say, if thou be as black as hell, if thou be as foul as the Stygian bog, if thou have sinned till thy sins cannot be counted, and if thy crimes be so heinous that infinite wrath is their just desert, yet come and look to those five wounds and to that sacred head once wounded, and to that heart pierced with the spear. There is life in a look at Jesus crucified. Wilt thou try it? As surely as God's word is true, if thou dost but glance thine eye at him who "died the just for the unjust" thou shalt be brought to God and reconciled, and that now—*now*—while sitting in that seat, ere yet the last word of this sermon shall be uttered: for whosoever believeth in him shall be saved. Like "as Moses lifted up the serpent in the wilderness, even so must the Son of man be lifted up: that whosoever believeth in him should not perish, but have eternal life." O that thou wouldst believe on Jesus now. We sometimes sing,

> "Venture on him: venture wholly,
> Let no other trust intrude.
> None but Jesus
> Can do helpless sinners good."[1]

But, sinner, it is not a venture. As surely as ever you cast yourself upon him he will be sure to save you. I will not multiply words, but I would if I thought words would draw you. I pray the blessed and eternal Spirit sweetly to influence your minds, young people, tonight—and old people, too, and middle-aged people, too—that you may have done with trying to do anything, or to be anything, in order to your

---

1 *Come, Ye Sinners, Poor and Needy* by Joseph Hart.

own salvation, and know that it was all done when Jesus bled and died, all finished when he cried "It is finished," and you have only to take believingly what he presents to you, and accept him as your all in all. God help you to do it!

The second reflection is this. *If Jesus Christ received some of us when we felt ourselves to be outcasts, how we ought to love him!* It does us good to look back to the hole of the pit whence we were digged. We get to be very top-lofty at times, my brethren. We are wonderfully big, are we not? Are not we experienced Christians now? Why, we have known the Lord these five-and-twenty years. Dear me, how important we are! And perhaps we are deacons of churches, or, at any rate, we have a class in the Sunday-school, and we pray in the prayer-meeting: considerable importance attaches to us, and we are high and mighty on that account. Ah! I have heard say of a man worth his thousands that once he had not a shirt to his back, and if he recollected what he sprang from he would not carry his head so high. I do not see much in that, but I do see something in this—that if we recollected the time when we were dead in trespasses and sins, when we had not a rag to cover us, when we were under God's frown, and were heirs of wrath even as others—if we recollected our lost and ruined state by nature, I am sure that we should not lift our heads so very loftily, and want to have respect paid to us in the church, or think that God ought not to deal so very hardly with us, as if we had cause for complaint. Dear friends, let us remember what we used to be, and that will keep us low in our own esteem. But, oh, how it will fire us with zeal to remember from what a depth he has lifted us up. Did Jesus save such a wretch as I was? Then for him would I live and for him would I die. This ought to be the utterance of us all. We ought to live in that spirit. God grant we may!

Then, again, let us always feel that *if the Lord Jesus Christ took us up when we were not worth having, we will never be ashamed to try and pick up others who are in a like condition.* We will not count it any lowering of our dignity to go after the most fallen of all. We will reckon that they are no worse than we were if we were viewed from a certain point, and we will therefore aim at their conversion, hope for it, and expect it. This lesson is peculiarly applicable to some Christians here present. Dear brothers and sisters, if you really feel yourselves to have been outcasts, and yet have been received into the divine family, and are now on the road to heaven, I ask you to pay every attention to any whom you meet with who are now what you were once. If you meet with any in great despair of soul, say, "Ah, I must be a comforter here, for I have gone through this; and I will never let this poor soul go till by God's help I have cheered him." If you meet with one who is an open sinner, perhaps you will have to say to yourself, "I was an open sinner too;" but if not, say, "My sins were more secret, but still they were as bad as his; and therefore I have hope of this poor soul, and will try whether he cannot be loved to Christ by me." Mark my expression—"loved to Christ," for this is the power we must use—sinners are to be loved to Christ. The Holy Spirit uses the love of saints to bring poor sinners to know the love of Christ. Search after them, and do not let them perish. May God put this resolve into your soul—"If there is anything that I can do in the name of Jesus, and with the power of the Holy Ghost upon me, that might save that soul, it shall be done; and, if that soul dies lost, when I hear the passing bell I will, God helping me, be able to say, 'I did set Christ before that soul. I did plead with that conscience. I did seek to bring that sinner to Jesus.'"

The outcast, when converted, should seek after his brother outcasts. Young man, did you ever swear? seek the conversion of swearers. Young man, have you been fond of the card-table? Have you been a frequenter of low resorts of pleasure? Then addict yourself to looking after persons of the same sort. George Whitefield says that after his own conversion his first concern was the conversion of those with whom he had taken pleasure in sin; and he had the privilege of seeing many of them brought to Christ. Have you been a man of business, and have you been associated in wrongdoing with others? Seek the salvation of those who were associated with you. It is a natural obligation which Christ imposes upon all of any special sort, that they should seek those of their own sort, and labor to bring them to repentance.

May God bless you, beloved. We shall soon be in heaven. I can see some here tonight who, owing to their age, cannot be long before they enter the glory of Christ; and others of us who are younger do not know, from feebleness of health, how long it may be before we see the face of the Beloved. But we would say of him tonight, what a blessed Savior he is, and what an infinity of love there must be in him ever to have revealed himself to such as we are. Oh, when shall we be near him, and worship him for ever and ever? Make no tarrying, O our Beloved!

PORTION OF SCRIPTURE READ BEFORE SERMON—PSALM 147.

AENEAS

LORD'S-DAY EVENING, JULY 16TH, 1876, METROPOLITAN TABERNACLE

Upon the occasion of the regular hearers vacating their seats to allow strangers to fill the house.

And it came to pass, as Peter passed throughout all quarters, he came down also to the saints which dwelt at Lydda. And there he found a certain man named Aeneas, which had kept his bed eight years, and was sick of the palsy. And Peter said unto him, Aeneas, Jesus Christ maketh thee whole: arise, and make thy bed. And he arose immediately. And all that dwelt in Lydda and Saron saw him, and turned to the Lord.—ACTS 9:32–35.

I may not hope that I shall see you all again, and so, as I have the opportunity of only preaching one sermon to you, I must make it as full as I can of *essence of gospel*, from beginning to end. We have heard of a chaplain who preached in a jail, who selected a subject which he divided into two heads. The first part was the sinner's disease; this he took for his topic on one Sabbath, and closed the sermon by saying that he should preach upon the sinner's remedy upon the following Sunday. Now, there were several of the prisoners hanged on the Monday, according to the custom of the bad old times, so that they did not hear that part of the discourse which it was most necessary for them to hear. It would have been well to have told out the great news of salvation at once to men so near their end, and I think that in every sermon, if the preacher confines himself to one subject, and leaves out essential gospel truth, under the notion that he will preach salvation by Jesus another day, he is very unwise, for some of his congregation may be dead and gone—alas, some of them lost—before he will have the opportunity of coming to the grand and all-important point, namely, the way of salvation. We will not fall into that evil tonight. We will try to shoot at the very center of our target, and preach the plan of salvation as completely as we can; and may God grant that his blessing may rest on it, the Holy Spirit working with it.

I shall only preach this one sermon to some of you: you will, therefore, have the greater patience with me, as I shall not inflict myself upon you again: but, if we are to have only one communication with each other, let us come to real practical business and waste no time tonight. A good deal of sermon-hearing is mere trifling; let us come to matter-of-fact preaching and hearing at this time. I am afraid that some sermon-preaching is playing too—fine words and oratorical fireworks, but no agony for souls. We mean business tonight. My heart will not be satisfied unless many of you who came in here without Christ shall go down those steps saved by his atoning blood. Bitter will be my disappointment if many do not lay hold of Jesus, and realize in their own souls Peter's words, "Jesus Christ maketh thee whole." I have faith in the great Physician that many of you will go away whole tonight, though sin-sick when you came into this house of prayer. Much supplication has gone up to heaven for this, and the Lord heareth prayer; and therefore do I reckon that miracles of healing will surely be wrought in this house on this occasion.

To the point, then. Peter came to Lydda, and found one who bore the classic name of Aeneas: no mighty warrior, however, but a poor paralyzed man, who had been confined to his bed for eight long years. Touched with a sight of the man's feebleness, Peter felt the impulse of the Spirit upon him; and, looking at him as he lay there, he said, "Aeneas, Jesus Christ maketh thee whole: arise, and make thy bed." Touched by the same Spirit who inspired the apostle, the man believed the message,—believed that Christ had healed him, at once rose and made his bed, and in an instant was perfectly restored.

Now let us hear something about this man. We are not to hear Virgil sing, "arms and the man," but we are to let Luke tell us of the man and his Savior.

I. In the first place, then, it is very clear that THE MAN WAS TRULY SICK. Had he not been *really sick*, the incident before us would have been all a piece of imposture—a feint and a pretence from beginning to end: but he was hopelessly infirm. He had been anxiously watched by his friends for eight years, and was so completely palsied that during all those years he had not left his bed, which had grown hard as a stone beneath him. Now, as there is no room for a great cure unless there is a great sickness, so there is no room for God's great grace unless there is great sin. Jesus Christ did not come into the world to save sham sinners, but real sinners; neither did he descend from heaven to seek those who are not diseased with sin, for the whole have no need of a physician, but he has come to seek those who are deeply diseased, and to give them real healing. This man's sickness was no imaginary ill, for he could not move; his hands and feet were quite paralyzed. If in any limb there was a measure of motion, it was only a tremulous quiver, which rather indicated growing weakness than remaining force. He was bereaved of all strength. Are you such by nature, my friend, in a spiritual sense? Certainly you are so; but have you found it out? Has the Spirit of God made you feel that you can do nothing aright apart from him, and that you are altogether ruined and palsied unless Jesus Christ can save you? If so, do not despair because you feel how terribly your soul is smitten; but, on the contrary, say to yourself, "Here is room for mercy in me. If ever a soul wanted healing, I do. Here is space for divine power to operate in me, for if ever a soul was weak and palsied, I am just that soul." Be thou cheered with the hope that God will make of thine infirmity a platform upon which he will display his power.

The man had been paralyzed *eight years*. The length of its endurance is a terrible element in a disease. Perhaps yours is no eight years' malady, but twenty-eight, or thirty-eight, or forty-eight, or seventy-eight, perhaps, eighty-eight years have you been in bondage under it. Well, blessed be God, the number of years in which we have lived in sin cannot prevent the mercy of God in Christ Jesus from making us whole. You have a very long bill to discharge, while another friend has but a short one, and owes comparatively little; but it is just as easy for the creditor to write *"paid"* at the bottom of the large bill as the smaller one. And now that our Lord Jesus Christ has made full atonement it is as easy for God to pardon the iniquities of eighty years as the sins of the child of eight. Be not despairing, then. Jesus Christ can make such as thou art whole, even though thy heart and thine understanding have been long paralyzed with sin.

The man's disease was one which was then reckoned to be, and probably is now, *entirely incurable*. Who can restore a palsied man? Aeneas could not restore himself, and no merely human physician had skill to do anything for him. Dear hearer, has the Spirit of God made you feel that your soul's wound is incurable? Is your heart sick? Is your understanding darkened? Do you feel your whole nature to have become paralyzed with sin, and is there no physician? Ah, I know there is none among men, for there is no balm in Gilead, there is no physician there; there never was, or else the daughter of my people would have been healed of her hurt long ago. There is no soul physician except at Calvary; no balm but in the Savior's wounds. If you feel that you are incurably soul-sick, and the case is desperate unless infinite mercy shall interpose, then I am glad that you are here tonight. I am glad that there is such a one as Aeneas present. Do you know that the most delightful task in the world is to preach to those who consciously need the Savior? Mr. Whitefield used to say that he could wish to preach all day and all night long to those who really knew that they wanted Christ. We are bound to preach to everybody, for our Master said, "preach the gospel to every creature" under heaven; but, oh, when we can get at a knot of hungry souls it is easy and pleasant work to feed them with the bread of heaven; and when hearts are thirsty it is sweet work to hand out the living water, for they are all eager to take it. You know, the great difficulty is that you can bring a horse to the water, but you cannot make him drink if he is not thirsty; and so you may set Jesus Christ before men, but if they do not feel their need of him they will not have him. You may preach in tones of thunder, or plead with accents of intense affection, but you cannot stir them to desire the grace which is in Christ Jesus, unless they feel their need of it. Oh, I am happy tonight—thrice happy—if anywhere in this house there is an Aeneas who is sick, and knows that he is sick; who knows his disease to be incurable, laments that he is palsied and can do nothing, and longs to be healed by divine power. He is the man who will welcome the glad news of the gospel of free grace. The man was really sick, and so are you, my hearer; your sins are great, your sinfulness of nature is grievous, and your case is beyond reach of human skill.

II. In the second place, THIS MAN, AENEAS, KNEW SOMETHING ABOUT JESUS; because, otherwise, when Peter said, "Jesus Christ maketh thee whole," Aeneas might have earnestly enquired what he meant, but could not intelligently have acted upon what he could not comprehend. He could not have believed what Peter said, because he would not have understood his meaning. Mere words, unless they appeal to the understanding, cannot be useful; they must convey light as well as sound, or they cannot breed faith. When Peter said, "Aeneas, Jesus Christ maketh thee whole," I have no doubt that Aeneas remembered what he had aforetime heard about Jesus Christ, and his wondrous life and death. Now, lest there should be one in this congregation who does not know Jesus Christ, and does not understand how it is that he is able to heal sin-sick souls, let us briefly tell the old, old story over again.

"Jesus Christ," translated into English, means a "Savior anointed." Who is he? He is the Son of the Highest, very God of very God; and when we were lost in sin he who is called the Son of God laid aside his most divine array, and came hither to be dressed like ourselves in this poor flesh and blood; in the manger he lay as an infant, and on a woman's breast he hung a feeble babe. The God who stretched forth the heavens like a tent to dwell in, and digged the deep foundations of the earth, came down to earth to take upon himself our nature and to be born of a woman. Oh, matchless stoop of unbounded condescension that the Infinite should be an infant, and the Eternal God should conceal himself within the form of a babe. This marvel was performed that we might be saved. Being here, the Lord of angels lived some thirty years or so amongst men; he spent the earliest part of his life as a carpenter's son obedient to his father, and he was throughout the whole of his earthly sojourn obedient to his father, God. Inasmuch as we had no righteousness, for we had broken the law, he was here to make a righteousness for us, and he did so. But there was also wanted an atonement, for we had sinned, and God's judgment demanded that there should be punishment for sin: Jesus stepped in as the Surety and the Substitute for the guilty sons of men. He bared his back to the lash of justice, and opened his breast to her lance, and died that sinners might live. The just for the unjust, he died that he might bring us to God:—

> "He bore, that we might never bear,
> His Father's righteous ire."

Now, when he had thus lived and died, they placed his body in the tomb, but he rose again on the third day, and he is yet alive; and by this man Christ Jesus, who is risen from the dead, is preached unto the nations the remission of sins. For after forty days this same Jesus, who had been dead and buried, rose into the heavens in the presence of his disciples, ascending till a cloud concealed him from their sight, and he now sits at the right hand of God, even the Father, pleading there the merit of his blood, making intercession for sinners that they may be reconciled to God. Now, brethren, this is the story that we have to tell you, with the addition that this same Jesus is coming again to judge the quick and the dead, for he is Lord of all. He is at this hour the Mediator appointed by the infinitely glorious Jehovah, having power over all flesh that he may give eternal life to as many as Jehovah hath given him, and this we beseech you to consider, lest when he comes as a judge you should be condemned at his bar. Aeneas had heard more or less of these great facts. The story of the incarnate God had come to his ears by some means or other, and Aeneas understood that though Jesus Christ was not in the room, and there was only Peter and a few friends there, and though Jesus Christ was not on earth, but was gone to heaven, yet his power on earth was the same as ever it was. He knew that Jesus could work miracles from heaven as well as when he was here below. He understood that he who healed the palsy when he was here, could heal the palsy now that he has risen to his throne; and so Aeneas believed in Jesus Christ from what he had heard, simply trusting in him for healing. By means of that faith Aeneas was made whole.

I will very earnestly dwell on that point for a second or two. I am persuaded that in this congregation all of you know the story of Jesus Christ crucified. You have heard it on the Sabbath from the pulpit. Your children sing it when they come home from the Sunday School. You have a Bible in every house, and you read the "old, old story" in the plain but sublime language of our own noble version; but, oh, if you have heard it and know it, how is it that you have not drawn from it the same inference that this poor paralyzed man did? How is it that ye have no faith? Jesus lives, he sits on Zion's hill, he receives poor sinners still. Jesus lives "exalted on high to be a Prince and a Savior, to give repentance unto Israel and remission of sins."[1] He can heal you now, and save you now as well as if you met him in the street, or saw him standing at your door knocking for admittance. I would to God that this inference were drawn by you all.

III. We have got so far: the man was sick, and the man knew something about Christ. And now came the most important point of all: THE MAN BELIEVED ON THE LORD JESUS.

Peter said to him, "Aeneas, Jesus Christ maketh thee whole." The man did not believe in Peter as the healer, for you notice Peter does not say anything about himself. Peter does not say, "As the head of the church, I, by power delegated to me, make thee whole." There is no allusion to any such claim, Peter preached too clear a gospel for that. That is the purest gospel which has the least of man in it, and the most of Christ. I charge you, men and brethren, do not listen to that teaching which sets the priest in front of the Savior, or even by the side of the Savior, for it is false and ruinous. Your forefathers, Englishmen, your forefathers bled and died that they might never submit to that vile superstition which is being now propagated by a

1 Acts 5:31.

considerable party in the Established Church of this once Protestant land! No man beneath the sky has any more power to save your soul than you have yourself, and if any presumptuous priestling tells you that he has, do not believe him, but despise his claims. An old woman asks me to cross her hand with a sixpence, and says that she will tell my fortune. I am not such a fool. And if another person dressed in habiliments, which are not quite so becoming to him as a red cloak is to an old woman, tells me that he can regenerate my child, or forgive my sins, I treat him with the same contempt and pity as that with which I treat the wicked hag. I believe in neither the one impostor nor the other. If ever you are saved you must be saved by Jesus Christ alone through your own personal belief in him; certainly not by the intervention of any man, or set of men, hail they from whatever church they will. God send that the Pope and the priesthood and all their detestable deceits may go down in this land, and that Christ may be exalted!

As this man had no faith in any supposed power coming from Peter, much less had he any faith in himself, neither did he look within himself for hope. He did not say to Peter, "But I do not feel strength enough to get well;" neither did he say, "I think I do feel power enough to shake off this palsy." He said neither the one nor the other. Peter's message took him off from himself. It was, "Aeneas, *Jesus Christ* maketh thee whole; it is not that thou hast stamina in thy constitution and rallying points about thy bodily system. No, Aeneas, thou art paralyzed; thou canst do nothing; but Jesus Christ maketh thee whole." That was what the man had to believe; and it is very much what you also, my dear hearer, must believe.

With his faith Aeneas had the desires which showed that it was not mere speculation, but solid practical believing; he anxiously wished to be made whole. Oh, that sinners anxiously wished to be saved! Oh, that yonder angry man wished to be cured of his bad temper! Oh, that yonder covetous man wished to be cured of his avarice! Oh, that yonder lustful man wished to be cured of his uncleanness! Oh, that yon drunkard wished to be cured of his excess! Oh, that men really wanted to get rid of their sins! But no. I never heard of men reckoning a cancer to be a jewel, but there are many men who look upon their sins as if they were gems, which they keep as hid treasure, so that they will sooner lose heaven than part with their lustful pleasures. Aeneas wanted to be made whole, and was ready to believe when Peter spoke to him about Jesus Christ.

And what did Aeneas believe? He believed—and may you believe the same!—first, that Jesus could heal *him*, could heal *him*, *Aeneas*. John Brown, do you believe that Jesus Christ can cure you? I do not care, John, what your faith is about your wife's case; it is about yourself that you want faith: Jesus Christ is able to save *you*—you, Aeneas; you, John Brown; you, Thomas; you, Sarah; you, Mary. He is able to save *you*. Can you grip that, and reply, "Yes, he is able to save *me?*"

And Aeneas believed that Jesus Christ was able to save him *there and then*, just as he was. He had not taken a course of physic; he had not been under galvanism to strengthen his nerves and sinews and prepare him to be cured, but he believed that Jesus Christ could save him without any preparation, just as he was, then, immediately, with a present salvation. When you think what Christ is, and what he has done, it ought not to be difficult to believe this. But truly God's power must be revealed before your soul will believe this unto salvation. Yet is it true that Jesus Christ can heal, and can heal at once. Whatever the sin is, he can cure it. I mentioned a whole set of sins just now. The scarlet fever of pride, the loathsome leprosy of lust, the shivering ague of unbelief, the paralysis of avarice,—he can heal all, and with a word, instantaneously, for ever, completely, just now. Yes, sinner, he can heal *you now*. Aeneas believed that. He believed, and, as he believed, Jesus did make him whole. Oh, I wish I could tonight so preach the gospel that my Lord and Master would lead many unbelievers to believe in him. O Holy Spirit, work thou with the word! Sinner, dost thou want forgiveness? Christ has wrought it out. Every sin that you have done shall be forgiven you for his name's sake if you trust Jesus to do it. Do you see your sins like a great army pursuing you? Do you think they will swallow you up quick? Jesus Christ, if you believe in him, will make an end of them all. You have read in Exodus how Pharaoh and his hosts pursued the tribes of Israel, and the people were terribly alarmed; but early in the morning they were no more afraid, for Miriam took her timbrel, and the daughters of Israel went forth with her in the dance; and they sang, "Sing unto the Lord, for he hath triumphed gloriously. The horse and his rider hath he thrown into the sea."[1] One of the most magnificent notes in that marvellous song was this, "The depths have covered them: there is not one of them left." The damsels took up the refrain, and sang, "Not one, not one, not one! The depths have covered them: there is not one of them left." Now, if you believe in Jesus, the whole army of your sins shall sink beneath the sea of his blood, and your soul shall sing, "The depths have covered them: there is not one of them, left." Such shall be your song tonight, if you are enabled to believe in Jesus Christ, God's crucified Son.

But do not think that we preach about the pardon of past sin only, because if a man could get his past sins pardoned, and go on as he did before, it would be so much the worse for him. Pardon of sin, without deliverance from its power, would be rather a curse than a blessing; but wherever sin is pardoned, God breaks the neck of its power in the soul. Mind, we do not tell you that Jesus Christ will forgive the past and then leave you to live the same life as before; but we tell you this: whatever the sin is that is now a disease to you, Jesus Christ can heal you of it. He can save you from the habit and power of evil doing and thinking. I will not attempt to go into details. There are odd people coming into the tabernacle on ordinary occasions, and so I dare say there may be tonight. How often has there come in a man to whom I might say, "Put out your tongue, sir. Ah, I see red spots, and black spots, for you are a liar and a swearer." Can my Master heal such a diseased tongue as that? Yes, trust thou him tonight, and he will make thee truthful, and purge thee from thy profanity. But here is another; I dare not describe him. Look at him! He has lived an unchaste life, and strong are his passions; and he says, "Can I ever be recovered from my vile desires?" Oh, sir, my Lord can lay his hand on that hot heart of thine, and cool it down to a sweet sobriety of chastity. And thou, fallen woman, do not think that thou art beyond his powers;

1 Exodus 15:1.

he shows himself mighty to save such as "the woman that was a sinner." Ah, if you are a slave to vile sins, Jesus can give perfect freedom from vicious habits. You young man there, you know that you have fallen into many sins which you dare not mention, which coil about your heart, and poison your life like serpents writhing within your conscience. My Lord can take them all out of the soul, and deliver you from the results of their fiery venom. Yea, he can make you into a new creature, and cause you to be born again. He can make you love the things which you once hated, and hate the things which you aforetime loved, and turn the current of your thoughts in quite another way. You see Niagara leaping down its awful height, and you say, "Who can stop this?" Ay, indeed, who can stop it? But my Master can, and if he speaks to the Niagara of your lust, and says, "Cease thy raging!" it will pause at once; yea, if he bids the waters of desire leap up instead of down, you shall be as full of love to Christ as once you were full of love to sin. He made the sun to stand still, and caused the moon to pause upon the hill of Gibeah; and he can do all things. Spake he not the world out of nothing? And can he not create new hearts and right spirits in the souls of men who have been far off from him by wicked works? He can do so, and blessed be his name he will: the world of mind is as much beneath his control as that of matter. If thou believest, O man, to thee I may say as Peter did to Aeneas, "Jesus Christ maketh thee whole."

IV. Well, now, let us pass on to notice, next, that the MAN WAS MADE WHOLE. There was no imposture about it; he was made whole, and made whole there and then. Just fancy, for a minute, what would have been the result if he had not been made whole. What dishonor it would have been to Peter! Peter said, "Aeneas, Jesus Christ maketh thee whole," but there lies Aeneas as palsied as before. Everybody would say, "Peter is a false witness." Well now, I will not say that the preacher of the gospel must see souls saved, or else he is a false witness. I will not say that, but I will say that if ever my ministry, under God, does not save souls I will give it up; for it seems to me that if we do not bring souls to Christ we preachers are just good for nothing. What are we if we do not turn many to righteousness? Reapers who never reap, soldiers who never win a battle, fishermen who take no fish, and lights which enlighten no one. These are sad but true comparisons. Do I address any unsuccessful minister? I would not speak harshly to him, but I would speak very severely to myself if I were in his case. I remember the dream of a minister. He thought that he was in hell, and being there, he was dreadfully distressed, and cried out "Is this the place where I am to be for ever? I am a minister." A grim voice replied, "No, it is lower down for unfaithful ministers, much lower down than this." And then he awoke. Ah, and if we do not agonize till souls are brought to Christ, we shall have to agonize to all eternity. I am persuaded of it: we must have men saved, or else we shall be like Peter would have been if he had said, "Jesus Christ makes thee whole," and the man had not been made whole,—we shall be dishonored witnesses.

What dishonor would have been brought upon the name of Jesus if the man had not been made whole. Suppose, my dear fellow sinner, you were to believe in Jesus Christ, and yet were not saved; what then? Oh, I do not like to suppose so, for it is almost a blasphemy to imagine it, but yet consider it for a moment. Believe in Jesus and not be saved! Then he has broken his word, or lost his power to save, either of which we are unwilling to tolerate for a minute. If thou believest in Jesus Christ, as surely as thou livest Jesus Christ has saved thee. I will tell thee one thing,—if thou believest in Jesus Christ and thou art damned, I will be damned with thee. Come! I will risk my soul on that bottom as surely as thou wilt risk thine, for if the Lord Jesus Christ does ever lose a soul that trusts him he will lose mine: but he never will, he never can:—

> "His honor is engaged to save
> The meanest of his sheep:
> All that his heavenly Father gave,
> His hands securely keep."

Rest ye in him and ye shall be saved, else were his name dishonored.

And suppose that, like Aeneas, you trusted Christ—if you were not saved, what then? Why, then the gospel would not be true. Shut up those churches, close those chapels, banish those ministers, burn those Bibles; there is no truth in any of them if a soul can believe in Jesus and yet not be saved. The gospel is a lie, and an imposture, if it be true that any poor sinner can put his trust in Jesus and not be healed of his sins; for thus saith the Lord of old, "Him that cometh to me I will in no wise cast out." This is his last word to his church, "Go ye into all the world and preach the gospel to every creature: he that believeth and is baptized shall be saved; he that believeth not shall be damned."[1] If men believing are not saved from the power of sin, then the gospel is not true, and we are sent on a fool's errand: but they *are* saved, blessed be the name of God, and the gospel is truth itself.

Oh, my dear hearer, fain would I urge thee to put thy trust in Jesus Christ tonight, by the experience which I and other believers have enjoyed; for some of us have relied on the name of the Redeemer, and he has saved us. We shall never forget the day, some of us, when we left off self-righteousness and believed in Christ to the salvation of our souls. The marvel was done in a minute, but the change was so great that we can never explain it, or cease to bless the Lord for it.

> "Happy day! Happy day!
> When Jesus washed my sins away."

I recollect the morning when salvation came to me as I sat in a little Primitive Methodist chapel under the gallery, and the preacher said, "That young man looks unhappy;" and added, "Young man, you will never find peace except you look to Christ;" and he called out to me, "Look!" With a voice of thunder he shouted, "Young man, look! Look now!" I did look, I turned the eye of faith to Jesus at once. My burden disappeared, and my soul was merry as a bird let loose from her cage, even as it is now as often as I remember the blessed salvation of Jesus Christ. We speak what we do know; ours is no hearsay or second-hand testimony; we speak what we have felt and tasted and handled, and our anxiety is that you may know and feel the same. Remember, my dear hearer, that the way to use the gospel is to put it to yourselves like this. What is your name? I said, "John Brown," just

1 Mark 16:15–16.

now, did I not? Suppose it is John Brown, then. Well, the gospel "He that believeth on the Lord Jesus Christ hath everlasting life." Then it means, "If John Brown believes on Jesus he has everlasting life." "He that believeth and is baptized shall be saved,"—"Then I, John Brown, believing and being baptized, shall be saved." Lay hold of it in that way. Perhaps you say, "But may I put my name to a promise, and appropriate it in that fashion?" Yes, you may, because there is nothing in the Bible to say that your name was left out from the list of those to whom the promise is made. If I were a beggar in the streets, and were very hungry, and I heard that there was a gentleman who was giving a good meal away, and that he had advertised that any beggar might come, I do not think I should say, "Well, my name is not down in his list." I should stop away when I found that he inserted an excluding clause, "Charles Spurgeon shall not have any of the food I distribute," but not till then. Until I read in black and white that he excluded me I should run the risk, and get in with the other hungry folk. Until he shut me out I would go. It should be his deed and not mine that kept me from the feast. Sometimes you say, "But I am not fit to go to Christ." The fittest way to go to Christ is to go just as you are. What is the best livery to wear when you go a-begging? I recollect some long time ago, when I lived not far from here, in the extremeness of my greenness, I gave a man who begged at the door a pair of patent leather boots. He put them on, and expressed great gratitude; but I met him afterwards, and I was not at all surprised to find that he had pulled them off. They were not at all the style of things to go about begging in. People would look at him and say, "What! you needing coppers while wearing those handsome boots? Your tale won't do." A beggar succeeds a deal better barefoot than in fine shoes. Rags are the livery of mendicants. When you go and beg for mercy at the hand of God, do not put on those pretty righteousnesses of yours, but go with all your sin and misery, and emptiness, and wretchedness, and say, "Lord, here am I. Thou hast said that Christ is able to save to the uttermost them that come unto God by him. I am a soul that wants saving to the uttermost, and here I am. I have come. Lord, save me."

Now, summing all up: this is what you have to do, sinner, in order to be saved tonight, simply believe in Jesus Christ. I saw a young woman from America in the vestry some little time ago who came in great concern of soul to know the way of salvation, and I said to her, "Do you not see it? If you trust Christ, you are saved." I quoted the Scriptures which teach this great truth and made them plain to her, until the Holy Spirit opened her eyes; light came on her face in a moment, and she said, "I do see it. I trust Christ with all my heart; and I am to believe that I am saved because I trust Jesus, and he has promised to save believers?" "Yes," I replied, "you are getting on the rock now." "I feel," she said, "a deep peace beginning in my soul, but I cannot understand how it can be, for my grandfather belonged to the old school Presbyterians, and he told me he was six years before he could get peace, and had to be put into a lunatic asylum, for he was so miserable." Ah, yes, I have no doubt such cases have happened. Some will go seventeen thousand miles round about merely to go across a street, but there is no need for it. There it is—"The word is nigh thee, on thy lip and in thy heart. If with thy heart thou wilt believe in the Lord Jesus Christ, and with thy mouth make confession of him, thou shalt be saved."[1] There is naught to be done; there is naught to be felt; these is naught to be brought. No preparation is wanted. Come just as you are, and trust Christ to save you out and out this night, and you shall be saved. God's honor and Christ's word are pledged to it.

V. This is the last thing. WHEN AENEAS WAS HEALED HE ACTED IN CONFORMITY THEREWITH. "Peter said unto him, Aeneas, Jesus Christ maketh thee whole: arise, and make thy bed." He did so. He rose directly and made his bed.

Now, if any of you say tonight, "I have believed in Jesus," remember you are bound to prove it. How prove it? Why, if you have believed in Jesus, you are made whole, and you are to go home and show people how whole you are. This man was palsied, and had been lying there prostrate eight years, and could never make his bed, but he proved he was healed by making his bed for himself. Perhaps here is a man who when he has entered his house has generally opened the door with an oath. If there is such a person here, and Christ saves

1 See Romans 10:8–9.

you—he will wash your mouth out for you. You will have done with profane language for ever. Your wife will be surprised when you go home to hear how differently you talk. Perhaps you have been used to mix with rough companions in your work, and you have talked as they have done: if Jesus Christ has made you whole, there is an end to all filthy speaking. Now you will talk graciously, sweetly, cleanly, profitably. In years gone by you were angry and passionate; if Jesus Christ has made you whole, you will be as tender as a lamb. You will find the old lion lifting his head and giving an occasional roar and a shake of his mane, but then he will be chained by the restraints of grace, while the meek and gentle lamb of the new nature will feed in pastures wide and green. Ah, if the Lord has saved you, the drunkard's ale-bench will have no more of you, for you will want better company than the seats of scoffers can afford you. If the Lord saves you, you will want to do something for him, to show your grateful love. I know this very night you will long to tell your children, and tell your friends, that Jesus Christ has made you whole. John Bunyan says that when he was made whole he wanted to tell the crows on the ploughed land about it. I do not wonder that he did. Tell anybody, tell everybody, "Jesus Christ has saved me." It is a sensation the like of which no man can imagine, if he has not felt it, to be made a new creature right away, in a moment. That surprises all who see it, and as people like to tell news—strange news—so does a new-born man long to go and tell others, "I have been born again: I have found the Savior."

Now, mark, you will have to prove that this is so by an honest, upright, consistent, holy life,—not, however, by being merely sternly honest. If Christ has saved you, he will save you from being selfish. You will love your fellow men; you will desire to do them good. You will endeavor to help the poor; you will try to instruct the ignorant. He who truly becomes a Christian becomes in that very same day a practical philanthropist. No man is a true Christian who is un-Christlike—who can live for himself alone, to hoard money or to make himself great. The true Christian lives for others: in a word, he lives for Christ. If Christ has healed you, gentle compassion will saturate your soul from this time forth and for ever. O Master, thou who didst heal men's bodies in the days of thy flesh, heal men's hearts tonight, we pray thee.

Still this word more. Somebody says, "Oh, I wish I had Christ!" Soul, why not have him at once? "Oh, but I am not fit." You never will be fit; you cannot be fit, except in the sense in which you are fit even now. What is fitness for washing? Why, being dirty. What is fitness for alms? Why, being in distress. What is fitness for a doctor? Why, being ill. This is all the fitness that a man wants for trusting in Christ to save him. Christ's mercy is to be had for nothing, bribe or purchase is out of the question. I have heard of a woman whose child was in a fever and needed grapes; and there was a prince who lived near, in whose hothouse there were some of the rarest grapes that had ever been grown. She scraped together the little money she could earn, and went to the gardener and offered to buy a bunch of the royal fruit. Of course he repulsed her, and said they were not to be sold. Did she imagine that the prince grew grapes to sell like a market-gardener? And he sent her on her way, much grieved. She came again; she came several times, for a mother's importunity is great; but no offer of hers would be accepted. At last the princess heard of it and wished to see the woman; and when she came the princess said, "The prince does not sell the fruit of his garden:" but, snipping off a bunch of grapes and dropping them into a little bag, she said, "He is always ready to give it away to the poor." Now, here is the rich cluster of gospel salvation from the true vine. My Lord will not sell it, but he is always ready to give it away to all who humbly ask for it; and if you want it come and take it, and take it now by believing in Jesus.

The Lord bless you for Christ's sake. Amen.

PORTION OF SCRIPTURE READ BEFORE SERMON—ISAIAH 55.

REST FOR THE LABORING

LORD'S-DAY EVENING, OCTOBER 22ND, 1876, METROPOLITAN TABERNACLE

The Tabernacle was on this night thrown open to strangers, all the regular congregation kindly vacating their seats.

Come unto me, all ye that labour and are heavy laden, and I will give you rest. Take my yoke upon you, and learn of me; for I am meek and lowly in heart: and ye shall find rest unto your souls. For my yoke is easy, and my burden is light.—MATTHEW 11:28–30.

Our Lord had just been declaring the doctrine of election, thanking the heavenly Father that he had chosen babes, though he had passed by the wise and prudent. It is very instructive that, close upon the heels of that mysterious doctrine, should come the gracious invitation of my text: as much as if the Lord Jesus would say to his disciples, "Let no views of predestination ever keep you back from proclaiming fully my gospel to every creature;" and as if he would say to the unconverted, "Do not be discouraged by the doctrine of election. Never let it be a stumbling-block in your way, for when my lips have said, 'I thank thee, O Father, that thou hast hid these things from the wise and prudent, and revealed them unto babes,'[1] I also proceed to speak to you in the deepest sincerity of heart and say, 'Come unto me, all ye that labor and are heavy laden, and I will give you rest.'"

I shall notice at the outset who it is that makes so large a promise

---

1 Matthew 11:25.

and gives so free an invitation. There are many quack doctors in the world, and each one of these cries up his own medicine. Who is this man who calls us so earnestly and promises rest so confidently? Is he an impostor too? Will he play us false? Does he boast beyond his ability? Ah, it cannot be thought so; for this man, this marvellous man, who promises rest to those who come to him, is also God. He is the Son of the Highest as well as the son of Mary, he is Son of the Eternal as well as Son of man: and he has power because of his divine nature to accomplish whatever he promises to perform. As a man, the Lord Jesus was noted for his truthfulness. From his lips never fell an equivocation. He never boasted beyond his ability, or led men to expect from him what he could not render. Why should he deceive? He had no selfish end to serve or ambition to gratify. Did he not come to tell men the truth? It was his errand, and he did it thoroughly. Believe him, then. As you are persuaded of the truthfulness of his character accept his teaching; and as you believe in his deity—if so you do believe, and I trust you do—believe in his ability to save, and at once trust your soul in his hands. If he be a mere pretender, do not come to him; but if indeed you believe my Lord and Master to be faithful and true, I beseech you attend at once to his call.

Where is he now? He is not here, for he is risen; but since he spake these words he has lost no power to save, but in a certain sense has gained in ability: for since he uttered those words he has died the death of the cross, by which he obtained power to put away the sins of men; he has also risen from the grave, no more to die, and he has gone up into the glory with all power given unto him in heaven and in earth. He is King of kings and Lord of lords; and it is in his name and by his authority that we proclaim to you the gospel of Christ, according to his words, recorded by the evangelist Mark: "All power is given unto me in heaven and in earth: go ye therefore and teach all nations, baptizing them in the name of the Father and of the Son and of the Holy Ghost."[1] It is an enthroned Redeemer who tonight invites you. See that ye refuse not him that speaketh. He is able to save them to the uttermost that come unto God by him, seeing he ever liveth

1 Matthew 28:18–19.

to make intercession for them; therefore doubt not his power to save you, but come to him at once and find rest unto your souls.

Jesus being the speaker, and his authority and ability being both clear, we shall now come to dissect the words, and may God grant that as we do so the Spirit of God may use every syllable, and press the truth home upon our hearts.

And, first, I notice here *a character which*, dear friend, I think *describes you*—the laboring and the heavy laden. Secondly, I notice *a blessing which invites you*—"I will give you rest." Thirdly, I notice *a direction which will guide you*—"Come unto me: take my yoke upon you: learn of me." And, fourthly, I notice *an argument which I trust may persuade you*—"I am meek and lowly in heart. My yoke is easy, and my burden is light."

I. First, then, here is a character which, no doubt, describes a considerable number of those here assembled—"ALL YE THAT LABOR AND ARE HEAVY LADEN."

The words look as if there were a great many such persons—*"all ye,"* and, indeed, so there are, for laboring and burden-bearing are the common lot of the sons of Adam. Laborers and loaded ones constitute the great mass of mankind, and the Lord Jesus invites them all without exception; high or low, learned or illiterate, moral or depraved, old or young—"all that labor and are heavy laden" are comprehended in his call. Some have ventured to say that this describes a certain *spiritual* character, but I fail to see any word to mark the spirituality of the persons; certainly I see not a syllable to limit the text to that sense. Brethren and sisters, it is not our wont either to add to or to take from the word of God knowingly, and as there is no indication here that these words are to be limited in their meaning, we shall not dare to invent a limit. Where God puts no bolt or bar, woe unto those who shall set up barriers of their own. We shall read our text in the broadest conceivable sense, for it is most like the spirit of the gospel to do so. It says—*"all* ye that labor," and if you labor, it includes you. It says—*"all* ye that are heavy laden," and if you are heavy laden it includes you, and God forbid that we should shut you out. Nay, God be thanked that no man can shut you out if ye be willing and obedient, and come to Christ, accepting his invitation and obeying his command.

To you, then, do we speak, "all ye that labor." Ho, ye who work so hard to earn a crust that your limbs are weary with your daily toil, come ye to Jesus, and if he give you no rest to your bodies, yet to your souls he will. Yea, even for your physical toil he is your best hope, for his righteous and loving teaching will yet alter the constitution of the body politic, till the day shall come when no man shall need to toil excessively to earn his share of the common food which the great Father gives for all his creatures. If ever rest from oppression and from excessive labor shall become the joyful lot of mankind, it will be found when the Son of David shall reign from pole to pole, and from the river even to the ends of the earth.

But hither come ye, ye that labor with mental labor—ye that are straining your minds and exhausting your spirits, ye who pine and pant after repose for your souls, but find it not! Perhaps you are laboring to enter into rest by formal religion—trying to save yourselves by rites and ceremonies—by attendance on this service and on that, making your life a pious slavery, that you may find *salvation* by the outward ordinances of worship. There is no salvation there. Ye weary yourselves with searching for a shadow. You seek for the living among the dead. Wherefore spend ye your labor for that which satisfieth not? Turn ye your thoughts another way. If ye come to Christ ye shall cease from the bondage of an external and formal religion, and shall find a finished righteousness, and a complete salvation ready to your hand.

O you that are trying by your good works to save yourselves, and doing no good works all the while; for how can that be good which you do with the sole view of benefiting yourselves? That selfish virtue which only seeks its own—is that virtue? Can that commend itself to God? But I know how you wear your fingers to the bone to spin a garment of your own righteousness, which, if it were spun, would be no more substantial than a spider's web, and no more lasting than the fading autumn leaves. Why do ye not cease from this fruitless toil? O you that hope for salvation by the works of the law, it is to you that Jesus speaks; and he says, "Come to me, and I will give you rest." And he can do it, too. He can at once give you a spotless righteousness: he can array you from head to foot with the garments of salvation. On the spot he can give you both of these, and so give you rest, ye laboring ones.

Some of you are laboring after *happiness*. You think to find it in gain—hoarding up your pence and your pounds and seeking for rest in the abundance of your beloved wealth. Ah, you will never have enough till you get Christ; but when you have him, you will be full to the brim. Contentment is the peculiar jewel of the beloved of the Lord Jesus. All the Indies could not fill a human heart: the soul is insatiable till it finds the Savior, and then it leans on his bosom and enters into perfect peace.

Perhaps, young man, you are laboring after *fame*. You despise gold, but you pant to obtain a great name. Alas, ambition's ways are very weary, and he who climbs the loftiest peak of honor finds that it is a slippery place, where rest is quite unknown. Young brother, take a friend's advice and care no longer for man's praise, for it is mere wind. If thou wouldst rise to a great name, become a Christian, for the name of Christ is the name above every name, and it is bliss to be hidden beneath it, and overshadowed by it. Christ will not make thee great among men, but he will make thee so little in thine own esteem that the lowest place at his table will more than satisfy thee. He will give thee rest from that delirious dream of ambition, and yet fire thee with a higher ambition than ever.

What is it you are laboring for? Is it after *knowledge?* I commend you: it is a good possession and a choice treasure. Search for it as for silver. But all the knowledge that is to be had from the zenith to the center of the earth will never satisfy your understanding, till you know Christ and are found in him. He can give rest to your soul in that respect by giving thee the knowledge of God and a sense of his love.

Whatever it is thou laborest after, come thou to Jesus, and he will give thee rest.

But the text speaks of some as *"heavy laden."* They are not merely struggling and striving, but they are burdened. They have a load to carry, and it is to these that Jesus says, "I will give you rest." Some carry a load of *sin*. I mean not all of you. Some of you think, perhaps, that you have no sin; but there are others who know that they have sinned; in the memory of the past they are full of fear, and looking, in the present, to their own condition and position, they feel uneasy and unhappy. Their grief has nothing to do with the house or with the barn, it is with their own selves that their burden begins and ends. "I have sinned," say they, "and how can I be forgiven?" This is the load they carry. Some carry a load of *sorrow* on the back of this load of sin—a daily fretting, worrying sorrow, from which they cannot escape: to such Jesus beckons, and he says, "I will take your sin from you, forgive you, and make you whiter than snow. I will take your sorrow from you too, or, if the sorrow abide with you, I will make you so content to bear it, that you shall thank God for the cross that you carry and glory in your infirmity because the power of Christ doth rest upon you." Loaded, then, with sin or sorrow, come to Jesus and he will give you rest.

Or, possibly, the load may be that of *daily care*. You are continually crying, "What shall I eat, and what shall I drink, and wherewithal shall I be clothed?" Oh what heavy hearts tread our streets! How many are scantily fed and scarcely clothed! What myriads go down Cheapside unhappy because they can see no provision for their commonest wants! Even to these Jesus says, "Come to me, and I will give you rest." He teaches the sweet art of casting our care on him who careth for us. He shows us that "man shall not live by bread alone, but by every word that proceedeth out of the mouth of God shall man live."[1] He has a way of making us content with little, till a dinner of herbs with his grace to season it becomes a greater dainty than the stalled ox of the rich man. Come ye to him, ye poverty-stricken, and he will teach you the science of joying and rejoicing under all circumstances. Even in a cottage with scanty comfort he will give you rest and true riches.

Or, the burden may happen to be one of *doubt*. You perhaps feel as if you could believe nothing, and are uncertain about everything.

1 Matthew 4:4.

This also is a crushing load to a thoughtful spirit. I, too, know what that means, for I have seen the firm mountains of my youth moved from their foundations and cast into a sea of questioning. I, too, have been loaded down with difficulties and scepticisms. From that burden I am delivered, for in that day in which I believed in Jesus—the man, the God—and cast myself at his dear feet to be his servant and believe his words and trust in him, then did the reeling earth stand fast, and heaven no longer fled away. I saw Jesus, and in him I found the pole of faith, the basis of belief. Believe in Jesus, and you will meet with a blessed rest of mind and thought, such as earth cannot afford elsewhere—a rest that shall be the prelude to the everlasting rest in heaven, where they know even as they are known.

So Jesus cries aloud tonight, to you who labor and to you who are loaded down with mighty burdens; he cries, and I beseech you have regard to the cry. Are you weary of life, young man? Christ will give you a new life, and teach you how to rejoice in him always. Are you disappointed? Has the world given you a slap in the face where you looked for a kiss? Come to my Lord. He will give new hopes that shall never be disappointed, for he that believeth in him shall not be ashamed nor confounded, world without end. Are you vexed with everybody, and most of all with yourself? Jesus can teach you love, and put you at your ease again. Does something fret and tease you from day to day? Come to my Master, and the vexations of the world shall gall you no longer. You shall reckon that these light afflictions, which are but for a moment, are not worthy to be compared with the glory which shall be revealed in you. Do you despair? Are you ready to fling yourself away? Do you wish that there was no hereafter? And, if you were sure there would be none, would you speedily make your own quietus? Would you afford short shrift to your soul, and end this mortal life at once? Ah! do not so: there are brighter days before you, since Jesus has met you, and new life will begin if you will come to my Master and sit at his feet. I will give you a hymn to sing, which shall grow sweeter every day you live:—

"Happy day, happy day,

> When Jesus washed my sins away:
> He taught me how to watch and pray,
> And live rejoicing every day.
> Happy day, happy day,
> When Jesus washed my sins away."[1]

I have spoken enough upon the character, which, I think, comprehends many here,—"All ye that labor and are heavy laden." I know how well it suited me once upon a time, and how glad I was to answer to the call of the text.

II. Now, secondly, the text speaks of A BLESSING WHICH INVITES YOU. "Come unto me," says Jesus, "and I will give you rest." "Rest! rest! rest!" I could keep on ringing that silver bell all the evening— "Rest! *rest!* REST!" "Ye gentlemen of England who live at home at ease," ye scarcely know the music of that word. The sons of toil, the mariners tossed upon the sea, the warriors in the battle, the men who labor deep in the mines—these know, as you do not, how sweet this music sounds. Rest! Rest! Rest! Rest for the weary body is the outward emblem of that inward blessing which Jesus Christ holds up tonight before the eyes of all laboring and heavy-laden souls. Rest— rest which he will give, which he will give at once—rest to the *conscience*. The conscience, tossed to and fro under a sense of sin, has no peace; but when Jesus is revealed as bleeding and suffering in the sinner's stead, and making full atonement for human guilt, then the conscience grows quiet. As Noah's dove lighted upon the ark, so conscience lights on Christ, and rests there for ever. No sin of yours shall trouble you when you have seen how it troubled Christ, how he took it on his shoulders and bore it up to the cross, and then flung it into the depths of the sea, never to be mentioned against you any more for ever.

Jesus gives rest to the *mind* as well as to the conscience. As I have said, the mind wanders to and fro, in endless mazes lost. It must believe something, but it knows not what. He who is the greatest unbeliever, generally believes the most; only he believes a lie. Incredulity and credulity are strangely near of kin; for he that believes not in God

1 *Oh Happy Day, that Fixed My Choice* by Philip Doddridge.

generally believes in himself, or believes in whatever his own dreams may shape: but he that taketh Christ, and resteth upon him, finds his mind no more disturbed: his thoughts rest, his judgment becomes satisfied, his brain is quiet.

Rest to the *heart,* too, is given by Jesus. Oh, there are choice and tender spirits in this world that want, above all things, something to love; these too often choose an earthly object, and lean on that reed till it breaks or turns into a piercing spear. O hearts that pine for love, here is a Beloved for you whom ye may love as much as ye will or can, and yet never be guilty of idolatry, nor ever meet with treachery. O broken heart, he will heal thee! O tender heart, he will delight thee! The love of Jesus is the wine of heaven, and he that drinks it is filled with bliss. Jesus can give rest to the palpitating heart. Ye sons of desolation, hasten hither! Daughters of despondency, gather to this call!

He can give rest, too, *to your energies.* O ye whose unabated strength seeks a worthy field of labor, do ye enquire, what shall we pursue? You want to be up and doing, but you have not found an object worthy of you. Oh, but if you follow after Jesus, and, in the love of God and in the love of man, cast aside selfishness, desiring only to be obedient to the great Father's will and to bring your fellow men into a gracious state, then shall ye find a noble and restful life. If ye be willing to give up life itself for God's glory as Jesus did—for you cannot well be his disciple if you do not, then shall ye find perfect rest unto your souls.

As for your *fears and forecasts* which now are troubled—he will turn them into hopes of endless glory. Dark forebodings of a future, you know not what—the sound of an awful sea, whose surf beats upon an invisible shore, and whose billows resound with sound of storm and everlasting tempest—from all this you shall be delivered. Jesus will give you rest from every fear. If ye will come to Jesus ye shall obtain rest in all ways, the rest of your entire manhood, rest such as shall unload you of your burdens and ease you of your labors: this is the rest which Jesus promises to you.

"Alas," cries one, "I wish I could attain to rest. That is the one thing needful to me; I should then become strong and happy; my mind would become clear, and I should be able to fight the battle of life, if I could but obtain rest." Yes, but you cannot have it unless you come to Christ. Not heaven itself could give you peace apart from Christ, nor can the grave's deep slumbers rest you unless you sleep in him. Rest! Neither heaven nor earth, nor sea and hades, none of them can afford you any trace of it until you come to the incarnate God, Christ Jesus, and bow at his feet. Then ye shall find rest to your souls, but not till then.

III. This brings me, next, to say that the text presents A DIRECTION TO GUIDE EVERY LABORING AND LADEN SOUL IN THE PURSUIT OF REST. I shall be sure to have your very deep attention to the directions which Jesus gives, for you all want to find rest. Oh, may the divine Spirit now lead you into the way of peace. If you follow our Lord's directions and do not find rest, then his word is not true. But his word *is* true. I invite you to try it, and urge you at once to accept his guidance and leadership.

The first direction is, *"Come unto me."* "Come unto me," said he, "and I will give you rest." Mark, it is not coming to a sacrament, coming to a church, or coming to a doctrine: it is coming to a *person* which is set before you—"Come unto *me."* You are to come to God in human flesh, the Deity himself dwelling among us, and taking our nature upon himself. You are to come to *him*. He does not bid you do anything or bring anything, he does not command you to prepare yourself, or advise you to wait; but he bids you come—come as you are—come now—come alone—come to him and to him only. Nobody here needs me to say that we cannot go to Christ, as to bodily going, for in his own actual person he is in heaven, and we are here below. The coming to him is mental and spiritual. Just as we may come in spirit to some great poet whom we never saw, or approach some renowned teacher whose voice we have never heard, so may we come in thought, in meditation, to Jesus, whom our eyes have never beheld. We are to come to him in some such fashion as the following words describe:—"I believe what God has revealed concerning thee, O thou wondrous person, that thou art God and man. I believe that thou hast died for human sin. I believe that thou art able to save, and

I think of thee and meditate upon thee daily: I do believe thee to be the Savior, and I trust thee to save me. I am troubled, and thou sayest, 'I will give thee rest.' I trust thee to give me peace, and I mean to follow thy directions till I find it. I ask thee to give me thy Spirit that I may enter into thy rest. As much as lieth in me I come to thee: oh, draw me while I come. Lord, I believe: help thou mine unbelief."

Now, mark, it is not merely to his teaching, or to his commandments, or to his church that you are to approach: it is *to himself* that you are to come; not merely to reading the Scriptures or to offering prayer, for if you put your trust in reading the Bible, or in a prayer, you have stopped short of the true basis of salvation. It is to *him*—a real person—a man and yet God—one who died and yet ever liveth, that you must draw near. You are to trust him. The more you know of him by the reading of his Word, the better you will be able to come: but, still, it is neither Bible reading, nor praying, nor chapel-going, nor church-going, nor anything else that you can do that will save you, unless you come to Him. This you can do if you are on the sea where the Sabbath bell never sounds. This you can do in a desert where there are no meetings of God's people. This you can do on the sick bed when you cannot stir a limb. You can go to Jesus by the help of his blessed Spirit, and you can say, "Lord, I believe in thee."

Well, that is the first thing, "Come unto me, and I will give you rest."

The next command is, *"Take my yoke upon you."* "Come," and then "take," that is to say, no man is saved by merely trusting himself with Christ, unless that trusting be of a living and practical kind. I sometimes explain this to my people as I will explain it to you. A celebrated doctor visits you when you are very ill, and he says to you, "Do you trust me?" You reply, "Yes, sir, wholly." "Well," says he, "if you trust me completely, and give your case over into my hands, I believe that I shall see you through this sickness." You assure him of your implicit faith in him and then he begins to question you. "What do you eat?" He lifts up his hands in horror, and he exclaims, "Why, my good man, you eat the very thing which feeds your complaint; you must not touch that any more, however much you like it; you must have simpler food, and more harmless diet." "Then," says he, "I will send you a little medicine, which you will take every three hours, according to the prescription. You are sure you trust me?" "Yes." "Then all will be well." He comes in a few days, and he says. "You seem worse, my friend. I fear that your disease has taken a stronger hold upon you than before. I do not understand how matters have taken this turn. Are you trusting me?" "Yes, doctor, trusting you entirely." "Well, what have you been eating?" And then you tell him that you have been eating just what you used to eat, and you have broken all his rules as to food. "Now," he says, "I see why you are worse. You are not trusting me. Have you regularly taken my medicine?" He looks at the bottle upon the table. "Why, you have not taken a single dose!" "No, sir, I tasted it and I did not like it, and so I left it alone." "How is this?" says the doctor, very much grieved, "my friend, you said that you trusted me implicitly?" "Yes, sir, so I do." "But I say you do not," says he, "and I will leave you. I insist upon it that I will not be responsible for your health if you mock me with such a pretended faith; for if you did believe me you would have done as I told you." Now, Jesus Christ never sent me, or any other minister, to preach to you and say, "Only believe, and you may live as you like, and yet be saved." Such preaching would be a lie. It is true that we say, *"only believe,"* but that *"only believing"* must be such a believing that you do what Jesus bids you; for Jesus has not promised to save you *in* your sins, but *from* your sins, just as a physician does not pretend to heal a man while he feeds his disease and refuses the remedy, but only promises that he will benefit him if the faith which he expects him to exercise shows itself to be a practical and real faith. Beware of a liar's faith; and that is a liar's faith which you pretend to get at a revival meeting, if you then go and live just as you did before.

> "Faith must obey her Maker's will,
>   As well as trust his grace.
> A gracious God is jealous still,
>   For his own holiness."

So Christ says, "Take my yoke," that is, "If you will be saved by me

I must be your Master, and you must be my servant; you cannot have me for a Savior if you do not accept me for a Lawgiver and Commander. If you will not do as I bid you, neither shall you find rest to your souls."

Then there is a third direction; and I pray you notice each one of these words; for failure about any one of them may cause you to miss peace. I remember when I was seeking the Lord, that before I came to peace I was made willing to be or to do anything the Lord Jesus chose to bid me do or be. Are you in such a state? Then listen, for Jesus says, *"Learn of me;"* that is to say, at first you do not know all his will, and perhaps you will do wrong; but then that will be in ignorance, and he will graciously wink at your fault. But he says, "Be my disciple; be my scholar; come and learn at my feet." Christ will not be your Savior if he is not to be your teacher. He will teach you very much at first, and a great deal more as you go on; and it is essential to your salvation that you have a teachable spirit even as a little child. You must be willing to drink in what Christ pours out for you. The promise is to those who are willing to become learners. This is the gospel, but it is not often preached as it should be: "Go ye into all the world, and *disciple* all nations," or "make disciples of all nations." Now, what are disciples but learners? You must be willing to be a learner, and say, "As I learn I will do, and as I am taught I will practise, trusting thee, O Jesus, to save me all the while. Not trusting to my doing or my learning, but trusting alone to thee; yea, both doing and learning because I do trust thee. Because thou art all my hope, therefore will I do as thou biddest me, if thou, O Lord, wilt help me." Come, young men, I am glad to see so many of you present here this evening. It is a good thing that you bear Christ's yoke in your youth. You must have some master, you know, and you will either be your own master, and you cannot have a worse; or you will get the devil for your master, or you will get the world for a master, and either of these will make dreadful drudges of you. But if you take Christ for a master, oh, then it is that you will find him to be your Savior, and you shall enter at once into rest, and that rest will grow; for, if you notice, my text first says, "I will *give* you rest;" and then it says, "you shall *find* rest;" that is to say, you shall find for yourselves a deeper and profounder enjoyment of life as you understand more fully the divine will and obtain more grace to put it into practice.

This is the sum and substance of the gospel. Yield thee, sinner, yield thee; yield thee to Jesus. O ye proud sinners, come and bow before my Lord. Down with your weapons of rebellion; lower the crest of your pride; unbuckle the harness of your self-glorying; and say, "Jesus, Master, only save me from the guilt and power of sin, and I will bless thee for ever and ever, and rejoice to obey thee as long as I live."

Now, what I have said is no make-up of mine. I have not altered my Master's conditions, or imported anything into the text that is not there. There it stands. "Come unto me: take my yoke upon you, and learn of me."

IV. Now the last thing—and I will not detain you much longer, is THE ARGUMENT TO PERSUADE YOU SO TO DO. And that argument is this: First, *the Master you are to serve is "meek and lowly in heart."* I confess there are some men whom I could not serve; proud, austere, domineering, one might sooner eat his flesh from the bone, than serve such tyrants. There have been despots in the world whom to serve was degradation; but when you look at Jesus Christ, whose whole being is love, gentleness, meekness, lowliness, oh, there are some of us who feel that his shoe latchets we are not worthy to unloose. We would count it heaven to be permitted to kiss his feet, or wash them with our tears, for he is such a glorious one that his beauty attracts us to him, he holds us spell-bound by his wondrous character, and we count it no slavery, but perfect liberty, to wear his yoke and carry his cross.

Have you never heard how he has been served by his disciples? Why, man, they have given up their lives for him gladly! Let Bonner's Coalhole and the Lollards' Tower and the stakes that stood at Smithfield tell how men have loved him. So loved him that they sang in the dark dungeon, and made it light with their joys; and clapped their hands in the fires, glad to be consumed that they might bear testimony for him! Have you never heard of old Polycarp, when they bid him deny his Master, saying, "Eighty and six years have I served him, and he never did me a displeasure, how can I now blaspheme my King that saved me?" Oh, he has bred such enthusiasm in his followers that neither the gridiron of St. Lawrence nor the wild bulls of Blandina have been able to prevent the saints from glorying in his name. They would have gone through hell itself to serve him, if it had been possible; for his love has had such power over them. Whatever we have to suffer for him he suffers with us. Alexander was a great master of men, and one of the reasons why all his soldiers loved him so enthusiastically was that, if they were upon a long march, Alexander did not ride, but tramped along in the heat and dust with the common soldiery; and when the day was hot, and they brought his majesty water, he put it aside, and said, "The sick soldiers want it more than I, I will not drink till every soldier has a draught." So is it with Christ, in all our afflictions he is afflicted, and he will not have joy until he gives joy to his people. Yea, he has done more than Alexander, for he emptied himself of all his glories, and gave himself to die upon the cross, and consummated the redemption of his people by his own agonies. Who would not follow one whose footprints show that he was crucified for his followers? Who would not rally to his banner, when you see that his hand which upholds it was pierced with nails, that he might redeem us from hell? On which of his disciples has he ever looked unkindly. Which of his redeemed has he ever cast away? To which of those that love him has he ever been unjust or ungenerous? Therefore I charge you all—and all his saints speak in me while I speak—take his yoke upon you, and learn of him, for he is meek and lowly in heart.

In the last place, *that which Christ asks you to do is no hard thing*. As he is not severe himself, so his commands are not hard, for he says, "My yoke is easy, and my burden is light." True there are some things which you now delight in of which Christ will say, "Have no more to do with them," but he will only forbid you that which injures you, and he will put something better in their place. He may call you to duties which will try you; but, then, he will give you such consolations that they will cease to be trials. In fact, the difficulties of following Christ are delightful to his hearty followers. They love difficulties, that they may show the sincerity of their confidence in their leader. Oh, my beloved friends, the service of the Lord Jesus Christ is no bondage. There are no chains to wear; there are no prisons to lie in; or, if there be any, they are not of his making, but are the devices of his enemies: Christ's ways are ways of pleasantness, and all his paths are peace. He calls you to that which is right, true, honest, loving, tender, heavenly. Who would not be willing to be called to this? He asks you only to give up that which is evil and displeasing in his sight, degrading to your own mind, and which stops the channels of peace and happiness to your soul.

Above all, it is no hard thing, surely, to believe in him. "Oh," says one, "that is just the point. Sometimes I cannot feel that Christ could forgive me." No, and do you know why? It is because you do not think enough of *him*, and think too much of yourself. If you sit down and think of your sin, you will soon feel as if pardon were impossible; but, when you turn and think of *him*, you will see at once how readily he is able to forgive. There is a homely illustration which I often use, and as I cannot think of a better, I must use it now. If you were to go tomorrow up and down London, right along from end to end, there would be quite a journey for you. Twelve, fourteen, fifteen, perhaps twenty miles you could go, and scarcely see a break in the houses. I would have you traverse the main roads and then go down the cross streets, lanes, alleys, and courts. After you had had a day of it you would say, "Dear, dear me, what a mass of people! how do they live?" And if you were nervous you might very soon come to feel, "I am afraid one of these days London will be starved. Here are nearly four millions of people! Lebanon would not be sufficient to find them cattle, nor Carmel and Sharon to supply them with sheep, for a single week. They will certainly be starved." I can imagine your becoming seriously apprehensive of a famine. Well, then, next Monday morning, we will have a fast horse, and we will go up to Copenhagen Fields, and see the live cattle; and then we will drive to Smithfield, and see the carcasses; and next we will go round to the markets, and see where the fish and the vegetables are sold; and when we have finished our tour of observation—which will take us at least two or three hours early in the morning; as you get out of the Hansom cab, I know what you will say to me, you will change your tone and say, "I am no longer afraid of the people's starving, but I am more afraid of the meat being wasted; I cannot think where all the people come from to eat all this. I am astonished to see such a mass of food. I should not wonder if tons of it should be spoiled. There cannot be people enough to eat it all." Your mind has suffered that sudden change, because you have changed your point of consideration. So now, if you think of sin, sin will seem a monstrous thing that never can be put away, and when you have reached that point it is time to think of the blood which cleanses us from it. Do think of sin till it bows you down, but do not think of it so as to despair. Turn your eye to Calvary's bloody tree, and see there the Son of God, in agonies of body and soul, pouring out his life for sinners. May the Holy Spirit give you a quick eye for the sufferings of Jesus. Oh, I have sometimes looked at Christ in that way till I have said, "The sin of a *world* might readily be put away so! Ay, Master, and if every star that decks the heavens were a world, and every world were as full of sinners as this earth is, yet, surely, no grander redemption for them all would be wanted than thy august sacrifice, O mighty Son of God!" John Hyatt, when he lay dying, was asked by one of his friends, "Mr. Hyatt, can you trust Jesus with your soul now?" and the good man answered, "Trust him with *one* soul? I could trust him with a million souls, if I had them." That is how I feel when I think of the death of my Lord Jesus, and it is what I want you who are troubled in spirit to feel. As you see him wounded, bleeding, dying, on the cursed tree, sinners, may you find your hearts believing that he suffered thus for you, and, as you do believe it, you will find rest unto your souls.

May God give that rest to every one of you tonight, for Christ's sake. Amen.

A CHEERY WORD IN
TROUBLOUS TIMES

DELIVERED AT THE METROPOLITAN TABERNACLE, NEWINGTON

*Wherefore, sirs, be of good cheer: for I believe God, that it shall be
even as it was told me.*—ACTS 27:25.

The presence of a brave man in the hour of danger is a very great
comfort to his companions. It is a grand thing to observe Paul
so bold, so calm, in the midst of all the hurly-burly of the storm, and
talking so cheerfully, and so encouragingly, to the crew and to the
soldiery and to the prisoners. You must have seen in many events in
history that it is the one man, after all, that wins the battle: all the
rest play their parts well when the one heroic spirit lifts the standard.
Every now and then we hear some simpleton or other talking against
a "one-man ministry," when it has been a one-man ministry from the
commencement of the world to the present day; and whenever you
try to have any other form of ministry, except that of each individual saint discharging his own ministry, and doing it thoroughly and
heartily and independently and bravely in the sight of God, you very
soon run upon quicksands. Recollect, Christian man, that wherever
you are placed you are to be *the* one man, and you are to have courage and independence of spirit and strength of mind received from
God, that with it you may comfort those around you who are of the
weaker sort. So act that your confidence in God shall strengthen the
weak hands and confirm the feeble knees, and your calm quiet look
shall say to them that are of a faint heart, "Be strong; fear not."

If you are to do this, and I trust you will do it, in the sick chamber, in the midst of the troubles of life, in the church, and everywhere else, *you must be strong yourself.* Take it as a good rule that nothing can come out of you that is not in you. You cannot render real encouragement to others unless you have courage within yourself. Now, the reason why Paul was able to embolden his companions was that he had encouraged himself in his God; he was calm, or else he could not have calmed those around him. Imagine him excited and all in a tremble, and yet saying, "Sirs, be of good cheer." Why they would have thought that he mocked them, and they would have replied, "Be of good cheer yourself, sir, before you encourage us." So my dear brothers and sisters, you must trust God and be calm and strong, or else you will not be of such service in the world and in the church as you ought to be. Get full, and then you will run over, but you can never fill others till you become full yourselves. Be yourselves "strong in the Lord, and in the power of his might,"[1] and then you will be as a standard lifted up to which the timid will rally.

At this time we are going to speak very little about Paul, but a great deal to ourselves. May God speak to us! May the Holy Spirit cheer our hearts, and lead us into the way of peace and power. *If Paul was strong it was because he believed God:* let us speak about that faith. Paul, being strong, spake words of good cheer to others: let us, in the second place, *see whether we cannot speak words of encouragement to our comrades in distress.* We will finish up with such words as God may give us.

I. First, then, PAUL WAS STRONG BECAUSE HE BELIEVED. Faith makes men strong—not in the head, but in the heart. Doubting people are generally headstrong—the Thomas-sort of people who obstinately declare that they will not believe unless they can have proofs of their own choosing. If you read certain newspapers, journals, quarterly reviews, and so on, you will see that the doubting people who are always extolling scepticism and making out that there is more faith in their doubt than in half the creeds, and so on, are particularly strong in the upper region, namely, in the head, only it is that sort of head-strength which implies real weakness, for obstinacy seldom

1 Ephesians 6:10.

goes with wisdom. They are always sneering at believers as a feeble folk, which is a clear sign that they are not very strong themselves; for evermore is this a rule without exception, that when a man despises his opponent he is himself the party who ought to be despised. When certain writers rave about "evangelical platitudes," as they commonly do, they only see in others a fault with which they are largely chargeable themselves. Anybody who glances at the sceptical literature of the present day will bear me out that the platitudes have gone over to the doubting side of the house. No people can write such fluent nonsense, and talk such absurdity, as the school of modern doubt and "culture:" they think themselves the wisest of the wise, but, professing to be wise, they have become fools, and I know what I say. It is true that the evangelical party had become flat and stale, but the other party have beaten us at that. They are more dull, more stale, and more unprofitable by far. When a man leaves faith he leaves strength; when he takes up with "liberal" views in religion, and does not believe anything in particular, he has lost the bone and sinew of his soul. It is true all round, in all things, that he who firmly believes has an element of power which the doubter knows nothing of. Even if a man be somewhat mistaken in what he believes, there is a power in his faith though it may in part be power for mischief: there is, however, in a believer a world of power for good if the right thing be believed. Paul was a believer in God, and so became strong in heart, and was on board the foundering vessel the center of hope, the mainstay of courage.

But notice that *Paul's faith was faith in God.* "I believe God," said he. Nobody else in the ship could see any hope in God. With the exception of one or two like-minded with Paul they thought that God had forsaken them, if indeed they thought of God at all. But there had that night stood by Paul's side an angel fresh from heaven, bright with the divine presence, and, strengthened by his message, Paul said, "I believe God." That was something more than saying "I believe *in* God:" this many do and derive but slender comfort from the belief. But "I believe *God*, believe *him*, believe his truthfulness, believe the word that he has spoken, believe his mercy and his power.

I believe God." This made Paul calm, peaceful, strong. Would to God that all professing Christians did really believe God.

Believing God, *he believed the message that God had sent him,* drank in every word and was revived by it. God had said "Fear not Paul, I have given thee all them that sail with thee." He believed it. He felt certain that God, having promised it, was able to perform it; and amidst the howling of the winds Paul clung to that promise. He was sure that no hair of any man's head would be harmed. The Lord had said the preserving word and it was enough for his servant. Has he said it, and shall he not do it? Has he spoken it, and shall it not come to pass? He believed God that it should be even as it was told him.

And he did that—mark you, dear friends—*when there was nothing else to believe in.* "I believe God," said he. He might have said to the centurion, if he had pleased, "I do not believe in the sailors: they are evidently nonplussed, and do not know what to do. We are driven before the wind, and their sails and tackle are useless. I do not believe in the men themselves, for they are plotting to get into the boat, and leave the ship and all in it to go to the bottom. We must have them on board, but still I have no trust in them, their help is of small account compared with the divine aid." He did not say "I believe in you, the centurion, that you can maintain military discipline, and so we shall have a better opportunity of escaping." No, the ship was breaking up. They had put ropes all round her, undergirding her; but he could clearly perceive that all this would not avail. The fierce Euroclydon was sweeping the vessel hither and thither, and driving her towards the shore: but he calmly said, "I believe God." Ah, that is a grand thing—to believe God when the winds are out,—to believe God when the waves howl like so many wild beasts, and follow one upon another like a pack of wolves all seeking to devour you. "I believe God." This is the genuine breed of faith—this which can brave a tempest. The common run of men's faith is fair-weather faith, faith which loves to see its beautiful image mirrored in the glassy wave, but is far away when the storm clouds are marshalling the battle. The faith of God's elect is the faith that can see in the dark, the faith that is calm in the tumult, the faith that can sing in the midst of sorrow, the faith that is brightest when everything around her is black as midnight. "I believe God," said he, when he had nothing else to believe in. "My soul, wait thou only upon God, for my expectation is from him."[1] Say thou, O my soul, "Though the earth be removed, and though the mountains be carried into the midst of the sea, yet will we not fear, for God is our refuge and strength, a very present help in trouble."[2]

> "God liveth still!
> Trust, my soul, and fear no ill;
> Heaven's huge vault may cleave asunder,
>   Earth's round globe in ruins burst;
> Devil's fellest rage may thunder,
>   Death and hell may spend their worst;
> Then will God keep safe and surely
> Those who trust in him securely:
>   Wherefore then, my soul, despair?
>   Mid the shipwreck, God is there."

Since the apostle Paul believed God thus truly and really, *he was not ashamed to say so.* He said openly to all those around him, "There shall not a hair of your heads perish, for I believe God." Now, it is not so easy to thrust out your faith and expose it to rough weathers, and to the hearing of rough men. Many a man has believed the promise but has not quite liked to say so, for there has been the whisper in his soul, "Suppose it should not come true, then how the enemy will rejoice! How those that listened to me will be saddened when they find that I was mistaken." Thus does the devil cause faith to be dumb, and God is robbed of his honor. Under the name of prudence there lurks an unbelieving selfishness. Brother, lend me your ear that I may whisper in it—"You do not believe at all." That is not the legitimate sort of believing. Genuine faith in God speaks out and says, "God is true, and I will stake everything on his word." It does not swallow its own words and keep its thoughts to itself; but when the time comes, and others are in difficulty and doubt, it cheers them by crying out, "I believe God." It is not ashamed to say, "The Lord Jesus, whose I

---

1 Psalm 62:5.
2 See Psalm 46:1, 2.

am and whom I serve, stood by me this night, and spoke with me, and I avow it." I would to God all Christians were prepared to throw down the gauntlet, and to come out straight; for if God be not true let us not pretend to trust him, and if the gospel be a lie let us be honest enough to confess it. But if it be true, wherefore should we doubt it and speak with bated breath? If God's promise be true why should we distrust it? What excuse is there for this hesitancy? "Oh," says one, "but that might be running great risks." Risks with God, sir? Risks about God's keeping his word? It cannot be. "Let God be true and every man a liar."[1] Let heaven and earth return to chaos and old night, but the Most High cannot break his word or run back from his promise. Therefore, O ye Pauls, if ye receive a message from the Most High, publish it abroad and let your faith be known.

I should like that little word to drop into the ears of some of you who think you love Christ, but have never told your love—you that are hiding in the background there. Come out and show yourselves!

As for you who have long avowed your Savior, do it more and more, and

> "Speak his word, though kings should hear,
> Nor yield to sinful shame."

II. Now, if we have any measure of the faith of Paul, let us try whether we cannot CHEER OTHERS AS PAUL DID. Let the language of the text be on our tongues, "Wherefore, sirs, be of good cheer: for I believe God, that it shall be even as it was told me."

First, you will meet with *seeking souls*. They have not found Christ yet, but they are hungering and thirsting after him. They are saying, "Oh that I knew where I might find him!" You that believe God are bound to speak comfortably to them, and say, "Sirs, be of good cheer: for I believe God, that it shall be even as it was told me." There is one that is sorrowing for sin. Go and tell him that sorrow for sin is sweet sorrow, and that no man should ever regret that he mourns his faults, but should be glad that God has enabled him to feel a holy grief, a penitential pain. Gotthold tells us that he was called one day to see a

1 Romans 3:4.

man who, when he entered his chamber, burst into many tears; and it was a long time before the good divine could discover what made him so unhappy. At last the man broke out, saying, "Oh, my sin, how I hate it! My sin, how I sorrow over it!" Whereupon Gotthold, who had been sad at the sight of his sadness, smiled and said, "Friend, thy sadness is my gladness. I never behold a happier sight than when I see a man sorrowing for his sin." "Oh," said the other, "say you so?" "Yes, indeed," said he; "there are many mourners who mourn for others, but blessed are they that mourn for themselves. There are many who are sorry because they cannot have their own will; but," said he, "there are few enough that sorrow because they have had their own will, and have disregarded the will of the Lord. I rejoice," said he, "for such as you are those for whom Jesus died. Come and trust him, for when there is sorrow for sin there will soon be joy for pardon." Now, whisper in the ears of those who are penitent. Tell the mourner that God has promised to turn his night into day, and his sackcloth into beauty.

Perhaps you will meet with another whose condition is that he is *pleading daily for mercy.* "Oh," saith he, "I have been praying, and praying, and praying. I cannot let a day pass without asking for forgiveness; but somehow my prayers seem to come back to me. I get no favorable replies." Brother, to a man in this plight you should speak up, and say, "Be of good cheer, friend, for I believe God, that it shall be even as he told me, and he told me this—'Ask, and it shall be given you: seek, and ye shall find: knock, and it shall be opened.'"[1] Tell the praying soul that praying breath was never spent in vain, and that in due time "he that asketh receiveth." To withhold your testimony will be cruelty to the seeking one, and a robbery of God, to whose honor you are bound to speak.

Possibly you will meet with another who is saying, "I am beginning now to *venture myself upon Christ.* I am desiring to believe; but oh! mine is such a feeble confidence. I think I trust him, but I am afraid I do not. I know there is no other Savior, and I do give myself to him; but still I am jealous of my heart, lest mine be not true faith." Tell that soul that Jesus has plainly said, "Him that cometh to me I

1 Matthew 7:7.

will in nowise cast out," and then say, "Be of good cheer: for I believe God, that it shall be even as he hath told me." Tell the trembling heart that Jesus never did yet reject one believer, however trembling might be his trust. Whosoever believeth in him is not condemned. Let the comfort you feel in coming to Christ yourself thus be handed on to other seekers, even as the disciples passed the loaves and fishes among the hungry multitudes.

Perhaps you will find one who says, *"I desire the renewal of my nature.* I am so sinful. I can believe in Christ for pardon, but my heart is terribly deceitful, and I feel such strong passions and evil habits binding me that I am sore afraid." Go and say to that soul, "His name is called Jesus, for he shall save his people from their sins." Tell that anxious one that the Lord can take away a heart of stone and give a heart of flesh. Say that Christ has come to bring liberty to the captives, and to set men free from the bonds of sin; and tell them that you believe God, that it will be even as he has told you; and he has told you, and you know it is true, that he will purge you from sin and sanctify you wholly. Any soul and every soul that comes trustingly to Jesus and rests in him shall find sanctification in him, so that sin shall be hated, avoided, and conquered.

I do not know how I shall manage it, but I wish that I could in two or three words say something that would make every Christian here look out after poor seeking souls with tenfold eagerness. I do not know what to say, except this. There is a brother the less in this house tonight. There was one here two Sabbaths ago who never needed me to tell him to sympathize with anxious souls. He was always up here in the great congregation looking out, and then down in the prayer-meeting below on the same errand. Many persons have been invited from this upper service to go down below, and have there been spoken with by him concerning the Lord Jesus. It was our dear brother Verdon, who was a mighty soul-hunter before the Lord, and he lived to seek after souls. He is gone, and my heart mourns him. Alas, my brother, when shall I ever again see such an one as thou wast? Now, I want each one of you to try to fill up his place. Keep your eye on any who seem to feel the power of the word, and then step up with an encouraging word, somewhat like that of the apostle, "Sirs, I believe God, that it shall be even as it was told me."[1]

Now, there is another set of people who are saved, but they are *Little-faiths*, and I want you strong-faith people to encourage them, by telling them that you believe God that it shall be even as it was told you. Some of these Little-faiths are conscious of very great inward sin. They thought when they believed in Christ that they would never feel any more conflicts: their notion was that they should be saved from the assaults of sin the moment they were born unto God. But now they discover that the old viper within is not dead. He has had a blow on the head, but he is not dead; they see lusts and corruptions moving within their hearts, and they cannot make it out. Go and tell them that you feel the same, but that, thanks be to God, he giveth you the victory through our Lord Jesus Christ. The poor young soul that is just struggling out of darkness into light, and beginning to contend with inward corruption, will be greatly comforted if you thus state your experience, and declare your faith in the ultimate issue.

In the case of some others of these Feeble-faiths, the trouble is that they are *vexed with outward temptation*. Many a young man says, "It is hard to be a Christian where I work." Many a young woman has to say, "Father and mother are against me." Others have to complain that all their associations in business tempt them to that which is evil, and that they have few to help them. Go and tell them of the Lord all-sufficient. Remind them that "He keepeth the feet of his saints."[2] Tell them to pray day by day, "Lead us not into temptation, but deliver us from evil."[3] Tell them that there is strength enough in Christ to preserve his own. Bid them hide under the shadow of his wings. You have done so, and found a happy shelter, and therefore you may confidently say to them, "Sirs, be of good cheer: for I believe God, that it shall be even as it was told me."

You will find others whose lamentation is, *"I am so weak. If I am a Christian yet I am good for nothing. I have little liberty in*

1 Acts 27:25.
2 1 Samuel 2:9.
3 Matthew 6:13.

prayer, or power to edify anybody. I think I am the most useless of all the family." Tell them that "He giveth power to the weak, and to him that hath no strength he increaseth might."[1] Tell them that the Lord does not cast away the little ones, but he "carrieth the lambs in his bosom, and doth gently lead those that are with young." Tell them of the faithfulness and tenderness of the Good Shepherd, and say, "Sirs, be of good cheer: weak as you are, the Lord's strength will sustain you; and as he has promised to preserve his own, and has evermore preserved me, do not doubt, for it shall be to you even as the Lord has told me." Perhaps they will say, "Ah, but *I am beset by Satan*. Blasphemous thoughts are injected into my soul. I am driven to my wits' end." Then tell them that the Lord enables his people to cry, "Rejoice not over me, O mine enemy, for though I fall yet shall I rise again."[2] Tell them that when the enemy cometh in like a flood, the Spirit of the Lord will lift up a standard against him. As they feel their danger, point them to their great protector, the Lord Jesus, who has come to destroy the works of the devil, and say, "You will conquer him, you will conquer him yet. The Lord will bruise Satan under our feet shortly. Sirs, be of good cheer: for I believe God, that it shall be even as he has told me."

There is much work for happy believers amongst the Feeble-minds, and the Miss Much-afraids, and the Mr. Despondencies, and the like; I earnestly hope that they will set about it.

Now, if you have performed these tasks, I commend to your attention a third class of persons, namely, *those who are greatly tried*. God has a very tried people abroad in the world. I learned a lesson the other day which, I think, I never can forget. I was asked after preaching a sermon to go and see a lady who suffered from rheumatism. Now, I know by bitter experience what rheumatism is, but when I saw one whose fingers and hands had all lost their form through pain, so that she was incapable of any motion beyond the mere lifting up of her hand, and the letting it fall again,—when I saw the pain marked on her countenance, and knew that for two-and-twenty years she had

1 See Isaiah 40:29.
2 Micah 7:8.

suffered an agony, then I said, "You have preached me a sermon upon patience, and I hope I shall profit by it. How dare I be impatient if you have to suffer so?" Now, if you go and see sick folk—and I suppose you do, and if not sickness comes to your own house—say to them, "Sirs, be of good cheer, for it shall be even as God has told me;" and what has he told me? Why, that he will support his people in the severest afflictions. "In six troubles I will be with thee, and in seven there shall no evil touch thee!"[1] Tell them that the Lord will bless his people's troubles, for "all things work together for good to them that love God."[2] Tell them that God will bring his people out of the trouble some way or other, for he has said, "Many are the afflictions of the righteous, but the Lord delivereth him out of them all."[3] And if you will tell them these precious things, believing them yourself—for that is the main point—having experienced the truth of them yourself, your testimony will comfort them. You will meet with some that have been bereaved, who have lost the light of their house, and have seen the desire of their eyes taken away with a stroke. Cheer them, and tell them of the sweet things that God has said concerning the bereaved. He is "the Judge of the widow, and the Father of the fatherless,"[4] and do you make a point of declaring your belief that he is so. You will meet with godly folks who are under testing trials. Many young people have to go through severe tests. I mean trials like this:—"Will you take this situation, young man? The wages are sufficient, are they not?" "Yes, sir, I should be well content, I do not think I shall get a better situation as far as money goes." "You understand that you will not have the Sabbath day to yourself and that we want no religion here." Now, young man, what do you say to that? Do not think twice about it, my friend, but say, "No; 'what shall it profit a man if he gain the whole world, and lose his own soul?'"[5] Speak right straight out, and do not be afraid to throw up the tempting offer. Many Christians can tell you, "to be of good cheer," for if you do this

1 Job 5:19.
2 Romans 8:28.
3 Psalm 34:19.
4 See Psalm 68:5.
5 Mark 8:36.

God will bless you. You shall have even in this life your recompense, as well as in the life to come, if you can be decided and steadfast to stand for God and keep his way. I could mention many Christians who would tell you that when they were tested the Lord helped them to stand fast, and that they have to bless him for it every day of their lives; whereas certain others have temporized and given way a little, and they have got out of God's ways, and have had to run from pillar to post all their lives long, and though they are still Christians yet they never enter into the joy of their Lord. O sirs, be of good cheer when you have to suffer for Christ's sake, for he is able to give you much more than you will ever lose by him, and above all he will give you peace of conscience, which is worth all the mines of California. Should you come under persecution, any of you, I hope you will be met by your fellow Christians who will tell you not to be afraid, for the Lord can make you increasingly to rejoice the more you are despised and calumniated. Believe you that, and you shall find it true.

And, O ye tried people of God, ye that have lost the light of his countenance, those of us who rejoice in God would come to you and bear witness that he has only forsaken you for a small moment, but he will return to you in the fullness of his mercy. We believe God that, whether the season be dark or light, and whether the road be rough or smooth, his heart is still the same, and he will not turn aside from the salvation of one of his chosen people.

Thus, dear friends, you have good scope for your faith to exercise itself in comforting others. Lay yourselves out in this delightful service.

I have yet another set of good folks to speak to. We have some Christian people about who tremble greatly for the ark of the Lord. I occasionally meet with good brethren, very good brethren, who are tempted to commit the sin of Uzzah—to put forth their hand to steady the ark because the oxen shake it; as if God could not protect his own cause. Some say that the good men are all dying: I have even heard that they are all dead, but I am not quite sure of it; and they ask as the fathers fall asleep, and one after another of the pillars of the house of God are taken away, what will become of the church?

What will become of the church? "My Father! My Father! The chariot of Israel and the horsemen thereof!"[1] What will become of the truth, the cause, and the church? You know the good Methodist woman's outcry at the funeral sermon when the minister said, "Now that this eminent servant of the Lord is departed we know of no one to fill his place. The standard-bearers are removed and we have none left at all to be compared with them. It seems as if the glory were departing and the faithful failing from among men." The worthy mother in Israel called out from the aisle. "Glory be to God, that's a lie!" Well, I have often felt inclined to say the same when I have heard a wailing over the absence of good and great men, and melancholy prophecies of the awful times to come, "Glory be to God, he will never let his church die out for want of leaders; he has a grand reserve somewhere." If all the men who preach the gospel today were struck down in the pulpit with apoplectic fits tomorrow, the Holy Spirit would still qualify men to preach the gospel of Jesus Christ. We are none of us necessary to him, nor is any mere man necessary to God. Do not get into that state of mind which makes you attach undue value to men or means. The salvation of souls is God's work, and if it be God's work it will go on. Be quite sure of that. There is no fear of any work falling to the ground which has Jehovah for its builder. In this church of ours at the Tabernacle we gradually lose our leaders, and I have heard it said, and I must confess that I have almost thought, "If So-and-so were gone nobody would ever fill her place or his place." Such earnest and holy individuals seem to be essential, and we feel that their removal would be fatal. Yet it is not so, dear friends; it is not so. Others arise, and God's work still goes on. Christians ought to be as confident as the heroic Spartans. The old men advanced in procession, and they said, "We *have been* brave," and they showed their scars: and then the strong men in the prime of their days followed and said, "We *are* brave," and they bared their arms for war. Then if anyone wondered what would happen when the old men were gone, and when the strong men were slain in battle, there came the boys and the striplings behind, and they said, "We *will be* brave, for we are Spartans!" I see

1 2 Kings 2:12.

my grey-headed brethren going off the stage, and I bless God that, though they do not say it, I can say it of them—"They have been brave." Blessed be God, we have also a good staff of active workers of whom I may say, though they must not say it, "They *are* brave." And yonder are the young soldiers coming on—the young men and the young women. I see in their very faces that they are smiling at the thought of being numbered with the hosts of Christ, and I am persuaded they mean to be brave, and to stand up for the good old cause, and for the bloodstained banner of Christ, even as their fathers have done. Instead of the fathers shall be the children: God make them far better soldiers than we have been. Brethren, do not let us be discouraged, for I believe God, that it shall be even as it was told me; "the Lord hath been mindful of us, he will bless us."

Many minds are in a state of great distress about the spread of error. I do not know what is going to happen to England according to the weeping prophets. The signs of the times are very bad, and the would-be prophets say that a dreadful storm is coming on. My barometer does not indicate anything of the kind, but theirs stands at "much rain," or "stormy." Not long ago I walked with a very excellent man, whose name I will not mention, because I think he must have been ill that morning. He told me that he believed that he should live to see the streets of London run with blood, on account of the unbridled democracy, the atheism, and the radicalism of the times. In fact, he thought that everything was out of joint, and we were going—I do not know where. It is not long ago, and I remember that I pulled him by the sleeve, and said, "But, my dear friend, God is not dead." Now, that is my comfort. God is not dead, and he will beat the devil yet. As surely as Jesus Christ won the victory on the cross, he will win the victory over the world's sin. It is true it is a hard time for Christianity, and infidels are fighting us with new arguments; but when I think of them I feel inclined to say what the Duke of Wellington said at Waterloo to the generals "Hard pounding, gentlemen! hard pounding! but we will see which will pound the longest." And so we say. It may be "hard pounding" for the Christian church, but we shall see who can pound the longest. Hitherto—these eighteen hundred years or more—the gospel gun has gone on pounding, and has neither been spiked nor worn out. As for our opponents, they have changed their guns a good many times. Our gospel cannon has blown their guns and gun carriages and gunners all to pieces; and they have had to set up new batteries every year or two. They change their modes, their arguments, their tactics, but we glory in the same cross as Paul did, and preach the same gospel as Augustine, and Calvin, and Whitefield, and the like. All along the testimony of Jesus Christ has still been the same. The precious blood has been exalted, and men have been bidden to believe in Jesus. Pound away, gentlemen! We shall pound the longest, and we shall win the day. If we believe God in that fashion, let us turn round to our discomfited brethren, and say to them, "Sirs, be of good cheer: for I believe God, that it shall be even as it was told me."

The last class that I shall notice will be our brethren and sisters who are laboring for Christ. Sometimes workers for the Lord get cast down. "I have taught a class for years," says one, "and seen no fruit." "I have been preaching at the corner of the street for months but have never heard of a conversion," says another. "I have been visiting the lodging-houses, but I have never met with a convert." Well, dear brother, do you think that you have preached Jesus Christ, and nothing has come of it? If you do, you must be a very unbelieving brother. I do not believe it for a moment. I believe God, that it shall be even as he has told me, and he has said, "My word shall not return unto me void, but it shall prosper in the thing whereto I sent it."[1] Perhaps you preach unbelievingly. Now, an unbelieving word is not God's word. If you preach confidently, and teach trustfully, believing in the power of the Spirit of God, and so exhibiting Jesus Christ to your children and to your hearers, there are sure to be results. The raindrops return not to heaven, and the snow flakes climb not back to the treasure-house, but water the earth, and make it bring forth and bud: and even so shall God's word be. It must prosper in the thing whereto he has sent it. Beloved brother, do not give up. Dear sister, do not be discouraged. Go on! Go on! If you do not see results today you must wait and work on, for the harvest will come. "He that goeth

1 See Isaiah 55:11.

forth and weepeth, bearing precious seed, shall doubtless come again rejoicing, bringing his sheaves with him."[1] Be not so cowardly as to say, "I will leave the work." You are not to win a battle in a moment, or reap a harvest as soon as you sow the seed. Keep on! "Be stedfast, immovable, always abounding in the work of the Lord, forasmuch as ye know that your labor is not in vain in the Lord."[2] We say this to you because we are confident ourselves, and would have you confident also. Sirs, be of good cheer. God has been true to us, and given us success; and we believe that it shall be to you even as he has told us.

III. Now, I have done the sermon, but I had intended, if time had held out, to give ONE OR TWO WORDS OF PERSONAL TESTIMONY TO THE FAITHFULNESS OF GOD by declaring that the Lord has always acted to me as he has promised me. I will give one or two.

When I was converted to God, as I read the Scriptures I found that believers ought to be baptized. Now, nobody around me saw things in that light: but it did not matter to me what they thought, for I looked at it carefully for myself. Parents, friends, all differed, but believers' baptism seemed to me to be scriptural, and, though I was a lad, God gave me grace to be honest to my conscience, and to follow the Lord in that respect as fully as I could. Have I had any cause to regret it? It seemed then that I might soon have grave cause for doing so, but I have had none: it has, on the other hand, often been a great comfort to my soul to feel that I did not trifle with my convictions. And I should like to urge you, young people, whether on that matter or any other, if you have received light from God, never to trifle with it. Follow the Lord fully, and I can say, as the result of actual experience, "Sirs, be of good cheer. No harm will come to you if you are faithful to God and to your consciences."

Again, when I came to London as a young minister, I knew very well that the doctrines which I preached were by no means popular, but I for that very reason brought them out with all the more emphasis. What a storm was raised! I was reading the other day a tirade of abuse which was poured upon me about twenty years ago. I must

---

1 Psalm 126:6.
2 1 Corinthians 15:58.

have been a horridly bad fellow, according to that description, but I was pleased to observe that it was not *I* that was bad, but the doctrines which I preached. I teach the same truths now; and after having preached them these four-and-twenty years or so, what can I say of the results? Why, that no man loses anything by bringing the truth right straight out. If he believes a doctrine, let him speak it boldly. Mr. Slapdash, as Rowland Hill called the bold preacher, will after all succeed. Let no minister say, "That is too Calvinistic, and Calvinism is at a discount; that is too nonconforming, and if you dare to speak against the Church of England somebody will be very vexed. Now, trim your sails. Preach smoothly. Whenever you have anything to say, polish it, and put it in such a neat way that nobody can object. As the great goddess Diana now a days is unsectarianism, try and be unsectarian, and all that is sweet and soothing and velvety and treacly, and you will succeed." Now, how has it turned out with me? I wish to bear this witness, not about myself, mark, but about the truth which I have preached. Nothing has succeeded better than preaching out boldly what I have believed, and standing to it in defiance of all opposition, and never caring a snap of the fingers whether it offended or whether it pleased. Young man, if you are beginning life now, I charge you begin so that you can keep on, with a straightforward, honest reliance in God, for be sure of this, the truth will reward those who love it, and all who lose for its sake are great gainers. Be steadfast in following your convictions. I cannot help saying it, because some of you, perhaps, are beginning to temporize a little. I would say to you, "Stand up straight, and tell out the truth, and then be of good cheer, for I believe God, that it shall be even as he has told me."

May God grant that this little personal testimony may tend to put backbone into certain Christians, for we have a molluscous company of professors about, who do not believe anything, but shape their creed according to the mind of the last person they meet. Go, dear brethren, and pray God to cleanse your hearts of that evil if you have ever indulged it. Believe God. Take every letter of his Book and hang to it as for dear life, and in little as well as in great things keep to the statutes and precepts and ordinances and doctrines of the Lord, as they are committed to you. As surely as you do this the Lord of Hosts will bless you. First rest in Jesus by a simple faith in him, and then treasure up his every word, and keep his every command. So shall the blessing of God be with you henceforth and for ever. May his Holy Spirit work this in you! Amen.

PORTION OF SCRIPTURE READ BEFORE SERMON—Acts 27:11–44.

A GREAT GOSPEL FOR
GREAT SINNERS

June 2ND, 1884, Metropolitan Tabernacle, Newington

This is a faithful saying, and worthy of all acceptation, that Christ Jesus came into the world to save sinners; of whom I am chief. Howbeit for this cause I obtained mercy, that in me first Jesus Christ might show forth all longsuffering, for a pattern to them which should here-after believe on him to life everlasting. Now unto the King eternal, immortal, invisible, the only wise God, be honour and glory for ever and ever. Amen.—1 TIMOTHY 1:15–17.

When Paul wrote this ever-memorable text, "This is a faithful saying, and worthy of all acceptation, that Christ Jesus came into the world to save sinners," he placed it in connection with himself. I would have you carefully notice the context. Twelfth verse:— "I thank Christ Jesus our Lord, who hath enabled me, for that he counted me faithful, putting me into the ministry; who was before a blasphemer, and a persecutor, and injurious: but I obtained mercy, because I did it ignorantly in unbelief. And the grace of our Lord was exceeding abundant with faith and love which is in Christ Jesus. This is a faithful saying, and worthy of all acceptation, that Christ Jesus came into the world to save sinners." You see, the apostle had spoken of himself, and then it was that the Holy Spirit put it into his mind to write of the glorious salvation of which he was so notable a subject. Truly it was a seasonable and suggestive connection in which to place this glorious gospel text. What he preached to others was to be seen in himself.

When I read to you the story of Saul's conversion, suppose I had finished it by making the remark, "This is a faithful saying, that Christ Jesus came into the world to save sinners," you would all have said, "That is true, and it is a natural inference from the narrative." Such a remark would have served as the moral of the whole story. It is an easy and a simple inference from such a conversion, that Christ Jesus must have come into the world to save sinners. See, then, why Paul uttered it in this particular place. He could not help bringing his own case forward; but when he did bring it forward it was to add emphasis to this declaration that Jesus Christ came into the world to save sinners. It is my conviction that our Lord in infinite wisdom intends that his ministers should themselves be proofs of the doctrines which they teach. If a young man, a very young man, stands up to tell you of the experience of an aged Christian, you say at once, "That may be very true, but *you* cannot prove it, for you are not an aged person yourself." If one who has been privileged in the providence of God to enjoy the comforts of life stands up to preach upon the consolations of the Spirit in poverty, you say, "Yes, that is very true, but you cannot speak from experience yourself." Hence the Lord likes his servants to have such an experience that their testimony shall have a man at the back of it. He would have their lives sustain and explain their testimonies. When Paul said that Christ came into the world to save sinners, his own conversion, his own joy in the Lord, were proof positive of it. He was a witness who had tasted and handled the good Word of life to which he witnessed.

Paul went to heaven years ago, but his evidence is not vitiated by that fact; for a truthful statement is not affected by the lapse of time. If a statement was made yesterday, it is just as truthful as if you were hearing it today; and if it were made, as this was, eighteen hundred years ago, yet, if true then (and nobody disputed it in Paul's day), it is true now. The facts recorded in the gospels are as much facts now as ever, and they ought to have the same influence upon our minds as they had upon the minds of the apostles. At this moment the statement that Jesus Christ came into the world to save sinners has Paul still at the back of it. "He being dead yet speaketh." Oh, you who are burdened with your sins, I want you to see Saul of Tarsus before you at this moment, and to hear him say, with penitent voice, in your presence, "The Lord Jesus came into the world to save sinners, of whom I am chief." Doubt not the statement, for the man is the evidence of it. He who saved Paul can save you: yea, he is willing now to display his power upon you. Be not disobedient to the heavenly message.

But, beloved, if we have not Paul in our midst to bear his personal witness we have still many living proofs: we have indisputable evidence in those that are still about us that it "is a faithful saying, and worthy of all acceptation, that Christ Jesus came into the world to save sinners." I could summon to this pulpit scores who were literally the blackest of transgressors, but they are washed, and sanctified, and so they are living arguments of the Lord's power to save. Many also are now present who could not be numbered by their fellow-men among the chief of sinners in certain aspects of the case, yet they most willingly put themselves down as the chief of sinners under some other way of viewing it, and they bear their testimony, as I do to-night, that Jesus is able to save unto the uttermost. I, who now stand before you, am a living witness that Christ Jesus can save sinners, and does save them still. The Lord has forgiven and justified me, and I have found grace in his sight. In my case, also, it is proven that it "is a faithful saying, and worthy of all acceptation, that Christ Jesus came into the world to save sinners; of whom I am chief." Oh, how I wish that my hearers would believe me! Many of you would accept any statement which I should make; why do you not accept this? You do not think me a liar,—why, then, do you not believe my testimony concerning Jesus? He is as ready to save today as he was of old. He is ready to save you if *you* will trust him.

The run of thought at this time will be, first, concerning those *who are the chief of sinners;* secondly, we will enquire *why God has saved them;* and thirdly, *what they say when they are saved.*

I. First, then, WHO ARE THE CHIEF OF SINNERS? Paul says that he was the chief. I think, however, that he was only one of the regiment. There are different classes of sinners, and some are greater and some less. All men are truly sinners, but all men are not equally sinners. They are all in the mire; but they have not all sunk to an equal depth in it. It is true they have all fallen deep enough to perish in sin, unless the grace of God prevent; yet there are differences in the degrees of guilt, and there will doubtless be differences in the degrees of punishment.

Some are the chief of sinners in the same way as the apostle Paul, for *they have persecuted the church of God.* Paul, who was then called Saul, had given his vote against Stephen; and when Stephen was stoned, he kept the clothes of them that murdered him. He felt that blood lying upon his soul long afterward, and he bemoaned it. Would not you, if you had been a helper at the murder of some child of God, feel that you were among the chief of sinners? If you had been willingly and wilfully, maliciously and eagerly, a helper in putting a man of God like Stephen to death, you would write yourself down as a sinner of crimson dye? Why, I think that I should say, "God may forgive me, but I will never forgive myself." It would seem such a horrid crime to lie upon one's soul. Yet this was merely a beginning. Saul was like a leopard, who, having once tasted blood, must always have his tongue in it. His very breath was threatening, and his delight was slaughter. He harassed the people of God: he made great havoc of the saints: he compelled them, he says, to blaspheme: he had them beaten in the synagogues, driven from city to city, and even put to death. This must have remained upon his heart as a dark memory, even after the Lord Jesus Christ had fully forgiven him. When he knew, as Paul did know, that he was a justified man through the righteousness of Jesus Christ, yet he must always have felt a smiting at his heart to think that these innocent lambs had been worried by him; that for no other reason but that they were lovers of the Crucified, he had panted for their blood. This matter of deadly persecution placed Saul head and shoulders above other sinners. This was the top-stone of the pyramid of his sin, "because I persecuted the church of Christ." I thank God that there is no man here who has that particular form of sin upon his conscience in having actually put to death or joined in the slaughter of any child of God. The laws of our country have happily prevented your being stained with that foul offence, and I bless the Lord that it is so. Yet if there should be such among those who are hearing these words, or among those who shall one day read them, I must confess that they are, indeed, numbered among the chief of sinners, and I pray God to grant that they may obtain mercy as Saul did.

But you can go very near to this; in all probability certain of you have done so. That husband who has threatened his wife so bitterly if she obeys her conscience, that man who has discharged his servant for no other reason but his fidelity to Christ, that landlord who has turned out his cottager from his home because he held a religious service beneath his roof, that man who has wilfully and maliciously slandered a servant of God, not because he did him any harm, but because he cannot bear to hear of any truly following after Christ— these are the people who must be reckoned among the chief of sinners. They have done no murder, but they have gone as far as they dare to go, and their heart is full of venom against the people of God: this is a grievous crime. Though it may seem a very small thing to grieve a pious child, or to vex a poor, godly woman, God does not think it so. He remembers jests and scoffs levelled at his little ones, and he bids those who indulge in them to take heed. You had better offend a king than one of the Lord's little ones. That poor man in the workshop, who has so hard a time of it with your jests and chaff, has a Friend in the heavens. That other man who, seeking the Lord, has found the cold shoulder in society, has an Advocate on high, who will not see him despised without espousing his cause. It may appear a trifle to make a saint the target of ridicule, but his Father in heaven does not think so. I know this, that many patient men will bear a great deal, but if you strike their children, their blood is up, and they will not have it. A father will not stand by to see his child abused, and the Great Father above is as tender and fond as any other father. You have seen among birds and beasts that they will put forth all their strength for their young: a hen, naturally very timid, will fight for her little chicks with all the courage of a lion. Some of the smallest of animals, and the least powerful, nevertheless become perfectly terrible when they are taking care of their offspring; and think you that the everlasting God will bear to see his children maligned, and slandered, and abused, for their following of him? Is the God of nature without natural affection? I trow not. You shall rue the day, sir, in which you took up arms against the people of God. Humble yourself before God on account of it, otherwise you will be numbered among the chief of sinners, and the chief of punishments shall be meted out to you.

I have no doubt that there may be some of that kind here; and, if there are, I can only pray that the story of Saul of Tarsus may be repeated in them by boundless grace. May they even yet come to preach the gospel which now they despise. It is no new thing for the priest to be converted to Christ. It is no new thing for the opposer to become the advocate, and to be all the better and more powerful a pleader because of the mischief which he formerly did. Oh that the Lord would turn his foes into friends! God send it! For Christ's sake may he send it now!

Further, among the chief of sinners we must of course reckon *those who are guilty of the coarser and grosser sins.* I will not occupy a moment in mentioning what they are, for it is a shame even to speak of them. God keep us from unchastity and dishonesty,—from any one of those sins which are censurable even under the head of common morality; for, if not—if we indulge in these—we shall certainly come by them to be numbered among the chief of sinners. I must, however, mention blasphemy and lewd speaking, because these are unhappily far too common. Does a man think that he can go on damning his own body and soul in so many words, and never provoke the Lord to anger? Does he dream that he can use foul and filthy words, and wicked oaths, without incurring sin? I believe that these things bring the blackest guilt on the conscience; for God has expressly said that he will by no means hold him guiltless that taketh his name in vain. It is true of every sin that God will not hold a man guiltless who does it; but it is especially said about this sin, because men are apt to fancy that words are of no great importance, or that God takes no notice thereof. Even the thoughtless or trifling repetition of the name of the Lord involves great sin, for thus a man taketh the sacred name in vain. Yet men trifle with that name in common conversation, and that with fearful frequency. There is no excuse for this wanton wickedness, because it brings neither profit nor pleasure to the person who so offends. What practical end can it serve? As George Herbert said long ago,

> "Lust and wine plead a pleasure, avarice gain:
> But the cheap swearer through his open sluice
> Lets his soul run for nought, as little fearing
> Were I an *Epicure*, I could bate swearing."

I am unable to frame an excuse for profane language: it is needless wilful wickedness. Men talk so as to horrify us: they chill our blood with fear lest God should take them at their word; and all for nothing at all. I would to God that every blasphemer here (if such there be, and I have no doubt that there are), would abandon that vile, inexcusable, useless habit, which lowers men in society, defiles them before God, and ensures their condemnation. Filthy speech puts those who are guilty of it among the chief of sinners, and to them will certainly be meted out a terrible vengeance in that day when God shall solemnly curse those who have so glibly cursed themselves. It will be an awful thing for the man who used profane imprecations to find out at last that his prayers were heard, and that they will be answered. O swearer, beware lest the Lord God hear thy prayers at once to thine everlasting confusion! Sit down at this moment in deep contrition, and weep to think of the many times in which thou hast defied the God of heaven, and uttered words of provocation against the God in whose hand thy breath is. Not yet has he cut thee down. Oh, wonder of mercy! Take heed to thyself. Above all, marvel that there should be mention of mercy for such a one as thou art.

Now, dear friends, there are other chiefs among sinners who do not go in for these grosser sins at all. Let me mention them, for in this line I shall have to place myself and many of you. Those are among the chief of sinners *who have sinned against great light*, and against the influences of holy instruction, and gracious example. Children of godly parents, who have been brought up and instructed in the fear of God from their youth, are among the chief of sinners if they turn aside from the way of life. When they transgress, there is a heavy weight about their fault, which is not to be found in the common sin of the children of the slums, or the arabs of the gutter. The offspring of the degraded know no better, poor souls, and hence their transgressions are sins of ignorance; but those who do know better, when they transgress, transgress with an emphasis. Their sin is as a talent of lead; and it shall hang about their necks like a millstone. I remember how this came home to my heart when I was convinced of my sin. I had not engaged in any of the grosser vices, but then I had not been tempted to them, but had been carefully guarded from vicious influences. But I lamented that I had been disobedient to my parents, proud in spirit, forgetful of God's commands: I knew better—knew better from the very first, and this put me in my own estimation among the chief of sinners. It had cost me much to do evil, for I had sinned against the clearest light. Especially is this the case when the possession of knowledge is accompanied by much tenderness of conscience. There are some of you unconverted people, who, when you do wrong, feel that you have done wrong, and feel it keenly too, even though no one rebukes you for it. You cannot be unjust, or hasty in temper, or faulty in speech, or break the Sabbath, or do anything that is forbidden, without your conscience troubling you. You know what it is to go to bed and lie awake in misery, after some questionable amusement, or after having spoken too frivolously. Yours is a tender conscience; do not violate it, or you will be doubly guilty. When God puts the bit into your mouth, if you try to get it between your teeth, and it does not check you at all, you must mind what you are at, for you may be left to dash onward to destruction. "He, that being often reproved hardeneth his neck, shall suddenly be destroyed, and that without remedy."[1] It puts men among the chief of sinners when against light and against conscience they deliberately choose the way of evil, and leave the commandments of the Lord.

Especially is it a grievous offence *to sin against the gentle checking of the Holy Spirit.* Have you not been sad offenders upon this

1 Proverbs 29:1.

point? You felt the other Sunday night that if you could once get out of the chapel, and get home, you would bow the knee in prayer; *but you did not.* You have felt like that many times, and you have shaken off the feeling; and now a sermon scarcely moves you: it had need be full of thunder and lightning to make you turn a hair. Truths which used to make you shake from head to foot scarcely affect you now. Take care, I pray you; for he that sins against the Holy Ghost may find himself water-logged by sin, so as to be no longer able to move his vessel towards the shores of salvation. Nothing hardens like the gospel when it is long trifled with. To lie asoak in the truth without receiving it into the heart is sure destruction. To die on holy ground is to die indeed. God grant that it may not be so with any here!

Yet if you be this day the chief of sinners, do not despair, nor turn away in sullen anger; for we are going to say to you, at this hour, in the name of the merciful God, that his Son, Jesus Christ, has come into the world to save sinners, even the very chief.

I think that I must put down those among the chief of sinners *who have led others into sin.* Ah, this is a sad, sad, sad, sad subject! If you have led others astray, if you yourself seek the Lord, and are saved, yet you cannot save them. If it be young persons whom you have polluted with evil, you cannot take the wretched stain out of their minds. You can leave off sowing the devil's seed, but you cannot gather up what you have sown, nor prevent its growing and ripening. Fire is easily kindled, but not so soon extinguished when it has taken hold upon the fuel. It is an awful fact that there may be souls in hell whom you have sent there! It was a wise penitential prayer of a converted man who had exercised influence for evil,—"Lord, forgive me my other men's sins." When you lead others to sin, their sins are to a large extent your sins. They do not cease to be the sins of those who commit them, but they are also the sins of those who promoted or suggested them by precept or example. A bad example, a lewd expression, an unholy life, may be the means of drawing others down to perdition; and those that destroy others, and so are soul-murderers, are among the chief of sinners. He who uses dagger or pistol to the body is abhorred; what shall we say of those who poison human minds, and stab at the heart of piety? These are guiltiest of the guilty. Woe unto them!

Especially must I rank him among the chief of sinners who has preached falsehood,—who has denied the deity of Christ—who has undermined the inspiration of Scripture—who has struggled against the faith, fought against the atonement, and done evil even as he could in the scattering of scepticism. He must take his place among the ringleaders in diabolical mischief: he is a master destroyer, a chosen apostle of the prince of darkness. Oh, that he might be brought by sovereign grace to be among the foremost teachers of that faith which hitherto he has destroyed! I think that we should do well as Christian people if we prayed more for any who make themselves notorious by their infidelity. If we talked less bitterly against them, and prayed more sweetly for them, good would come of it. Of political argument against atheists we have had enough, let us carry the case into a higher court, and plead with God about them. If we use the grand artillery of heaven by importunate prayer, we should be using much better weapons than are commonly employed. God help us to pray for all false teachers that they may be converted to God, and so display the omnipotence of his love.

I shall not say more upon this mournful matter, for, indeed, I have only mentioned these examples in the hope that some here present may confess, "I am sorry to say that the preacher means me. Under some aspect or other I must take my place among the chief of sinners."

II. Now, secondly, WHY ARE THE CHIEF OF SINNERS SO OFTEN SAVED? The Lord Jesus Christ, when he went into heaven, took with him one of the chief of sinners as a companion: the dying thief entered Paradise the self-same day as our Lord. After our Lord Jesus had gone to heaven, so far as I know, he never did save more than one person by his own immediate instrumentality; and that one person was this very apostle Paul, who has given us our text. To him our Lord spake personally from heaven, saying, "Saul, Saul, why persecutest thou me?"[1] To him he revealed himself by the way, and called him to be his apostle, even to this man who truthfully called himself the chief of sinners. It is wonderful to think that it should be so: but grace

1 Acts 22:7.

delights in dealing with great and glaring sin, and putting away the crying crimes of great offenders.

The Lord Jesus not only saved the chief of sinners, but he was related to some of them by blood. Look through the long line of our Lord's genealogy. You know that doctrine, the last invention of Rome, concerning the immaculate conception of the Virgin Mary. I am going to tell you a doctrine which is about as far apart from that as the east is from the west. In the genealogy of our blessed Lord we find the names of certain of the chief of sinners. Three women especially hold a position in it, who were each notorious for sin. Not many women are mentioned, but among the first is Tamar, guilty of incest. The next is Rahab the harlot, and a third is Bathsheba the adulteress. This is a crooked pedigree, an ancestral tree whose branches are more than a little gnarled and twisted. Admire the condescension of our Lord in coming of such a stock. He came *of* sinners, because he came *for* sinners. According to the flesh he comes of sinners that sinners may come to him. There was mixed in the veins through which flowed his ancestry the blood of Ruth the Moabitess, a heathen, brought in on purpose that we Gentiles might see how truly he was bone of our bone, and flesh of our flesh. I say not that there was any defilement in his humanity, God forbid; for he was not born after the manner of men, so as to be polluted in that fashion; but still I say that his genealogy includes many great sinners in order that we may see how closely he allied himself with them, how thoroughly he undertook their cause. Read the roll of his ancestry, and you will see that David is there, who cried, "Against thee, thee only, have I sinned;"[1] and Solomon, who loved strange women; and Rehoboam, his foolish son; and Manasseh "who shed innocent blood very much,"[2] and worse men than they, if worse could be. Such sinners as these are in the genealogy of the Savior of sinners. "He was numbered with the transgressors."[3] He was called "The friend of publicans and sinners."[4]

---

1 Psalm 51:4.

2 2 Kings 21:16.

3 Isaiah 53:12.

4 Matthew 11:19.

It was said of him, "This man receiveth sinners, and eateth with them."[1] Still he delights to save great sinners. O my hearer, it will delight him to save *you!*

Why does he do it? The apostle says, in the sixteenth verse, "For this cause I obtained mercy, that in me first Jesus Christ might shew forth all longsuffering."[2] What, is that his reason for saving a sinner? It is that he may show in that sinner his long-suffering, revealing his patience and forgiveness. In a great sinner like Paul he shows *all* his long-suffering, not little grains of it, nor portions of it, but *all* his long-suffering. Is Jesus Christ willing to show forth all his long-suffering? Does he delight to unveil all his love? Yes; for remember that he calls his mercy his riches: "he is rich in mercy." I do not find that he calls his power his riches, but he calls his grace his riches, "in whom we have redemption through his blood, the forgiveness of sins, according to the riches of his grace." Oh, dear friends, the Lord, who is rich in mercy, seeks a treasury in which to put his riches; he wants a casket for the sacred jewelry of his love; and these atrocious criminals, these great offenders, these who think themselves black as hell, these are the very men in whom there is space for his rare jewels of goodness. Where sin has abounded there is elbow-room for the infinite mercy of the living God. Ought you not to be encouraged, if you feel yourself greatly guilty, that God delights to show forth all his patience by saving great sinners? Will you not at once seek that *all* long-suffering may be shown in your case? Believe on the Lord Jesus, and it shall be so.

And what does Paul say next? He says that the Lord saved him *for a pattern* to them which should hereafter believe on him to life everlasting. For a pattern. It means for a type or specimen. Paul was a "proof before letters." The first prints of an engraving are sharp and clear, and therefore they are very valuable: they exhibit the productive power of the plate at its highest point, before the surface is worn down in the least degree. Paul was one of the proof-engravings taken off the plate in the earliest days, and under the most favorable

1 Luke 15:2.
2 1 Timothy 1:16.

circumstances for bringing out every line of grace. All God's long-suffering was seen in him for a pattern. I would to God that we could put some of you under that same engraved plate, and issue more impressions at this very hour; for the plate is not worn out: the type that God uses is as new as ever. When a printer sets his type, he sends to the author a sheet to let him see what the type is, and he calls it his proof. So also Paul was God's proof—one of the first taken off by the glorious machinery of grace to let us all see what God has to say to us concerning long-suffering love. That printing-machine is at work at this very moment: it is making impressions at this hour, most clear, sharp, and readable. I would to God that some great sinner here would be like the paper laid under the type to take the impression of almighty grace. A grand edition of the Work of Love was issued before Paul was printed off, and published; I refer to the time when Peter preached at Pentecost. Many large and splendid editions have been issued from that press since. I see before me a whole library that God has printed in this house—the proofs that God has taken of late years from the old standing type; but Paul stands at the head of the list as a fine first proof of what God can do.

Then God can save *me*. I came to that conclusion a year ago, and putting it to the test, I found it true. Dear fellow sinners, come to the same conclusion! Who are you? No, I do not ask you to tell me. I do not want to know. God knows. But I want you to come to this conclusion,—"If Paul is a specimen of saved ones, then why should not I be saved? If Paul had been unique, a production quite by himself, then we might justly have doubted as to ourselves; but since he is a pattern, we may all hope to see the Lord's long-suffering repeated in ourselves." Nowadays, by the Parcels' Post, people are sending you patterns of all sorts of things, and many articles are bought according to sample. When you buy from a pattern you expect the goods to be like the pattern. So God sends us Paul as a pattern of his great mercy to great sinners. He thus says, in effect,—"That is the kind of thing I do. I take this rough, bad material of the chief of sinners, and I renew it, and show forth all my mercy in it. This is what I am prepared to do with you." Poor soul, will you not accept the mercy of

God? Enter into this salvation business with the Lord, that you, too, like the apostle, being a sinner, may become like him in obtaining the glorious salvation which is in Christ Jesus, who came into the world to save sinners. I am talking very plainly and simply to you; but if you love your own souls you will be all the better pleased to listen. I do not want to amuse you, but to see you saved. Do, I pray you, bend your minds to this subject, and learn that there is good hope for the worst of you if you will cry unto the Lord.

That is why Jesus saves those who have most grievously erred, that he may display them as specimens of what his grace can do.

"But I belong to such a wicked family," cries one. Oh, yes; and many have been saved who belonged to the most depraved and degraded of families. They have entered into relationship with Christ, and their own base condition has been swallowed up in his glory. The children of criminals when converted belong to the family of God. "To as many as received him, to them gave he power to become the sons of God, even to them that believe on his name."[1]

"Oh, but I have indulged in such horrible vices." This is a sad confession, but it does not doom you to despair, for the blood of Jesus washes away the worst of filth. Blasphemers, adulterers, drunkards, thieves—"such," O ye saints—"such were some of you, but ye are washed, but ye are sanctified;" and why should not others of like character be washed and sanctified too?

III. I must close by dwelling a moment on the third head, which is this—WHAT THE CHIEF OF SINNERS SAY WHEN THEY ARE SAVED. What they say is recorded in the text. It reads like a hymn:—"Now unto the King eternal, immortal, invisible, the only wise God, be honor and glory for ever and ever. Amen." See, the first word is *"Now."* As soon as ever they are saved they begin praising the Lord. They cannot endure to put off glorifying God. Some one might whisper to them, "You will praise God when you get to heaven." "No," replies the gracious soul, "I am going to praise him now. *Now* unto the King eternal, immortal, invisible, be glory for ever and ever." Grateful love cannot be restrained, it is like fire in the

1 John 1:12.

bones. Our heart would break for love if it could not find a means of expressing itself at once.

Does another person whisper, "When you praise God, do not be too long about it. Leave off as soon as you have moderately praised and adored. Do not be for ever engaged in the work of praise." "No," says the saved man, "I cannot have done while life lasts,—'To him be honor and glory *for ever and ever.'*" Not only for ever: that might seem to be long enough; but "for ever and ever." It is a redundant expression, such as enthusiasm delights to use: it indicates a sort of double eternity. The saved sinner can never have enough of glorifying the Lord; he will praise him throughout eternity. As soon as a man is cleansed from sin, he is clothed with praise. A new song is put into his mouth, and he must sing it: he cannot help doing so. There is no stopping him.

Notice what titles Paul here heaps together. First, he calls the Lord Jesus Christ *a King*. "Now unto the King eternal." Or apply it to God the Ever-Blessed, in his sacred unity, if you will: he calls the Lord King, for he would give him the loftiest name, and pay him the lowliest homage. He calls him a King, for he had found him so; for it is a king that distributes life and death, a king that pardons rebels, a king that reigns and rules over men. Jesus was all this to Paul, and much more, and so he must needs give him the royal title: he cannot speak of him as less than majestic. If Jesus is not King to all the world, at least he is King to the man whose sins have been forgiven him. "Now," says he, "unto the King eternal be honor and glory for ever and ever."

See how he puts it, "the King *eternal.*" Not a king that will lose his kingdom; not a king who will cease to reign, or abdicate, or die. Oh, dear brethren, the King that pardoned Paul is a King today, equally mighty to save. Eighteen hundred years after his great deed of grace to the chief of sinners he is still a King.

> "Jesus sits on Zion's hill:
> He can save poor sinners still."

He sits upon the throne of mercy in the sovereignty of his grace, in the splendor of his love, in the majesty of his power, passing by iniquity, transgression, and sin. Will you not bow before him? Here at this moment I pause to do him reverence,—Glory be to the Lord Jesus, for he is the King eternal!

Then he calls him the King *immortal*. He is the King that ever lives by his own power, and is therefore able to give life to dead souls. Blessed be the name of the Savior that he died for sinners, but equally blessed be his name that he ever liveth to make intercession for sinners, and is therefore able to save unto the uttermost them that come unto God by him. The quickened, raised-up spirit cries aloud, "Glory be unto the King immortal, for he has made me immortal by the touch of his life-giving hand!" Because he lives, we shall live also. Our life is hidden in him, and throughout eternity we shall reign with him.

Then Paul styles him the King *invisible;* for as yet we see not all things put under him, and his reign is perceived rather by faith than by sight. The Lord Jesus is to mortal eyes invisible, and therefore our service must be rendered by the spirit rather than through the senses. He must be trusted if we are to draw near to him, and we must say of him, "whom having not seen we love." An unseen Lord, who can only be known to our faith, has saved us, and will save us, world without end. We have not a King that we have seen or touched, or whose voice we have audibly heard; but ours is a King who is invisible, and yet moveth to and fro among us, mighty to save. Thanks be unto the Holy Spirit for giving us eyes of faith to see him that is invisible, and hearts to trust and to rest upon an invisible Lord!

"Now, now, now, now, now, now, now," that is the word for every saved soul. *Now* unto the King eternal, immortal, invisible, be endless glory. Do you not respond to the call by immediate praise? Do you not say, "Awake up my glory! Awake, psaltery and harp?" Oh, for a seraph's coal to touch these stammering lips! As a sinner saved by my Lord and King, I would fain pour out my life in a continual stream of praise to my redeeming Lord.

Furthermore, our apostle speaks of *the only wise God*. He is so wise that he saves great sinners to make them patterns of his mercy; so wise that he takes bigots and persecutors to make them into apostles;

so wise that he makes the wrath of man to praise him, and the very wickedness of man he uses as a foil to set forth the brightness of the glory of his grace. Unto the only wise God, wise enough to turn a lion into a lamb, wise enough to make a sinner a saint, a persecutor a preacher, an enemy a friend—to him be glory. Oh, the wisdom of God in the plan of redemption! It is a deep unfathomable. Compared with it there is no wisdom elsewhere, and God is seen to be "only wise."

To him *be honor and glory for ever and ever. Amen.* Unto him be glory on earth and glory in heaven, honor from all of us poor imperfect beings, and glory from us when he shall have made us perfectly meet to behold his face. Come, lift up your hearts, ye saved ones! Begin at once the songs which shall never cease. The saints shall never have done singing, for they remember that they were sinners. Come, poor sinner, out of the depths extol him who descended into the depths for you! Chief of sinners, adore him who is to you the Chief among ten thousand, and the Altogether Lovely! You black sinners, who have gone to the very brink of damnation by your abominable sins, rise to the utmost heights of enthusiastic joy in Jesus your Lord! Put your trust in the Lord Jesus Christ, and all manner of sin and of blasphemy shall be forgiven unto you; and at the receipt of such a pardon you shall burst out into new-made doxologies to God your Savior. "Come now, and let us reason together, saith the Lord: though your sins be as scarlet, they shall be as white as snow; though they be red like crimson, they shall be as wool."[1] O ye guiltiest of the guilty, the apostle Paul speaks to you, and stands before you as the bearer of God's white flag of mercy. Surrender to the King eternal, and there is pardon for you, and deliverance from, the wrath to come. Thirty-five years Paul lived in sin. Twenty years after that, when he was older than I am, he wrote these words, "This is a faithful saying, and worthy of all acceptation, that Christ Jesus came into the world to save sinners; of whom I am chief." Is there not some thirty-five years' old fellow here tonight who had better turn over a new leaf? Is there not some woman here of that age who has had more than enough of sin?

1 Isaiah 1:18.

Is it not time that you turned unto the Lord and found a new and better life? Turn them, Lord: turn them, and they shall be turned! Make them live and they shall live unto thee, world without end. Amen and Amen.

PORTION OF SCRIPTURE READ BEFORE SERMON—Acts 9:1–31.

THE BEST STRENGTHENING
MEDICINE

LORD'S-DAY, JUNE 21ST, 1891, AT THE METROPOLITAN TABERNACLE

Out of weakness were made strong.—HEBREWS 11:34.

Those who out of weakness were made strong are written among the heroes of faith, and are by no means the least of them. Believers "quenched the violence of fire, escaped the edge of the sword, out of weakness were made strong." Who shall tell which of the three grand deeds of faith is the greatest? Many of us may never have to brave the fiery stake, nor to bow our necks upon the block, to die as Paul did; but if we have grace enough to be out of weakness made strong, we shall not be left out of the roll of the nobles of faith, and God's name shall not fail to be glorified in our persons.

Brethren, as believers in the Lord Jesus, *we are called to two things*, namely, to do and to suffer for his name's sake. Certain saints are summoned to active marching duty, and others are ordered to keep watch on the walls. There are warriors on the field of conflict, and sentries in the box of patience.

Both in doing and in suffering, if we are earnest and observant, *we soon discover our own weakness.* "Weakness" is all we possess. "Weakness" meets us everywhere. If we have to work for the Lord, we are soon compelled to cry, "Who is sufficient for these things?" and if we are called to suffer for him, our weakness, in the case of most of us, is even greater: many who can labor without weariness cannot suffer without impatience. Men are seldom equally skilled in the use of the two hands of doing and bearing. Patience is a grace which is rarer and harder to come at than activity and zeal. It is one of the choicest fruits of the Spirit, and is seldom, found on newly-planted trees. The fact soon comes home to us that we are weak where we most of all desire to be strong.

Our longing is to be able both to do and to suffer for our Lord, and to do this we *must have strength from above, and that strength can only come to us through faith.* I have read you this glorious eleventh of Hebrews, which describes the mighty men of faith, the men of renown. They accomplished all their feats by a power which was not in them by nature. They were not naturally strong either to do or to suffer. If they had been, they would not have required faith in God; but being men of like passions with ourselves, they needed to trust in the Lord, and they did so. They were quite as weak as the weakest of us; but by their faith they laid hold on heavenly strength until they could do all things. There was nothing in the range of possibility, or, I might say, nothing within the lines of impossibility, which they could not have performed. They achieved everything that was necessary in the form of service, and they bore up gloriously under the most fearful pressure of suffering, simply and only by faith in God, who became their Helper. You and I may be very weak at this time, but *we can be made strong out of just such weakness.* We need not wish to have any strength of our own, for by faith we can reach to any degree of power in the Lord. We can have all imaginable strength for the grandest achievements desirable, if we have faith in God. Upon this simple but most practical matter I am going to speak to you at this time. We all wish to be strong. Medicines, embrocations, foods, baths, and all sorts of inventions are advertised as means of increasing strength. We are all in heavenly things so weak, that the idea of being made strong should be very attractive to us. Let us learn, then, how others "out of weakness were made strong," and let us follow on to enjoy their privilege by copying their conduct.

Let me ask you to note, first, *faith makes men strong for holy doing;* and, secondly, *faith makes men strong for patient suffering.* We shall go over the ground which I marked out in my introduction.

I. To begin with: FAITH MAKES MEN STRONG FOR HOLY DOING.

Here, indeed, all our strength must come to us by faith in the thrice-holy God.

The first duty of a Christian man is *to obey God*. Obedience is hard work to proud flesh and blood; indeed, these ingrained rebels will never obey through our own efforts. By nature we love our own will and way; and it goes against the grain for us to bring ourselves into such complete subjection as the law of the Lord requires. "Thou shalt love the Lord thy God with all thy heart, and with all thy soul, and with all thy mind."[1] Who among us has done this? Who among us can do this, unless a power outside of himself shall come to his aid? Faith alone takes hold of the divine strength; and only by that strength can we obey. Hence faith is the essential point of holiness. Ah, my dear friend! if you start on the voyage of life, by divine grace, with the resolve that you will follow the track marked down on the chart by the Lord your God, you will find that you have chosen a course to which the Lord's hand alone can keep you true. The current does not run that way. Before long you will find that the wind is dead against you, and the course to be followed is hard to keep. What will you do then if you have not faith? When duty is contrary to your temperament, what will you do without faith? When it involves loss of money, or ease, or honor, what will you do then if you have no faith? If you believe that God is the Rewarder of them that diligently seek him, you will persevere; but not else. Suppose the right course should expose you to ridicule, cause you to be spoken of as a fanatic, or mocked at as a hypocrite, or despised as a fool, what can you do without faith? If you trust the living God, you will do the right, and bear the loss or the shame; but if your faith fail you, self-love will create such respect for your own good name, such fear of ridicule, such unwillingness to be singular, that you will slide from your integrity, and choose a smooth and pleasing road. Though you may think it a very ordinary thing to obey God in all things, you will find that a man had need to set his face like a flint in order to keep the right road; and the only way in which he will be able to hold on his way will be by having faith in God. Let him say, "God commands, and therefore

1 Matthew 22:37.

I must do it;" and he will be strong. Let him feel, "God commands, and therefore he will bear me through;" and he will be strong. Let him say, "God commands, and he will recompense me;" and he will be strong. We are not saved *by* obedience, for obedience is the result of salvation. We are saved by faith, because faith leads us to obey. Faith is weakness clinging to strength, and becoming strong through so doing. Faith in God made the cripple at the temple gate stand, and walk, and leap, and praise God; and even so does faith make our sin-crippled manhood obey the will of the Lord with exultation.

Taking another view, we would remark that faith makes us strong *to fulfil the relationships of life.* We are not alone by ourselves, and we can neither live nor die apart, for God has linked us with others. We either curse or bless those around us. If we have faith in God, we shall bless our children, as Isaac and Jacob blessed their sons. Faith leaves a legacy of benediction to its heirs. If you have faith in God, you may bless your brothers while you live, as Joseph did: faith has housed many a family which else had starved. If you have faith in God, you can lead others out of the bondage of sin, and through the wilderness world, as Moses led the children of Israel; for faith is a great guide. But you can do nothing aright for others without faith in God for yourself and them. Do I address a wife who has a godless husband? Have faith in God about him. Do not try to deal with your husband otherwise than by faith in God. If you attempt his conversion apart from heavenly power, you might as well try to take leviathan with a hook! Dear father, have you children who are unruly, irreligious, defiant? Do the young men refuse to be advised? Are your girls light and trifling? Go to God in prayer and faith. He that knows the care of a household knows how easily a parent can do serious mischief with his children by his very efforts to do them good. One parent is too indulgent, another is too severe. Take the children to God, take them to God, I pray you. It is here that your strength lies. Strength to do right at the head of a household must come by divine gift; and that gift will only be placed in the open hand of faith. If we believe for our whole house, the promise will be fulfilled to us and to our house; for it is made to faith. May faith enable us each one, like David, to bless our household!

Do I speak to a youth here who fears God, and who lives in an ungodly family? Do you feel bewildered as to how to behave yourself? Orders are given you which cause you great searchings of heart. You have to question in your inmost soul whether you can conscientiously do as your employer requires. I beseech you, have faith, in God that he will direct you, and have faith also to follow that direction when you receive it. It is a very perilous spot, that beginning of life, when the youth first leaves the home of piety, and finds himself where the fear of God is not in the place. If, as a decided believer, he takes his stand, and if he is firm and steadfast for his God, he will make a man, and his after years will be bright and useful; but if he begins to give way a little, and if he tries to trim his sail to the wind, he will never attain to a holy character. We read of the children of Ephraim that, being armed, and carrying bows, they turned back in the day of battle; and therefore they were never to be relied on in the time of war. He who is not firm at starting is cutting out for himself a poor pattern of life. That which begins with shamefacedness, equivocation, hesitation, and compromise will ripen into apostasy. Such a wretched faith has no influence on the man's self, and it will have no influence upon others. Father, mother, husband, wife, sister, brother, servant, master—whatever your relation, I beseech you, if you feel weak in the discharge of your duty, exercise faith in God about it, and out of weakness you shall be made strong.

There is a high and blessed duty and privilege—I will call it both—which is to every Christian the necessity of his life, and that is *to pray*. Can you pray, my brother? If you know how to pray, you can move heaven and earth. Can you pray, my brother? Then you can set almighty forces in operation. You can suffer no need, for everlasting supplies await the hand of prayer: "Ask, and it shall be given you."[1] You cannot miss your way, for you shall be guided in answer to prayer. You shall hear a voice behind you, saying, "This is the way, walk ye in it."[2] "O sir," you say, "I cannot pray prevailingly." Then you are not like Jacob, good at wrestling. You cannot take hold upon

---

1 Matthew 7:7.
2 Isaiah 30:21.

the angel, and win the victory. Do you feel in prayer as if the sinew of your strength were shrunk, and your knee out of joint? Well, then, let me bring the text before you. Out of this weakness in prayer you can only be made strong *by faith*. Believe in God, and you will prevail with God. Believe in his promise, and plead it. Believe in his Spirit, and pray by his help. Believe in Jesus, who makes intercession; for through him you may come boldly to the throne of grace. Faith alone can confirm feeble knees. "According to your faith be it unto you." To pray without faith is formality; nay, it is vanity. To be weak in prayer is a disease which will bring on many other maladies. Seek faith to become Masters of the Art of prayer. I would rather be Master of the Art of prayer than M.A. of both universities. He who knows how to pray has his hand on a leverage which moves the universe. But there is no praying without believing. If thou believest not, thou mayest be heard—it is more than I can promise thee; but if thou believest, *thou shalt* be heard, for God refuses no believing prayer. To refuse to keep his own promise when it is pleaded would be to falsify his word, and change his character; and neither of these things can ever be. Have thou strong confidence: "He that spared not his own Son, but delivered him up for us all, how shall he not with him also freely give us all things?"[1] Jesus said, "If ye then, being evil, know how to give good gifts unto your children, how much more shall your Father which is in heaven give good things to them that ask him?"[2] Believe in prayer, and you will pray believingly. Some do not think that there is much in prayer. Poor souls! The Lord teach them better! O my brothers, believe up to the hilt in prayer, and you will find it to be the most remunerative work on earth! He that trades with God in prayer enters upon a business whereof the merchandise is better than silver or gold. Prayer makes us "rich towards God," and this is the best of riches; but it must be believing prayer. "Let him ask in faith, nothing wavering." Hast thou a poor, faint heart in this sacred exercise? Be assured that only by faith out of this weakness canst thou be made strong.

It may be that certain of my hearers feel that they cannot attain

---

1 Romans 8:32.
2 Matthew 7:11.

to the matters I have mentioned, for they are as yet battling to reach the position of servants and pleaders. Faith is the great force which is needed by those whose principal work is *to overcome sin*. When God began with many of us, he found us very low down beneath the flood of evil. It may be that an awful temper broke over us in surging waves. We have to rise superior to it. Possibly he found us plunged in the great deeps of an evil habit. Was it drunkenness? Was it gambling? What was it? It had to be left beneath; we were called to rise out of it. Some are permitted to sink a long way down in sin; and when God begins with them, they have a desperate ascent even to reach common morality; what must the conflict be before they attain to spirituality and holiness? It is hard for those to rise to the surface who have been plunged in the deeps. If a man has been sunk down in black waters full of filth, a thousand fathoms deep, and if he has been long imprisoned in dark caves where no light has come, what a wondrous power would that be which should raise him to the sunlight! The Spirit of God comes to many when they are in much the same condition; and what a work it is to bring up from the horrible midnight, and to give strength to rise out of the inky waters! I have seen many a soul wearying to ascend; receiving a little light, and a little more light, and a little more light; but yet far from being clear of the dark waters of iniquity. Dear straggler, you will never overcome sin except by faith in Jesus Christ. Trust him! Trust in the precious blood: that is the great sin-killer. Trust his pierced hands to pierce the hands of your lusts. Trust his wounded side to smite through the heart of your evil desires. Your hope lies there: where Jesus died, where Jesus rose again, where Jesus has gone into the glory. You may resolve to overcome a sin, and, perhaps, any one sin you may conquer for a time; but sin itself, as a force, in all its armies, is never to be overcome, save through the blood of the Lamb. You will never be able to cut down this huge upas tree except with the axe of Christ's atoning sacrifice. Take that, and every blow will tell, but no other instrument will avail. God strengthening you, you shall out of weakness be made strong to overcome sin, though it be backed by the world, the flesh, and the devil. Entrenched in your nature though your sins may be, you will drive out these Canaanites, and free your heart from their dominion.

I have often met with persons awakened by divine grace to see the evil of a certain act, and they have said, "I do not know how I shall ever break off the habit;" yet they have very easily escaped from it. I remember one who was very foul-mouthed, and used oaths habitually. I hardly think that, for years, he had spoken without ill language; and yet, from the moment he turned unto the Lord, he never used an oath, and he also noted that he never had a temptation so to do. I remark that the particular form of sin known as blasphemy is one of the first to die, and to be buried out of sight. Other sins die hard, but this is shot through the head by true repentance and faith in Jesus. Some sins cling to a man like the fabled tunic of Hercules, which could not be torn away, but burned into his flesh and bone, whatever he might do. How long a well-beloved habit lingers at the door after the heart has given it a bill of divorce! As a dog, which is chased away from the house, returns again and again to its former master, so does an evil lust turn again even to the soul that loathes it. How weak we are in this matter! How slow to cut off right hands, and pluck out right eyes! But yet it must be done; and only faith can do it, by calling in the aid of the Almighty One. Trust you in Christ to overcome by his Spirit that which he has put away by his death. In him we shall find succor, and by faith out of weakness we shall be made strong.

I change the run of my discourse altogether by remarking that there is another thing that falls to the lot of Christian men, a matter of the very first importance: namely, *to spread the gospel.* "Yes," says one, "I own that it is an urgent service to make known to others what the Lord has done for me: but, somehow, I cannot discharge my conscience by fully doing as I would. I tried the other day to say a good word, and I am afraid that I made a failure of it. I stammered a good deal, and I said little that I thought to say, and some things which seemed to weaken what I did say. I resolved, the other day, that I would see a man whom I had known, and tell him that I was a changed character; but when I reached his house, I drifted into other talk, and went the way in which he led me. I could not come to the point." Many would make a similar confession if they made a clean breast of it. Many of the truest children of God are at first possessed by a dumb spirit; and it needs the Lord Jesus to cast it out. But do you not think that we are too apt to attempt to spread the gospel in our own strength; and need we wonder if we break down? If we were by faith to begin, humbly waiting upon the Lord for words, and taking hold upon divine strength, might we not accomplish far more than we now do? I have heard of one brought to Christ, who was a very great sinner—of so stiff a neck that he never would be approached by anybody who aimed at his conversion. He hated the very mention of religion. He answered all appeals very coarsely. But one of his neighbors felt forced to go to him very early in the morning, and to say to him, "I beg your pardon for intruding so early, but I lay awake all last night thinking about you; and I cannot rest till I tell you something." He answered, "What were you thinking about me for? I don't want any of your thoughts." "Oh," said the other, "I felt so sorry to think that, if you were to die, you would die without hope, that I was obliged to come to you." The bearish man grumbled, "Mind your own business." "But," said the other, "it is my own business. I think my heart will break unless I see you saved." All the answer was, "Go away with you. Don't come here with your cant." The brother went home weeping; but he was not the only one who felt his heart breaking. The bearish one went away from his forge, and said to his wife, "I can always answer these religious fellows. I do not care for your parsons a bit; but that neighbor of ours has been in here, and he says he shall break his heart unless I am converted; *and that beats me.*" He was beaten. Out of a sort of kindly pity for his neighbor's weak-mindedness, with a mixture of an unacknowledged feeling on his own account, he went to hear the preaching of the Word, and was brought to Jesus.

"But," says one, "I know if I were to try to speak to any of my neighbors, I should break down." Friend, I am not careful in that matter, nor need you be. If you are in real earnest, you might possibly do more by a break-down than by anything else. Only break the ice, and begin; and you shall find my text to be true in your case also, and out of weakness you, too, shall be made strong. God does not need your strength: he has more than enough of power of his own. He asks your weakness: he has none of that himself, and he is longing, therefore, to take your weakness, and use it as the instrument in his own mighty hand. Will you not yield your weakness to him, and receive his strength?

Permit me to speak to some aspiring spirit here, and say,—Dear friend, would you like *to do something great for God?* Have you heard the motto of our early missionaries: "Attempt great things for God?" Does that thought burn within your heart? Do you long to be of some use? "Oh, yes," says one, "I would attempt great things for God, but I am terribly weak." Make the attempt by faith in God; for it is written, "Out of weakness were made strong." If you feel incapable, throw yourself upon the infinite capacity of God. So long as you are willing to be used, so long as God has given you an anxiety and travail of spirit for the souls of others, you need not fear; but may with faith get to work in all your feebleness, for as your day your strength shall be. Has not the Lord said, "My grace is sufficient for thee: for my strength is made perfect in weakness?"[1] And is not that word true?

I would make one more application of my text, which is capable of being used in a thousand directions. "Out of weakness were made strong:" this will be experienced *in bearing witness for the truth of God.* Suppose that you are called to testify for truth in the midst of those who doubt, disbelieve, or even deride it. You look to those who agree with you, and they are lukewarm; you turn to old associates, and they do not share your concern. Friends tell you that you are making much ado about nothing, or that you are uncharitable, narrow-minded, and bigoted. I need not repeat the accusations; they have been so often hurled at myself that I know them by heart. They say, "The man was born too late; he is behind the age; he fights for a worn-out creed; he is out of place in a world of progress." What then? Is there anything galling to you in all this? Indeed there is, unless faith is strong; and then the bullets turn to pellets, and the stones are soft as sponges. When they talk to you like that, do not begin bristling up, and declaring that, after all, you are as wise and as strong as your

---

1 2 Corinthians 12:9.

opponents, though that may readily be the case; but accept all their remarks upon your folly and weakness, and say to yourself, "Out of weakness were made strong." Hold you to God's Word by faith, and you will be strong. God will vindicate his own cause; but it may be his way to let error prevail for a while. Bide your time when the cause is an eternal one, for you can afford to do so. If we had been in Egypt at the time when Pharaoh started out to follow the Israelites to the Red Sea, if we had been clothed with all power, we should have stopped Pharaoh's chariots and horses before they quitted Egypt, and thus we should have nipped his enterprise in the bud. We should have taken off the chariot wheels at once, so that they could not follow after the children of Israel. That is what we should have done; but Jehovah did something better. He suffered the Egyptians to pursue, and overtake, and threaten to divide the spoil; and he allowed them in their pride to go down after Israel into the depths of the sea. Then, and not before, he overthrew them, so that Israel sang, "The horse and his rider hath he thrown into the sea."[1] This was a grand thing for the tribes in their after journeys through the wilderness. The timid Israelites would always have been afraid that Pharaoh would follow them and capture them; but when the forces of Egypt and all her chosen captains were drowned beneath the waves, all fear of them was gone for ever. The victory was complete. Meanwhile, the tremendous blow made their future antagonists in Canaan to tremble. In the conflict with evil, we would overcome it early, and put it to the rout at the first attack; but it may be that God will allow error to proceed further, and let it seem to triumph, so that by its own presumption it may place itself where it may be the more effectually crushed, never again to afflict the church. It is for us in our weakness to go forward as the Lord leads us; and the day of the resounding timbrels and the twinkling feet will come in due time, and Jehovah will be magnified when even humble maidens "sing unto the Lord, for he hath triumphed gloriously." Be steadfast, unmovable. Never mind the craft, policy, and number of the foe. God's time is best. He knows better than we do when to strike for victory. Out of weakness we shall be made strong, if we fully

1 Exodus 15:1.

rely upon the faith "once for all delivered to the saints."[1]

I would entreat you each one to make an application of the text to yourself in every work of faith, and labor of love, in which you may be engaged.

II. Now, beloved friends, suffer me a few words upon the other cheering fact, namely, that FAITH MAKES MEN STRONG FOR PATIENT SUFFERING. The patience of hope is a very important part of Christian life, and faith is the essence of it.

Many are called to suffer much *in daily life*. Ah me! what a world of misery there is in this great city, among even good and gracious people! A man might study London till he turned his brain. The poverty and the suffering of even godly people in London would be a subject too harrowing for those of you who have specially tender hearts. Let us not forget those members of Christ's mystical body that are in the fire: "his feet are like unto fine brass, as if they burned in a furnace."[2] Few, if any, are without sorrow, and many saints have a double portion of grief in their pilgrimage. Sitting here with your brethren in Christ, you look very cheerful; but I may be addressing those whose life is one protracted struggle for existence. Assuredly, you will not hold out without true faith, and much of it. You must endure, "as seeing him who is invisible."[3] You must joy in God, or you will not joy at all. Earthly comforts are not yours; but if you grasp the spiritual and the eternal you will not repine. If in this life only you had hope, you would be of all men most miserable; but having that hope, you are among men most happy. The solitary place shall be glad for you, and the desert shall rejoice and blossom as the rose. Commend me to firm faith for power to bear the daily cross. He that believeth hath everlasting life, and the joys which come of it. Trust thou in thy God, in his love to thee, in his care of thee, and then thou shalt be as the lilies, which toil not, and spin not, and yet are clothed; or as the ravens, which have no store, and yet are fed. Behold thou, by faith, the heaven prepared for thee, and know of a certainty that

1 Jude 1:3.
2 Revelation 1:15.
3 Hebrews 11:27.

thou wilt soon be there among the angels; and thou wilt defy cold, and hunger, and nakedness and shame, and everything else. Thy faith out of weakness shall make thee strong.

Certain saintly ones are called to bear *great physical pain*, and I commend to them, from practical experience, the power of faith in God under acute agony. This is the sweetest support in the presence of a threatened operation. How grim those surgeon's lancets seem! Ah me! I knew a patient once—I know her still—who, when the lancets had been used upon her, caused the doctor's case of instruments to be filled up with roses! God alone can help you to fill up with roses that grim memory of danger and suffering. Oh, how sweet to feel that, if God has sent diseases to your house, he has made them a chariot in which benedictions have been brought to you! Go not to wine for comfort in the hour of depression. Above all things, dread the intoxicating cup in all its forms. You need not even appeal to friends for consolation. What do they know about your inward sorrow? There are seas of suffering which the sufferer must navigate alone. No other sail is within sight. Scan the horizon, and nothing is to be seen but wave after wave. Now is the hour for faith in the great Lord, who holds even lonely seas in the hollow of his hand. He knows thy poor body, and he permits it to be frail, and permits thy heart to be trembling, because he will glorify himself in his tenderness to thy weakness, wherein he will make thee strong. JEHOVAH ROPHI is his name: "The Lord that healeth thee." Give thyself up to him, and thou shalt yet sing of his lovingkindness and tender mercies.

But there are other forms of suffering than these of daily life and of bodily pain. Possibly I speak to some who are suffering the evils of *persecution*. No cruel tyrant can burn believers now, nor even cast them into prison for Christ's sake; but there are ways enough for the seed of the serpent to show its enmity to the seed of the woman. "Trials of cruel mockings" are common yet. There are many ways in which the devil's whip can reach the back of the child of God. Persecution is still abundant, and many a man's foes are of his own household. I will rehearse no stories of Christian women with jeering husbands, nor of godly youths who endure scoffing, and far worse; but many a house is still a place of martyrdom. Gracious sufferers, may the Lord keep you from anger and unkindness! By faith alone can you bear persecution, and turn it to account for the good of others. Do not attempt to escape by yielding what is right and true; but ask the Lord to help you to stand fast for him. If it be true that the Lord has his martyrs still, let it be seen that they are as brave as ever. Not now do they gather in the great amphitheater, where sits the emperor in state, with all the proud citizens of Rome in the nearer gallery, tier on tier, and the multitude up yonder, gazing with their cruel eyes into the vast arena below. Not now do I see them lift up the great iron door, and let loose the monsters that come forth roaring, hungry for their prey. Not now do I see, standing in the middle, a man and his wife and children, all unarmed. Not now do I hear the shouts of the mob, as they exult that Christians are given to the lions. This is all over. Christ, in his suffering members, has conquered Caesar and pagan Rome; for out of weakness believers were made strong. A softer spirit has come over the human mind; but there is as much enmity against God as ever; and now it finds a less public arena, and a meaner mode of torture. Today, the tried one suffers alone, and misses the encouragement of Christian eyes. At times he has to feel that it were better for him to fight with beasts at Ephesus than to bear the taunts, and threats, and slanders of ungodly kinsfolk. My sister, my brother, have faith in God in your hidden sorrow! Cry to him in the secret of your soul, and you will bear your load; yes, you will bear it calmly, and you will win those who hate you. Of your secret martyrdom angels will be spectators, and Christ will suffer in you—wherefore, fear not. Out of weakness you shall be made strong by faith.

We have among us those who are not exposed to persecution, but have to stand against *assaults of unbelief.* That which believers in past ages have accepted as truth, is not believed in many places nowadays; and so it comes to pass that one brings to us a bit of sceptical science which he has picked up from Huxley or Tyndall; another comes with a criticism that he has found in some of the modern divines, who are the devil's instruments for spreading infidelity; and a third appears with a vile blasphemy from one of the coarser assailants of religion, and each one demands an immediate answer to his quibble, or his difficulty. Do they really expect that we are to answer, on the spur of the moment, every objection that they are pleased to raise? I confess that I do not believe that one human brain is capable of answering every objection that another human brain could raise against the most obvious truth in the world. Do not try to answer cavillers; but if you do, mind that faith is your weapon. If you take the wooden sword of your own reasoning, you may easily be beaten. Believe for yourself, because God has said it; and speak as the Lord guides you. Fix it in your mind, "This is God's Book. This is his infallible revelation, and I believe it against every argument that can possibly be urged against it. Let God be true, but every man a liar." This will be sure defensive ground; but if you get off that rock, you will soon find yourself sinking or staggering. For an offensive weapon, take "the sword of the Spirit, which is the word of God;" and if this does not serve your turn, nothing will. Have a thorough, and entire, and child-like faith in the revelation of the Most High, and you will be made strong in those mental conflicts for which in yourself you are so weak.

Again, it may be that I am speaking to sad ones who suffer under *mental depression*. Some of us are by constitution inclined to that condition. I have sometimes envied those good people who are never excited with joy, and consequently seldom or never despond. "Along the cool, sequestered vale of life they hold the even tenor of their way."[1] Happy people! At the same time, when I rise, as upon eagle's wings, in joyous rapture, I feel right glad to be capable of the blissful excitement. Yet if you soar to the skies, you are very apt to drop below the sea-level. He that can fly, can faint. Elijah, after he had slain the prophets of Baal, was found fleeing into the wilderness from the face of Jezebel. If you are so constituted that you rise and fall; if you are a creature that can be excited, and that can be depressed; and worse still, if you happen to have been born on a foggy day, and to have swallowed so much of that fog that you have found it shading your spirit many a time ever since; then you can only be strong by faith. If you are one of those plants which seldom bloom with bunches

1 *Elegy Written in a Country Churchyard* by Thomas Gray.

of bright flowers, but have your blossoms hidden and concealed, be not disquieted. If you are never mirthful, and seldom able to call yourself joyful—the only cure for depression is faith. Settle this in your heart: "Whether I am up or down, the Lord Jesus Christ is the same. Whether I sing, or whether I sigh, the promise is true, and the Promiser is faithful. Whether I stand on Tabor's summit, or am hidden in the vale of Baca, the covenant standeth fast, and everlasting love abideth." Be assured, beyond all questioning, that he that believeth in the Lord Jesus is not condemned. Believe in him, though you see no flashes of delight nor sparkles of joy. We are safe, because we are in the City of Refuge, and not because we are, in ourselves, ill or well. If you will stand firm in Christ Jesus, even in your weakness you will be made strong.

It may be that certain of you are called to suffer in your minds, not because of any wrong thing in yourselves, but *for the sake of others*. Some years ago, I preached a sermon to you from the text, "My God, my God, why hast thou forsaken me?"[1] and in a mournful degree I felt what I preached, as my own cry. I felt an agony of spirit, for I was under an awful sense of being forsaken of God, and yet I could not understand why I was surrounded by such thick darkness. I wished to clear myself if any sin remained upon me, but I could not discover any evil which I was tolerating. When I went back into the vestry, I learned the secret of my personal distress, for there was an elderly man in a horror of great darkness, who said to me, "I have never before met with any person who has been where I am. I trust there is hope for me." I bade him sit down, and I talked with him. I saw him afterwards, and I hope I conducted him from the verge of insanity into the open, healthy place of peace through believing. I fear I should never have touched his case if I had not been in the miry clay myself. Then I understood why I must feel like one forsaken. The Lord was leading me where I should be taught to know my man, and should be made willing to sit side by side with him in the dark prison-house, and lend him a hand to escape. Since then, in presenting myself to my Lord for service, I have said to him, "Make

1 Psalm 22:1.

me useful to the doubting and the feeble-minded. I do not bargain for comfort, and peace, and joy, if I can be more helpful to thy poor, weary children without them. Place me where I can best answer thy purpose by being made to sympathize with thy troubled people. I only want to bring them to heaven, to the praise of the glory of thy grace; and as for me, let me rejoice or suffer, as best suits their case." For this a man must have faith in God; and he must be sure that his trials, endured through his office, will have great recompense of reward. If you are chosen to be a leader and a helper, or a mother in Israel, be satisfied to endure hardness with the full belief that it is all right, and that God will not only bring you through, but will also bless somebody else by the means of your tribulations.

My time is ended, although I had much more to say. I can only pray the Lord to give you to believe in him. If I should never again have the pleasure of speaking for my Lord upon the face of this earth, I should like to deliver, as my last confession of faith, this testimony— that nothing but faith can save this nineteenth century; nothing but faith can save old England: nothing but faith can save the present unbelieving church: nothing but firm faith in the grand old doctrines of grace, and in the ever-living and unchanging God can bring back to the church again a full tide of prosperity, and make her to be the deliverer of the nations for Christ: nothing but faith in the Lord Jesus can save you or me. The Lord give you, my brothers, to believe to the utmost degree, for his name's sake! Amen.

PORTION OF SCRIPTURE READ BEFORE SERMON—HEBREWS 11.
HYMNS FROM "OUR OWN HYMN BOOK"—531, 533, 682.

CHRIST'S HOSPITAL

Lord's-day Evening, March 9th, 1890, Metropolitan Tabernacle

He healeth the broken in heart, and bindeth up their wounds.
                                                    —Psalm 147:3.

Often as we have read this Psalm, we can never fail to be struck with the connection in which this verse stands, especially its connection with the verse that follows. Read the two together: "He healeth the broken in heart, and bindeth up their wounds. He telleth the number of the stars; he calleth them all by their names." What condescension and grandeur! What pity and omnipotence! He who leads out yonder ponderous orbs in almost immeasurable orbits, nevertheless, is the Surgeon of men's souls, and stoops over broken hearts, and with his own tender fingers closes up the gaping wound, and binds it with the liniment of love. Think of it; and if I should not speak as well as I could desire upon the wonderful theme of his condescension, yet help me by your thoughts to do reverence to the Maker of the stars, who is, at the same time, the Physician for broken hearts and wounded spirits.

I am equally interested in the connection of my text with the verse that goes before it: "The Lord doth build up Jerusalem: he gathereth together the outcasts of Israel." The church of God is never so well built up as when it is built up with men of broken hearts. I have prayed to God in secret many a time, of late, that he would be pleased to gather out from among us a people who should have a deep experience, who should know the guilt of sin, who should be broken and ground to powder under a sense of their own inability and unworthiness; for I am persuaded that, without a deep experience of sin, there is seldom much belief in the doctrines of grace, and not much enthusiasm in praising the Savior's name. The church needs to be built up with men who have been pulled down. Unless we know in our hearts our need of a Savior, we shall never be worth much in preaching him. That preacher who has never been converted, what can he say about it? And he who has never been in the dungeon, who has never been in the abyss, who has never felt as if he were cast out from the sight of God, how can he comfort the many who are outcasts, and who are bound with the fetters of despair? May the Lord break many hearts, and then bind them up, that with them he may build up the church, and inhabit it!

But now, leaving the connection, I come to the text itself, and I desire to speak of it so that everyone here who is troubled may derive comfort from it, God the Holy Ghost speaking through it. Consider, first, *the patients and their sickness:* "He healeth the broken in heart." Then, consider, *the Physician and his medicine*, and for a while turn your eyes to him who does this healing work. Then, I shall want you to consider, *the testimonial to the great Physician* which we have in this verse: "He healeth the broken in heart, and bindeth up their wounds." Lastly, and most practically, we will consider, *what we ought to do* towards him who healeth the broken in heart.

I. First, then, consider THE PATIENTS AND THEIR SICKNESS. They are broken in heart. I have heard of many who have died of a broken heart; but here are some who live with a broken heart, and who live all the better for having had their hearts broken; they live another and a higher life than they lived before that blessed stroke broke their hearts in pieces.

There are many sorts of broken hearts, and Christ is good at healing them all. I am not going to lower and narrow the application of my text. The patients of the great Physician are *those whose hearts are broken through sorrow*. Hearts are broken through disappointment. Hearts are broken by bereavement. Hearts are broken in ten thousand ways, for this is a heart-breaking world; and Christ is good at healing all manner of heart-breaks. I would encourage every person here, even though his heart-break may not be of a spiritual kind, to make an application to him who healeth the broken in heart. The text does not say "the spiritually broken in heart," therefore I will not insert an adverb where there is none in the passage. Come hither, ye that are burdened, all ye that labor and are heavy laden; come hither, all ye that sorrow, be your sorrow what it may; come hither, all ye whose hearts are broken, be the heart-break what it may, for he healeth the broken in heart.

Still, there is a special brokenness of heart to which Christ gives the very earliest and tenderest attention. He heals *those whose hearts are broken for sin.* Christ heals the heart that is broken because of its sin; so that it grieves, laments, regrets, and bemoans itself, saying, "Woe is me that I have done this exceeding great evil, and brought ruin upon myself! Woe is me that I have dishonored God, that I have cast myself away from his presence, that I have made myself liable to his everlasting wrath, and that even now his wrath abideth upon me!" If there is a man here whose heart is broken about his past life, he is the man to whom my text refers. Are you heart-broken because you have wasted forty, fifty, sixty years? Are you heart-broken at the remembrance that you have cursed the God who has blessed you, that you have denied the existence of him without whom you never would have been in existence yourself, that you have lived to train your family without godliness, without any respect to the Most High God at all? Has the Lord brought this home to you? Has he made you feel what a hideous thing it is to be blind to Christ, to refuse his love, to reject his blood, to live an enemy to your best Friend? Have you felt this? O my friend, I cannot reach across the gallery to give you my hand; but will you think that I am doing it, for I wish to do it? If there is a heart here broken on account of sin, I thank God for it, and praise the Lord that there is such a text as this: "He healeth the broken in heart."

Christ also heals *hearts that are broken from sin.* When you and sin have quarrelled, never let the quarrel be made up again. You and sin were friends at one time; but now you hate sin, and you would be wholly rid of it if you could. You wish never to sin. You are anxious to be clear of the most darling sin that you ever indulged in, and you desire to be made pure as God is pure. Your heart is broken away from its old moorings. That which you once loved you now hate. That which you once hated you now at least desire to love. It is well. I am glad that you are here, for to you is the text sent, "He healeth the broken in heart."

If there is a broken-hearted person anywhere about, many people despise him. "Oh," they say, "he is melancholy, he is mad, he is out of his mind through religion!" Yes, men despise the broken in heart, but such, O God, thou wilt not despise! The Lord looks after such, and heals them.

Those who do not despise them, at any rate avoid them. I know some few friends who have long been of a broken heart; and when I feel rather dull, I must confess that I do not always go their way, for they are apt to make me feel more depressed. Yet would I not get out of their way if I felt that I could help them. Still, it is the nature of men to seek the cheerful and the happy, and to avoid the broken-hearted. God does not do so; he heals the broken in heart. He goes where they are, and he reveals himself to them as the Comforter and the Healer.

In a great many cases people despair of the broken-hearted ones. "It is no use," says one, "I have tried to comfort her, but I cannot do it." "I have wasted a great many words," says another, "on such and such a friend, and I cannot help him. I despair of his ever getting out of the dark." Not so is it with God; he healeth the broken in heart. He despairs of none. He shows the greatness of his power, and the wonders of his wisdom, by fetching men and women out of the lowest dungeon, wherein despair has shut them.

As for the broken-hearted ones themselves, they do not think that they ever can be converted. Some of them are sure that they never can; they wish that they were dead, though I do not see what they would gain by that. Others of them wish that they had never been born, though that is a useless wish now. Some are ready to rush after any new thing to try to find a little comfort; while others, getting worse and worse, are sitting down in sullen despair. I wish that I knew who these were; I should like to come round, and say just to them, "Come, brother; there must be no doubting and no despair tonight, for my text is gloriously complete, and is meant for you. 'He healeth the broken in heart, and bindeth up their wounds.'" Notice that fifth verse, "Great is our Lord, and of great power; his understanding is infinite." Consequently, he can heal the broken in heart. God is glorious at a dead lift. When a soul cannot stir, or help itself, God delights to come in with his omnipotence, and lift the great load, and set the burdened one free.

It takes great wisdom to comfort a broken heart. If any of you have ever tried it, I am sure that you have not found it an easy task. I have given much of my life to this work; and I always come away from a desponding one with a consciousness of my own inability to comfort the heart-broken and cast-down. Only God can do it. Blessed be his name that he has arranged that one Person of the Sacred Trinity should undertake this office of Comforter, for no man could ever perform its duties. We might as well hope to be the Savior as to be the Comforter of the heart-broken. Efficiently and completely to save or to comfort must be a work divine. That is why the Holy Spirit has undertaken to be the Comforter; and Christ, through the Divine Spirit, healeth the broken in heart, and bindeth up their wounds with infinite power and unfailing skill.

II. Now, secondly, we are going to consider THE PHYSICIAN AND HIS MEDICINE: "He healeth the broken in heart, and bindeth up their wounds." Who is this that healeth the broken in heart?

I answer, that *Jesus was anointed of God* for this work. He said, "The Spirit of the Lord is upon me, because he hath anointed me to preach the gospel to the poor; he hath sent me to heal the broken-hearted." Was the Holy Spirit given to Christ in vain? That cannot be. He was given for a purpose which must be answered, and that purpose is the healing of the broken-hearted. By the very anointing of Christ by the Holy Spirit, you may be sure that our Physician will heal the broken in heart.

Further, Jesus was *sent of God* on purpose to do this work: "He hath sent me to heal the broken-hearted." If Christ does not heal the broken-hearted, he will not fulfil the mission for which he came from heaven. If the broken-hearted are not cheered by his glorious life and the blessings that flow out of his death, then he will have come to earth for nothing. This is the very errand on which the Lord of glory left the bosom of the Father to be veiled in human clay, that he might heal the broken in heart; and he will do it.

Our Lord was also *educated* for this work. He was not only anointed and sent; but he was trained for it. "How?" say you. Why, he had a broken heart himself; and there is no education for the office of comforter like being placed where you yourself have need of comfort, so that you may be able to comfort others with the comfort wherewith you yourself have been comforted of God. Is your heart broken? Christ's heart was broken. He said, "Reproach hath broken my heart; and I am full of heaviness."[1] He went as low as you have ever been, and deeper than you can ever go. "My God, my God, why hast thou forsaken me?"[2] was his bitter cry. If that be your agonized utterance, he can interpret it by his own suffering. He can measure your grief by his grief. Broken hearts, there is no healing for you except through him who had a broken heart himself. Ye disconsolate, come to him! He can make your heart happy and joyous, by the very fact of his own sorrow, and the brokenness of his own heart. "In all our afflictions he was afflicted." He was "tempted in all points like as we are," "a man of sorrows and acquainted with grief." For a broken heart, there is no physician like him.

Once more, I can strongly recommend my Lord Jesus Christ as the Healer of broken hearts, because he is so *experienced* in the work. Some people are afraid that the doctor will try experiments upon them; but our Physician will only do for us what he has done many times before. It is no matter of experiment with him; it is a matter of experience. If you knock tonight at my great Doctor's door, you will, perhaps, say to him, "Here is the strangest patient, my Lord, that ever

1 Psalm 69:20.
2 Matthew 27:46.

came to thee." He will smile as he looks at you, and he will think, "I have saved hundreds like you." Here comes one who says, "That first man's case was nothing compared with mine; I am about the worst sinner who ever lived." And the Lord Jesus Christ will say, "Yes, I saved the worst man that ever lived long ago, and I keep on saving such as he. I delight to do it." But here comes one who has a curious odd way of broken-heartedness. He is an out-of-the-way fretter. Yes, but my Lord is able to "have compassion on the ignorant, and on them that are out of the way." He can lay hold of this out-of-the-way one; for he has always been saving out-of-the-way sinners. My Lord has been healing broken hearts well nigh nineteen hundred years. Can you find a brass-plate anywhere in London telling of a physician of that age? He has been at the work longer than that; for it is not far off six thousand years since he went into this business, and he has been healing the broken in heart ever since that time.

I will tell you one thing about him that I have on good authority, that is, he never lost a case yet. There never was one who came to him with a broken heart, but he healed him. He never said to one, "You are too bad for me to heal;" but he did say, "Him that cometh to me, I will in no wise cast out."[1] My dear hearer, he will not cast you out. You say, "You do not know me, Mr. Spurgeon." No, I do not; and you have come here tonight, and you hardly know why you are here; only you are very low and very sad. The Lord Jesus Christ loves just such as you are, you poor, desponding, doubting, desolate, disconsolate one. Daughters of sorrow, sons of grief, look ye here! Jesus Christ has gone on healing broken hearts for thousands of years, and he is well up in the business. He understands it by experience, as well as by education. He is "mighty to save." Consider him; consider him; and the Lord grant you grace to come and trust him even now!

Thus I have talked to you about the Physician for broken hearts; shall I tell you what his chief medicine is? It is his own flesh and blood. There is no cure like it. When a sinner is bleeding with sin, Jesus pours his own blood into the wound; and when that wound is slow in healing, he binds his own sacrifice about it. Healing for

1 John 6:37.

broken hearts comes by the atonement, atonement by substitution, Christ suffering in our stead. He suffered for every one who believeth in him, and he that believeth in him is not condemned, and never can be condemned, for the condemnation due to him was laid upon Christ. He is clear before the bar of justice as well as before the throne of mercy. I remember when the Lord put that precious ointment upon my wounded spirit. Nothing ever healed me until I understood that he died in my place and stead, died that I might not die; and now, today, my heart would bleed itself to death were it not that I believe that he "his own self bare our sins in his own body on the tree." "With his stripes we are healed,"[1] and with no medicine but this atoning sacrifice. A wonderful heal-all is this, when the Holy Ghost applies it with his own divine power, and lets life and love come streaming into the heart that was ready to bleed to death.

III. My time flies too quickly; so, thirdly, I want you to consider THE TESTIMONIAL TO THE GREAT PHYSICIAN which is emblazoned in my text. It is God the Holy Ghost who, by the mouth of his servant David, bears testimony to this congregation tonight that the Lord Jesus heals the broken in heart, and binds up their wounds. If I said it, you need no more believe it than I need believe it if you said it. One man's word is as good as another's if we be truthful men; but this statement is found in an inspired Psalm. I believe it; I dare not doubt it, for I have proved its truth.

I understand my text to mean this: *he does it effectually*. As I said last Thursday night, if there is a person cast down or desponding within twenty miles, he is pretty sure to find me out. I laugh sometimes, and say, "Birds of a feather flock together;" but they come to talk to me about their despondency, and sometimes they leave me half desponding in the attempt to get them out of their sadness. I have had some very sad cases just lately, and I am afraid that, when they went out of my room, they could not say of me, "He healeth the broken in heart." I am sure that they could say, "He tried his best. He brought out all the choicest arguments he could think of to comfort me." And they have felt very grateful. They have come back

---

1 1 Peter 2:24.

sometimes to thank God that they have been a little bit encouraged; but some of them are frequent visitors; I have been trying to cheer them up by the month together. But, when my Master undertakes the work, "He *healeth* the broken in heart," he not only tries to do it, he does it. He touches the secret sources of the sorrow, and takes the spring of the grief away. We try our best; but we cannot do it. You know it is very hard to deal with the heart. The human heart needs more than human skill to cure it. When a person dies, and the doctors do not know the complaint of which he died, they say, "It was heart disease." They did not understand his malady; that is what that means. There is only one Physician who can heal the heart; but, glory be to his blessed name, "He healeth the broken in heart," he does it effectually.

As I read my text, I understand it to mean, *he does it constantly.* "He healeth the broken in heart." Not merely, "He did heal them years ago;" but, he is doing it now. "He *healeth* the broken in heart, and *bindeth up* their wounds." What, at this minute? Ten minutes to eight? Yes, he is doing this work now. "He healeth the broken in heart," and when the service is over, and the congregation is gone, what will Jesus be doing then? Oh, he will still be healing the broken in heart! Suppose this year 1890 should run out, and the Lord does not come to judgment, what will he be doing then? He will still be healing the broken in heart. He has not used up his ointments. He has not exhausted his patience. He has not in the least degree diminished his power. He still healeth. "Oh, dear!" said one, "if I had come to Christ a year ago, it would have been well with me." If you come to Christ tonight, it will be well with you, for "he healeth the broken in heart." "I fear that I have sinned away my day of grace," says one. "He healeth the broken in heart." I do not know who was the inventor of that idea of "sinning away the day of grace." If you are willing to have Christ, you may have him. If you are as old as Methuselah—and I do not suppose you are older than he was—if you want Christ, you may have him. As long as you are out of hell, Christ is able to save you. He is going on with his old work. Because you are just past fifty, you say the die is cast; because you are past eighty, you say, "I am too old to be saved now." Nonsense! He *healeth*, he *healeth*, he is still doing it, "he healeth the broken in heart."

I go further than that, and say that *he does it invariably*. I have shown you that he does it effectually and constantly; but he does it invariably. There never was a broken heart brought to him that he did not heal. Do not some broken-hearted patients go out at the back door, as my Master's failures? No, not one. There never was one yet that he could not heal. Doctors are obliged, sometimes, in our hospitals to give up some persons, and say that they will never recover. Certain symptoms have proved that they are incurable. But, despairing one, in the divine hospital, of which Christ is the Physician, there never was a patient of his who was turned out as incurable. He is able to save to the uttermost. Do you know how far that is—"to the uttermost?" There is no going beyond "the uttermost," because the uttermost goes beyond everything else, to make it the uttermost. "He is able also to save them to the uttermost that come unto God by him." Where are you, friend "Uttermost?" Are you here tonight? "Ah!" you say, "I wonder that I am not in hell." Well, so do I; but you are not, and you never will be, if you cast yourself on Christ. Rest in the full atonement that he has made; for he healeth always, without any failure, "he healeth the broken in heart, and bindeth up their wounds."

As I read these words, it seems to me that *he glories in doing it*. He said to the Psalmist, by the Holy Spirit, "Write a Psalm in which you shall begin with Hallelujah, and finish with Hallelujah, and set in the middle of the Psalm this as one of the things for which I delight to be praised, that I heal the broken in heart." None of the gods of the heathen were ever praised for this. Did you ever read a song to Jupiter, or to Mercury, or to Venus, or to any of them, in which they were praised for binding up the broken in heart? Jehovah, the God of Israel, the God of Abraham, Isaac, and Jacob, the God and Father of our Lord and Savior Jesus Christ, is the only God who makes it his boast that he binds up the broken in heart. Come, you big, black sinner; come, you desperado; come, you that have gone beyond all measurement in sin; you can glorify God more than anybody else by believing that he can save even you! He can save you, and put you among the children. He delights to save those that seemed farthest from him.

IV. This is my last point: consider WHAT WE OUGHT TO DO.

If there is such a Physician as this, and we have broken hearts, it goes without saying that, first of all, *we ought to resort to him*. When people are told that they have an incurable disease, a malady that will soon bring them to their grave, they are much distressed; but if, somewhere or other, they hear that the disease may be cured after all, they say, "Where? Where?" Well, perhaps it is thousands of miles away; but they are willing to go, if they can. Or the medicine may be very unpleasant or very expensive; but if they find that they can be cured, they say, "I will have it." If anyone came to their door, and said, "Here it is, it will heal you; and you can have it for nothing, and as much as ever you want of it;" there would be no difficulty in getting rid of any quantity of the medicine, so long as we found people sick. Now, if you have a broken heart tonight, you will be glad to have Christ. I had a broken heart once, and I went to him and he healed it; healed it in a moment, and made me sing for joy! Young men and women, I was about fifteen or sixteen when he healed me; I wish that you would go to him now, while you are yet young. The age of his patients does not matter. Are you younger than fifteen? Boys and girls may have broken hearts; and old men and old women may have broken hearts; but they may come to Jesus, and be healed. Let them come to him tonight, and seek to be healed.

When you are about to go to Christ, possibly you ask, "How shall I go to him?" Go by prayer. One said to me, the other day, "I wish that you would write me a prayer, sir." I said, "No, I cannot do that, go and tell the Lord what you want." He replied, "Sometimes I feel such a great want that I do not know what it is I do want, and I try to pray, but I cannot. I wish that somebody would tell me what to say." "Why!" I said, "the Lord has told you what to say. This is what he has said: 'Take with you words, and turn to the Lord: say unto him, Take away all iniquity, and receive us graciously.'"[1] Go to Christ in prayer with such words as those, or any others that you can get.

---

1 Hosea 14:2.

If you cannot get any words, tears are just as good, and rather better; and groans and sighs and secret desires will be acceptable with God.

But add faith to them. *Trust the Physician.* You know that no ointment will heal you if you do not put it on the wound. Oftentimes, when there is a wound, you want something with which to strap the ointment on. Faith straps on the heavenly heal-all. Go to the Lord with your broken heart, and believe that he can heal you. Believe that he alone can heal you; trust him to do it. Fall at his feet, and say, "If I perish, I will perish here. I believe that the Son of God can save me, and I will be saved by him; but I will never look anywhere else for salvation. 'Lord, I believe; help thou mine unbelief!'"[1] If you have come as far as that, you are very near the light; the great Physician will heal your broken heart before very long. Trust him to do it now.

When you have trusted in him, and your heart is healed, and you are happy, *tell others about him.* I do not like my Lord to have any tongue-tied children. I do not mean that I want you all to preach. When a whole church takes to preaching, it is as if the whole body were a mouth, and that would be a vacuum. I want you to tell others, in some way or other, what the Lord has done for you; and be earnest in endeavoring to bring others to the great Physician. You all recollect, therefore I need not tell you again, the story that we had about the doctor at one of our hospitals, a year or two ago. He healed a dog's broken leg, and the grateful animal brought other dogs to have their broken legs healed. That was a good dog; some of you are not half as good as that dog. You believe that Christ is blessing you, yet you never try to bring others to him to be saved. That must not be the case any longer. We must excel that dog in our love for our species; and it must be our intense desire that, if Christ has healed us, he should heal our wife, our child, our friend, our neighbor; and we should never rest till others are brought to him.

Then, when others are brought to Christ, or even if they will not be brought to him, be sure to *praise him.* If your broken heart has been healed, and you are saved, and your sins forgiven, praise him. We do not sing half enough. I do not mean in our congregations;

1 Mark 9:24.

but when we are at home. We pray every day. Do we sing every day? I think that we should. Matthew Henry used to say, about family prayer, "They that pray do well; they that read and pray do better; they that read and pray and sing do best of all." I think that Matthew Henry was right. "Well, I have no voice," says one. Have you not? Then you never grumble at your wife; you never find fault with your food; you are not one of those that make the household unhappy by your evil speeches, "Oh, I do not mean that!" No, I thought you did not mean that. Well, praise the Lord with the same voice that you have used for complaining. "But I could not lead a tune," says one. Nobody said you were to do so. You can at least sing as I do. My singing is of a very peculiar character. I find that I cannot confine myself to one tune; in the course of a verse I use half-a-dozen tunes; but the Lord, to whom I sing, never finds any fault with me. He never blames me, because I do not keep to this tune or that. I cannot help it. My voice runs away with me, and my heart too; but I keep on humming something or other by way of praising God's name. I would like you to do the same. I used to know an old Methodist; and the first thing in the morning, when he got up, he began singing a bit of a Methodist hymn; and if I met the old man during the day, he was always singing. I have seen him in his little workshop, with his lapstone on his knee, and he was always singing, and beating time with his hammer. When I said to him once, "Why do you always sing, dear brother?" he replied, "Because I always have something to sing about." That is a good reason for singing. If our broken hearts have been healed, we have something to sing about in time and throughout eternity. Let us begin to do so to the praise of the glory of his grace, who "healeth the broken in heart, and bindeth up their wounds." God bless all the broken hearts that are in this congregation tonight, for Jesus' sake! Amen.

EXPOSITION OF PSALM 147

This is one of the Hallelujah Psalms; it begins and ends with "Praise ye the LORD." May our hearts be in tune, that we may praise the Lord while we read these words of praise!

Verse 1. *Praise ye the LORD:*

It is not enough for the Psalmist to do it himself. He wants help in it, so he says, "Praise *ye* the LORD." Wake up, my brethren; bestir yourselves, my sisters; come, all of you, and unite in this holy exercise! "Praise ye the LORD."

1. *For it is good to sing praises unto our God; for it is pleasant; and praise is comely.*

When a thing is good, pleasant, and comely, you have certainly three excellent reasons for attending to it. It is not everything that is good that is pleasant; nor everything that is pleasant that is good; but here you have a happy combination of goodness, pleasantness, and comeliness. It will do you good to praise God. God counts it good, and you will find it a pleasant exercise. That which is the occupation of heaven must be happy employment. "It is good to sing praises unto our God," "it is pleasant," and certainly nothing is more "comely" and beautiful, and more in accordance with the right order of things, than for creatures to praise their Creator, and the children of God to praise their Father in heaven.

2. *The LORD doth build up Jerusalem:*

Praise his name for that. You love his church; be glad that he builds it up. Praise him who quarries every stone, and puts it upon the one foundation that is laid, even Jesus.

2. *He gathereth together the outcasts of Israel.*

Praise him for that. If you were once an outcast, and he has gathered you, give him your special personal song of thanksgiving.

3. *He healeth the broken in heart, and bindeth up their wounds.*

Praise him for that, ye who have had broken hearts! If he has healed you, surely you should give him great praise.

4. *He telleth the number of the stars; he calleth them all by their names.*

He who heals broken hearts counts the stars, and calls them by their names, as men call their servants, and send them on their way. Praise his name. Can you look up at the starry sky at night without praising him who made the stars, and leads out their host?

5. *Great is our Lord, and of great power: his understanding is infinite.*

Praise him, then; praise his greatness, his almightiness, his infinite wisdom. Can you do otherwise? Oh, may God reveal himself so much to your heart that you shall be constrained to pay him willing adoration!

6. *The* Lord *lifteth up the meek:*

What a lifting up it is for them, out of the very dust where they have been trodden down by the proud and the powerful! The Lord lifts them up. Praise him for that.

6. *He casteth the wicked down to the ground.*

Thus he puts an end to their tyranny, and delivers those who were ground beneath their cruel power. Praise ye his name for this also. Excuse me that I continue to say to you, "Praise ye the Lord," for, often as I say it, you will not praise him too much; and we need to have our hearts stirred up to this duty of praising God, which is so much neglected. After all, it is the praise of God that is the ultimatum of our religion. Prayer does but sow; praise is the harvest. Praying is the end of preaching, and praising is the end of praying. May we bring to God much of the very essence of true religion, and that will be the inward praise of the heart!

7. *Sing unto the* Lord *with thanksgiving; sing praise upon the harp unto our God:*

"Unto *our* God." How that possessive pronoun puts a world of endearment into the majestic word "God!" "This God is our God." Come, my hearer, can you call God your God? Is he indeed yours? If so, "Sing unto the LORD with thanksgiving; sing praise upon the harp unto our God."

8. *Who covereth the heaven with clouds, who prepareth rain for the earth, who maketh grass to grow upon the mountains.*

They did not talk about the "laws of nature" in those days. They ascribed everything to God; let us do the same. It is a poor science that pushes God farther away from us, instead of bringing him nearer to us. HE covers the heaven with clouds, HE prepares the rain for the earth, HE makes the grass to grow upon the mountains.

9. *He giveth to the beast his food, and to the young ravens which cry.*

Our God cares for birds and beasts. He is as great in little things as in great things. Praise ye his name. The gods of the heathen could not have these things said of them; but our God takes pleasure in providing for the beasts of the field and the birds of the air. The commissariat of the universe is in his hand: "Thou openest thine hand, and satisfiest the desire of every living thing."

10. 11. *He delighteth not in the strength of the horse: he taketh not pleasure in the legs of a man. The LORD taketh pleasure in them that fear him, in those that hope in his mercy.*

Kings of the olden times rejoiced in the thews and sinews of their soldiers and their horses; but God has no delight in mere physical strength. He takes pleasure in spiritual things, even in the weakness which makes us fear him, even that weakness which has not grown into the strength of faith, and yet hopes in his mercy. "The Lord taketh pleasure in them that fear him, in those that hope in his mercy."

12. *Praise the LORD, O Jerusalem; praise thy God, O Zion.*

Let whole cities join together to praise God. Shall we live to see the day when all London shall praise him? Shall we ever, as we go down these streets, with their multitudes of inhabitants, see the people standing in the doorways, and asking, "What must we do to be saved?" Shall we ever see every house with anxious enquirers in it, saying, "Tell us, tell us, how we can be reconciled to God?" Pray that it may be so. In Cromwell's day, if you went down Cheapside at a certain hour of the morning, you would find every blind drawn down; for the inmates were all at family prayer. There is no street like that in London now. In those glorious Puritan times, there was domestic worship everywhere, and the people seemed brought to Christ's feet. Alas, it was but in appearance in many cases; and they soon turned back to their own devices! Imitating the Psalmist, let us say, "Praise the Lord, O London; praise thy God, O England!"

13. *For he hath strengthened the bars of thy gates; he hath blessed thy children within thee.*

As a nation, we have been greatly prospered, defended, and supplied; and the church of God has been made to stand fast against her enemies, and her children have been blessed.

14, 15. *He maketh peace in thy borders, and filleth thee with the finest of the wheat. He sendeth forth his commandment upon earth: his word runneth very swiftly.*

Oriental monarchs were very earnest to have good post arrangements. They sent their decrees upon swift dromedaries. They can never be compared with the swiftness of the purpose of God's decree. "His word runneth very swiftly." Oh, that the day would come when, over all the earth, God's writ should run, and God's written Word should be reverenced, believed, and obeyed!

16. *He giveth snow like wool:*

Men say, "*it*" snows; but what "*it*" is it that snows? The Psalmist rightly says of the Lord, "HE giveth snow." They say that, according to the condition of the atmosphere, snow is produced; but the believer says, "He giveth snow like wool." It is not only like wool for whiteness; but it is like it for the warmth which it gives.

16. *He scattereth the hoar frost like ashes.*

The simile is not to be easily explained; but it will often have suggested itself to you who, in the early morning, have seen the hoar frost scattered abroad.

17. *He casteth forth his ice like morsels: who can stand before his cold?*

None can stand before his heat; but when he withdraws the fire, and takes away the heat, the cold is equally destructive. It burns up as fast as fire would. "Who can stand before his cold?" If God be gone, if the Spirit of God be taken away from the church, or from any of you, who can stand before his cold? The deprivation is as terrible as if it were a positive infliction. "Who can stand before his cold?"

18. *He sendeth out his word, and melteth them: he causeth his wind to blow, and the waters flow.*

The frozen waters were hard as iron; the south wind toucheth them, and they flow again. What can God not do? The great God of nature is our God. Let us praise him. Oh, may our hearts be in a right key tonight to make music before him!

19. *He sheweth his word unto Jacob, his statutes and his judgments unto Israel.*

This is something greater than all his wonders in nature. The God of nature is the God of revelation. He hath not hidden his truth away from men. He hath come out of the eternal secrecies, and he hath showed his word, especially his Incarnate Word, unto his people. Let his name be praised.

20. *He hath not dealt so with any nation:*

Or, with any other nation. He revealed his statutes and his judgments to Israel; and since their day, the spiritual Israel has been privileged in like manner: "He hath not dealt so with any nation."

20. *And as for his judgments, they have not known them.*

Even today there are large tracts of country where God is not known. If we know him, let us praise him.

20. *Praise ye the LORD.*

Hallelujah! The Psalm ends upon its keynote: "Praise ye the LORD." So may all our lives end! Amen.

HYMNS FROM "OUR OWN HYMN BOOK"—386, 537, 587.

Made in the USA
Middletown, DE
21 July 2022

69493234R00130